THE CHANGING COMMONWEALTH

Issued under the joint auspices of:

The Royal Institute of International Affairs
The Australian Institute of International Affairs
The Canadian Institute of International Affairs
The Indian Council of World Affairs
The New Zealand Institute of International Affairs
The Pakistan Institute of International Affairs
The South African Institute of International Affairs

The Institutes of International Affairs in the Commonwealth, and the Indian Council of World Affairs, are precluded by their rules from expressing, as Institutes, an opinion on any aspect of international or Commonwealth affairs. Any opinions expressed in this book are, therefore, purely individual.

THE
CHANGING
COMMONWEALTH

Proceedings of the Fourth Unofficial
Commonwealth Relations Conference
Held at Bigwin Inn, Ontario, Canada,
September 8-18, 1949

Edited by
F. H. SOWARD
Director of International Studies,
University of British Columbia

Foreword by
R. M. FOWLER
Chairman of the Conference,
and President of the Canadian Institute
of International Affairs

Issued under the auspices of the
Canadian Institute of International Affairs

OXFORD UNIVERSITY PRESS
TORONTO
1950

Oxford University Press, Amen House, Toronto

LONDON   GLASGOW   NEW YORK   MELBOURNE

WELLINGTON   BOMBAY   CALCUTTA   MADRAS   CAPE TOWN

Geoffrey Cumberlege, Publisher to the University

Printed in Canada
by
THE HUNTER ROSE CO. LIMITED

To
EDGAR TARR

CONTENTS

CONTENTS

PREFACE

As Recorder of the Fourth Unofficial Commonwealth Relations Conference it was my task to prepare for publication this volume, containing a digest of the various delegation papers distributed before the Conference, and a summary of the proceedings. To attempt to do so in reasonable compass may lead to excessive compression of discussions or to an unequal balance of emphasis in summarizing points of view. If these dangers have been avoided, it is largely due to the accuracy and industry of the précis writers and round table recorders at the Conference who were tireless in their efforts to secure an accurate record of the discussions. It is a pleasure to acknowledge the work of the précis writers, Messrs. H. R. Horne, P. R. Hyndman, A. S. McGill, and K. D. McIlwraith, and of the recorders, Miss Lucy Sutherland (United Kingdom), Messrs. Alexander Brady (Canada), George Caiger (Australia), Nicholas Mansergh (United Kingdom), John F. Northey (New Zealand), and E. A. G. Robinson (United Kingdom). I am especially indebted to Dr. Nicholas Mansergh, who has read the whole of the manuscript and has offered many valuable suggestions, and to Mr. Robinson, who scrutinized carefully the economic sections, which owed so much to his work as author of a delegation paper and as recorder. My thanks are also due to the Messrs. Brady and McInnis who, with Dr. Mansergh, constituted the editorial committee, and to Mr. J. D. Gibson, who read the economic sections. As on former occasions my friend and colleague, Dr. W. L. Macdonald, of the Department of English of the University of British Columbia, has greatly helped me by pointing out flaws in style and presentation. I am under great obligation to Mrs. F. Sutherland for her prompt and careful typing of

the manuscript. Dr. C. C. Lingard and Mr. M. R. D. Vos of
the Canadian Institute of International Affairs have been most
co-operative in editing the manuscript for the publishers. Lastly,
I wish to acknowledge the aid of the University of British
Columbia in providing stenographic assistance. It only remains
to add that, for such errors of fact and opinion as have survived
this careful screening, I am solely responsible.

F. H. SOWARD

University of British Columbia,
April 1950

INTRODUCTION

This is the age of conferences, committees, congresses and
endless discussion. In most cases, these meetings are widely and
intensively publicized; their deliberations form the basis for news
reports, the comments of newspaper columnists, and intensive
discussions in magazine articles and books. More often than
not, the results are negligible or, at best, disappointing. Why,
then, should there be yet another conference? Why, in the
unanimous opinion of those who attended it, was the 1949
Commonwealth Relations Conference a valuable and successful meeting?

The answers to these questions may lie in the nature of these
Commonwealth Relations Conferences. They are unofficial and
therefore do not start with predetermined positions and views.
They are informal and can thus bring out in discussion individual and divergent view-points. They are private and therefore
a delegate can voice his personal and, at times, his tentative,
opinions without fear of public commitment. The object of
these Conferences is to bring together representative and differ-
ing points of view from each of the member nations of the
British Commonwealth. There is considerable advance preparation of factual material describing the political, economic, and
military position of each nation, but there is no attempt to
formulate a national party line. Frank and informal discussion
of a detailed agenda extends over a period of ten days, and by
this interchange of personal view-points, representative and
frequently influential individuals are able to return to their
countries with a greater knowledge and understanding of the
national problems of other Commonwealth nations and even
of the problems of their own countries.

There is perhaps another reason why these conferences, organized by non-political, non-partisan Institutes of International Affairs, have been successful and valuable. They do not try to do too much. In fact they do not try to do anything, except provide greater knowledge and understanding of the problems discussed for those who participate. In the modern world, the problems of international relations are so large and complex that they discourage the participants from the outset by their mere magnitude. The attempt to reach solutions of world problems must, nevertheless, be made at large official conferences. But it is valuable, at times, to lower the sights and aim at problems which, while they are complex and vague enough, are more within human grasp.

The first three Commonwealth Relations Conferences organized by the Institutes—at Toronto, at Lapstone, and at London—each in their different ways contributed to the development of the nature and functioning of the Commonwealth. It is possible to look back over the history of the last twenty years and trace the influence of the discussions at these three conferences on the course of development of Commonwealth relations. This influence was not the result of decisions taken at the conferences, for there were none, but came from the knowledge and understanding gained by delegates in conference discussions which were subsequently translated into domestic policies in which the delegates had a part. And that may well be the best and most effective way to influence national and international policies, for it is founded on personal conviction rather than on agreement or compromise.

The fourth Commonwealth Conference, held in September 1949 at Bigwin Inn, Ontario, promises to have a similar influence on future Commonwealth relations. Those who can speak with experience of other conferences rate it the best of the series. Generally the delegations were strong and representative of their countries. The preparatory papers were valuable in launching the discussions, and the arrangements were competently handled. This fourth conference was distinguished by the unanimous willingness of all delegations to refrain from discussion of forms and technicalities of Commonwealth relations. There was, in the words of Professor Mansergh, a general recognition of a "widening sense of community" between the members of the Commonwealth which produced "a striking consensus of opinion about the inner nature of the Commonwealth, the outward means by which its co-operation may be made effective, and the high purposes which it serves in the contemporary world."

The Canadian Institute of International Affairs is happy that it was able to act as host to this important conference. It is greatly indebted to five generous Canadians—Mr. J. S. McLean, Mr. J. W. McConnell, Mr. H. R. MacMillan, Mr. Garfield Weston, and Mr. John David Eaton—whose substantial contributions to the Conference Fund made it possible to hold the meetings in the pleasant and retired atmosphere of Bigwin Inn. I wish also to express the appreciation and indebtedness of the Canadian Institute to Professor F. H. Soward, whose duties as Conference Recorder were discharged with such great distinction during the meetings at Bigwin Inn, and whose labours have continued through the past year in the preparation of a pamphlet summary of the Conference and of the official record contained in this volume.

The final note in this introduction must be one of great sadness and personal loss to members of the Canadian Institute and indeed to members of all international organizations throughout the Commonwealth. There were many who contributed to the success of the Fourth Commonwealth Conference, but I am sure everyone will agree that a great share of the credit for its success should go to Mr. E. J. Tarr, who died suddenly this month in Winnipeg. He was a past president of the Canadian Institute and was the only delegate who attended all four of the Conferences. His guidance and advice were invaluable both during the last Conference and throughout the months of preparation for it. To him this volume is respectfully dedicated.

R. M. FOWLER
President
Canadian Institute of International Affairs

Montreal, Quebec,
November 1950

PART I

A SURVEY OF THE PREPARATORY PAPERS

1

National Attitudes Towards the Commonwealth and Foreign Policies

In their plans for the Bigwin conference the Committee on Arrangements and Agenda followed the precedent of previous meetings and asked each National Institute of International Affairs to submit a preparatory paper on its country's policies in advance of the Conference. Somewhat optimistically it was hoped that a single paper would prove sufficient for that purpose. These papers were designed as a background for the opening discussion on "The Position of the Members of the Commonwealth in the Post-War World." The Committee suggested that they should normally contain "an account of the changes which the war and the post-war settlement have brought about, together with an appreciation of the present political, economic and strategic position, drawing particular attention to the development since the 1945 Conference and to present day problems and attitudes." As it turned out, it did not prove possible for all the delegations to submit such papers or, in most cases, to confine their submission to a single paper. But the list of preparatory papers[1] does indicate how much pertinent information and descriptions of national attitudes were available as a background for the Conference. Submissions ranged from published

---

[1] See Appendix C. "Canada and the Commonwealth," by Alexander Brady, "Strategy and Policy in the Defence of Canada," by Eric Harrison, and "Canada and the North Atlantic Treaty," by a Winnipeg Study Group, were published in the *International Journal*, Vol. IV, No. 3 (Summer, 1949). Ceylon, Ireland and New Zealand did not forward preparatory papers. During the Conference the Irish delegation circulated copies of an address at Chatham House in February, 1949, by the Minister for External Affairs on "Anglo-Irish Relations," and a government pamphlet "Working with Europe" on Ireland's co-operation in the Marshall Plan. The New Zealand delegation provided a list of reference material drawn mainly from publications of the Department of External Affairs and the quarterly, *Pacific Affairs*.

volumes, such as *The Commonwealth and the Nations* by Nicholas Mansergh (London, 1948), included in the United Kingdom set of papers, and *Canada's Economy in a Changing World* edited by J. D. Gibson (Toronto, 1948), to reprints of articles, reports and questionnaires. Australia followed most closely the Committee's instructions and produced a compact mimeographed paper of seventy-seven pages, in four parts, which discussed "Economic Problems," "Political Developments Since 1939," and "Strategic Problems," and included a suggestive essay on "The Future of the British Commonwealth." As was to be expected there were marked variations of interest and emphasis in the data papers. Canada submitted a report by a study group in Winnipeg on "Canada and the North Atlantic Treaty." Pakistan thought it advisable to include a special paper on "The Genesis of Pakistan." India included in her papers one on "Racial Discrimination," while South Africa devoted one to her relations with the United Nations. It is possible, however, to sum up the preparatory papers under four headings: National Attitudes Towards the Commonwealth, Foreign Policies, Strategy, and Economic Problems.

National Attitudes Towards the Commonwealth

On the whole the preparatory papers unconsciously obeyed the admonition of the Chairman of the Canadian Delegation to the Third Unofficial Commonwealth Conference at London in 1945. During his remarks at the opening ceremony at Chatham House, Mr. E. J. Tarr, K.C., had then exhorted his colleagues, "Let us now with great solemnity and all respect duly embalm and tuck away in some forgotten crypt beyond all possibility of resurrection, the word 'status' in so far as it is used in an intra-Commonwealth sense."[2] The remarkable succession of events in the past decade of Commonwealth history had made irrelevant what Professor Mansergh has described as "blind, unprofitable discussions about nationality, about secession, about symbolism." Irish neutrality in 1939 and departure from the Commonwealth a decade later, Indian independence in 1947 and subsequent decision to become a Republic but to seek approval from her sister nations for remaining within the Commonwealth—a deci-

[2] Richard Frost (ed.), *The British Commonwealth and World Society* (London, 1947), p. 149.

sion endorsed by the Prime Ministers' Conference of April, 1949 —the emergence of Pakistan as an independent state still free to make up its mind as to retention of Commonwealth membership, Ceylon's appearance in 1948 by deliberate choice as an equal partner with the other Commonwealth countries, Burma's peaceful secession from the Commonwealth—these were events which contradicted the arguments of the rigid logicians of the twenties and thirties and confounded the advocates of a unitary empire.

On one problem of metaphysics there was still room for controversy. What is meant by describing the Crown as "the symbol of their free association" and the King as "the symbol of free association of its independent member nations"? These phrases appeared in the Declaration of the Commonwealth Prime Ministers of April, 1949, which recorded India's wish to remain in the Commonwealth as a Republic and endorsed that policy. Were they, as Prime Minister St. Laurent had told the Canadian House of Commons, simply a "new demonstration of the traditional capacity of the Commonwealth to strengthen its unity of purpose while adapting its organization and procedure to changed circumstances"? Did they create a new function for the King as "Head of the Commonwealth"? The first point of view would appear to have been that shared by the United Kingdom, Canada, Australia and New Zealand, all of whom made no special reference to the Declaration in their preparatory papers. On the other hand India, Pakistan and South Africa felt obliged to comment on the new situation, and their observations are of considerable significance.

In discussing "The New Shape of the Commonwealth" in a delegation paper, a South African is greatly concerned lest the Prime Ministers' Declaration of April, 1949, should be regarded as simply making India "an exception in a monarchical association . . . without much more significance than as a concession to whim or idiosyncrasy." Such an interpretation, he felt, would be an evasion of reality as was, in his opinion, the Balfour Declaration of 1926.[8] By stressing the organic nature of the

[8] It is significant that an Australian who holds quite different views on the nature of the Commonwealth comments in the Australian paper on the Balfour Declaration as "a masterpiece of ambiguity framed with a view to maintaining the existing practice by a series of formulae covering incompatible positions."

Commonwealth in such a mystical fashion as could not appeal to those who do not possess "a breezy, hearty, bull-necked and bone headed imperialism" it contributed, according to him, to the growth of republican sentiment in Ireland, India and Palestine. What the author sees in the April Declaration is a late flowering of the policy which General Hertzog carried out in South Africa in 1934. Then, in securing the adoption of the Union Status Act and its corollary, the Royal Executive Functions and Seals Act, the Prime Minister had asserted the indivisibility of allegiance to South Africa and the divisibility of the Crown, in contradiction to the theory of "a common allegiance to the Crown" which is affirmed in both Balfour Declaration and the Statute of Westminster. To underline this concept the South African Parliament, under General Hertzog's leadership, deliberately chose a different date from that selected by the other Commonwealth countries for the abdication of King Edward VII and accession to the throne of George VI. By so doing it made clear the South African position "that the King for purposes of reigning in and over the Union is created by our statutes." As a consequence the writer argues:

A South African Crown resting firmly in the affections and the intellectual assent of the South African people has nothing to fear from any change in the Commonwealth's structure.

For them the Crown is not a symbol of common allegiance or proof of the existence of an alien overlord but "a living dynamic creation óf our own statecraft." In keeping with that belief the Commonwealth cannot be a monarchical association united by a common allegiance to the Crown, in which India is to be an eccentric exception, but a group of "sister states existing separately in their own right, in their own self-reliance, and in the light of their own verities." Whether the partner governments are kingdoms or republics is not of great significance so long as they are free partners in what the writer prefers to call a "concord of Nations." In this association, as Prime Minister Malan stressed in London, the Crown does not possess a vestige of "functional reality." Unless this attitude is understood and accepted elsewhere, there is a real danger that not only those Afrikaans who look back with nostalgia to the days of the

Calvinistic Boer Republics, but those Europeans who have more recently settled in South Africa and are much nearer "to American Republican ideas than to the British Monarchy" will turn away from the Kingdom of South Africa created by General Hertzog and support a Republic devoid of all connection with the Commonwealth. That would be, says the writer, simply "a dark day for South Africa."

India is completely in agreement with South Africa in rejecting any concept of organic unity for the Commonwealth and in affirming that by the April Declaration the King acquires no new powers as "Head of the Commonwealth." Prime Minister Nehru is quoted as saying on his return from London:

It had been made perfectly clear that the King had no functions at all. He had a certain status but the Commonwealth itself as such had no body, it had no organization to function, and the King also could have no function.

The writer of the article on "India and the Commonwealth" suggests that the phrase "as head of the Commonwealth" was ". . . inserted with a view to avoid complications in international law and to enable India to treat the members of the Commonwealth and *vice versa* as something better than foreign nations with whom exist treaties with the Most Favoured Nation Clause." The Indian view of membership in the Commonwealth is a pragmatic one based upon the world situation and the political dangers in South Asia. There is a realization, says the Indian author,

that economic and defence considerations require India to continue her membership of the Commonwealth—at least for some years to come.

Again Prime Minister Nehru is clear upon that point, as in his speech to the Indian Constituent Assembly on May 16, 1949:

We join the Commonwealth obviously because we think it is beneficial to us and to other causes in the world that we wish to advance. Other countries of the Commonwealth want us to remain there because they think it is beneficial to them. It is mutually understood, that it is to the advantage of the nations in the Commonwealth, and therefore, they join, but, at the same time, it is made perfectly clear that each country goes its own way. It may be that way sometimes goes so far as to make the Commonwealth link break. Well then, it breaks and there the matter ends.

The Indian position differs slightly from the South African in that it was necessary for the Government leaders to modify the position of Purna Swaraj, or complete independence, which they had taken in 1930. That policy, which remained unchanged until August, 1947, when the independence of India was conceded by the United Kingdom and her position in the Commonwealth left for future arrangement, arose largely from the bitterness of the struggle in India. But it also reflects resentment against the absence of complete racial equality in the Commonwealth. As the paper states bluntly:

The ruthless policy of racial discrimination, segregation and repatriation of Asians followed by the Government of South Africa has created a strong anti-Commonwealth sentiment in the country.

The early realization that complete freedom of action was compatible with membership in the Commonwealth, and the practical considerations previously described, among which should also be included the fact that Pakistan would probably continue to remain in the Commonwealth, persuaded the Indian statesmen to seek the solution of continuing membership and a republican form of government. There is no hint in the Indian paper of any appreciation of the previous rejection by South Africa of the theory of "common allegiance to the Crown." Irish precedents appear to have been studied closely, but the writer of the Indian paper does not differentiate specifically between the views of South Africa and New Zealand on the position of the Crown. He does point out, however, that the Indian precedent leaves the way open for South Africa and Pakistan to choose also to become republics and remain in the Commonwealth.

It is also important to note that the Indian paper emphasizes the fact that India retains full membership in the *Commonwealth*, not the *British* Commonwealth. The April Declaration referred to the British Commonwealth of Nations in the opening paragraph when describing the situation before India chose to become a republic but on six subsequent occasions the word "Commonwealth" only is used. Although Mr. Attlee later declared that everyone was free to use what nomenclature he wished, it is the Indian view that the omission of the word "British" is intentional. It reflects the fact that India is herself a mother country and not a colony peopled by British settlers and sharing to the full British culture.

What India accepts is "free co-operation among free, equal, and independent members in the pursuit of peace, liberty and progress." The ideal of free co-operation is threatened, in the view of the Indian writer, by the policy of racial discrimination that is still being followed, especially in South Africa and also, although this point is not clarified, by "the religious basis on which the state of Pakistan is being built."

The author of the paper on "Pakistan and the Commonwealth" agreed with his South African and Indian colleagues in rejecting the concept of organic unity. He believes in the divisible nature of the Crown and comments that while it is true that Pakistan owes allegiance to the Crown ". . . the Crown in respect of Pakistan is distinct from the Crown in the United Kingdom." He never uses the phrase "British Commonwealth," and concurs in the reminder that with the Asian countries entering into full Commonwealth partnership it is unrealistic to talk of "a common way of life" or "like-minded" nations. But having gone that far with the Indian and South African writers the author then reveals some interesting divergencies of opinion and some different variations on the Commonwealth theme. To Pakistan the elimination of allegiance to the Crown as a characteristic of Commonwealth association is not to be taken as lightly as it was in the South African paper. On the contrary, since it destroyed the distinctive character of the Commonwealth "as a closely-knit association," it is to be regretted. It is true that the Commonwealth states continue to proclaim common objectives of peace, liberty and progress, but these ideals are not peculiar to themselves. They are also the ideals of the United Nations and could be the objectives of other associations of states. The fact remains, the writer argues, that "the club rules have now changed beyond recognition." As an illustration of the changes in the club rules which particularly concerned Pakistan the paper cites the new habit of calling upon "outsiders" to mediate in Commonwealth disputes.

The most recent illustration of this occurred in the handling of the Kashmir dispute between India and Pakistan. When Pakistan appealed to the other Commonwealth countries for assistance in solving the series of difficulties of which this was the latest and most serious ". . . the reply that she received from them was 'non possumus'." Accordingly the question came under the jurisdiction of the Security Council. In describing these events the paper asks pertinently,

How can an association of states such as the Commonwealth is, that cannot adjust its own internal differences, that cannot check aggression by one of its members against a fellow-member, be depended upon to present a united front to an outside aggressor? . . . It is not sufficient to say, "The Commonwealth affords protection against the naughty boy from outside, even though it does not afford protection against the naughty boy inside."

With this situation in mind he suggests that the other Commonwealth countries "must counsel India to moderate her policy towards her Moslem citizens" and must evolve a new policy of which the essence must be ". . . to treat Pakistan more fairly and to give a military guarantee of the Indo-Pakistan frontiers." He admits these policies are a departure from past practice but replies that there have been recently more fundamental changes ". . . and the one here urged is ancillary to those changes." These difficulties, desires, and disappointments are bound to colour the decision of Pakistan as to the continuance of membership in the Commonwealth. The maker of Pakistan, the late Mr. Jinnah, is quoted as being inclined to having his country "a willing member of the Commonwealth," but there is no definite obligation to stay in the Commonwealth. Prime Minister Liaquat Ali Khan pointed out after his return from London that those who wished Pakistan to be a friendly partner in the Commonwealth should give concrete proof of their own sincerity. As the paper summarizes the Pakistan point of view ". . . Pakistan will remain in the Commonwealth, if it will do unto her, what it would have her do unto it. Otherwise she will not."

In the introduction to the Australian paper the editor begins his comments on the future organization of the Commonwealth by quoting Mr. Menzies' summary of the problem when he was out of office:

We must now once and for all, decide whether the British Commonwealth is to remain as an organic structure in which there must be some permanent binding element which preserves unity, or whether it is to broaden out into a merely functional association, an alliance between otherwise separate and independent nations.

So far as Australia and Britain are concerned there is a community of feeling which is only paralleled by the relationship of New Zealand to Britain. As another Australian puts it,

. . . we regard Britain and Australia as one community sharing the same way of life, pursuing the same ideals and, not the least important fact, being one folk.[4]

This sentiment was well expressed by the Prime Minister, Mr. Curtin, when he visited England in 1944 for the Prime Ministers' Conference and said that he represented "seven million Britishers." Similarly, in the Australian and New Zealand parliaments the unity of the British Commonwealth is taken for granted and no politician would risk his political future by challenging it. Because of this identity of feeling, which it is appreciated India and Pakistan could not be expected to share, there is in the Australian paper a suggestion, more implicit than explicit, that it may be necessary for the Commonwealth to develop on more than one level, with the United Kingdom, Australia and New Zealand forming the most compact group, Canada and South Africa coming next, and India, Pakistan and Ceylon forming the outer ring. As the paper suggests:

Those parts of the Empire with ethnic ties might desire a solidarity of policy and a degree of co-operation which the others would not want. It is important that the presence of these others should not frustrate the desire for co-operation which the British members possess.

On the other hand no support is advanced for the concept of federal union, even as applied to the first-mentioned group. Co-operation in the Commonwealth, it is agreed, must develop

[4] The last census showed that in the two largest Australian states 99.5 per cent. of the population are of British descent.

along functional lines and recognize regional interests, as has already been demonstrated in the North Atlantic Pact, to which only the United Kingdom and Canada are committed, or the Anzac Pact of 1944. One Australian writer appears concerned that the next challenge to the security of the Commonwealth may not be so clearly recognizable as its predecessors of 1914 and 1939 and may find the Commonwealth less cohesive.

Success in a modern war depends on sound foreign policy and long-term preparation, and it is by no means certain that the necessary degree of co-operation exists to enable us to face another test.

For that reason he favours the closest degree of co-operation among those Commonwealth members who will unhesitatingly fight if the safety of one with whom they are spiritually in sympathy is threatened. He does not think that economic ties are as strong or as effective as spiritual ones in holding Commonwealth states together. Nor is he content with the existing Commonwealth machinery of consultation. In his paper on "The Future of the British Commonwealth" the author advocates a Commonwealth Secretariat, as Prime Minister Curtin and Lord Bruce have previously suggested, and points out that it has been endorsed by all Australian parties. However his proposal is not shared by all Australians. The editor states that:

There is a growing body of opinion which feels that, given the varying levels of association and tradition within the Commonwealth, the creation of a Secretariat is inadvisable. There is a clear division within the Commonwealth which is not geographical, and this could bring a differentiation in practice between members which would weaken cohesion and result in disintegration. A formal centripetal movement amongst some members might accelerate a centrifugal movement amongst others . . . . It is believed that the proposed functions of a Secretariat could best be performed by government to government consultation, by the creation of a series of *ad hoc* committees (of which some twenty already exist) rather than by the creation of any specialised permanent and formal machinery.

But, apart from the question of the secretariat, there is in Australia the fullest agreement on "close functional collaboration" in the Commonwealth. There is also the same unity of

opinion that "Australia cannot contract out of the Commonwealth." Probably because of this view the Australian paper is
inclined to suspend judgment on the Declaration of April, 1949.
In the view of its editor it is

. . . too early to tell whether the recent formula worked out in
London will be, like the Balfour Declaration, anything more than
what Sir Owen Dixon described as "a disorderly collection of
abstract nouns."

The Canadian attitude towards the Commonwealth is described as being influenced by two basic circumstances which will
remain operative in the future as they are today. These are
proximity to the United States, with which Canada is linked
by powerful economic ties and cultural forces, and by what
Dr. Brady's paper on "Canada and the Commonwealth" calls
"the character of her composite nationality." The desire to
maintain a balance between the United States and Great Britain
which geography and environment make necessary is appreciated
by all thoughtful Canadians and is reflected in the restrained
and cautious pronouncements on Commonwealth relations by
responsible Canadian politicians. They are, to quote the Canadian paper ". . . concerned with an American attachment as
well as a Commonwealth one, and . . . ever anxious to avoid
open conflict between the two." The fact that almost one-third
of the Canadian population is of French origin greatly reduces
the strength of "the call of the blood" which is so clearly
manifest in Australia and New Zealand. For French Canadians
association with Britain has meant in the past preservation of
language and guarantees of essential rights, and protection
against absorption by the United States. It has also meant
involvement in "the vortex of European militarism" and "im-
perialistic wars" with which they feel Canada has no direct
concern. The fact that some twenty per cent of the population
are of European origin other than British or French further
dilutes in Canada the sentimental attachment to the Commonwealth. The attitude of these two non-British groups to the
Commonwealth is generally summed up as

friendly to Canada's membership in it, appreciative of its role in
the world, but somewhat disturbed in mind by any strong emphasis

on what they would regard as an ultra-imperial or intra-Commonwealth ideal.

Wartime experience and post-war developments have hastened national maturity and greatly modified the sense of isolation. They have not appreciably changed the attitude towards the Commonwealth which is based upon what has become "the accepted Canadian tradition . . . that the Commonwealth should not involve formal commitments although it does involve moral responsibilities." In keeping with this tradition official policy remains as it was before 1939, ". . . abundant and intimate consultation within the Commonwealth without commitment and on the basis of national autonomy." The government's position was summarized by Mr. St. Laurent before he became Prime Minister. In 1947 he told an audience at the University of Toronto that in seeking to preserve the Commonwealth as an instrument of co-operation for our common good:

. . . we should continue to resist as in the past, efforts to reduce to formal terms or specific commitments this association which has demonstrated its vitality through the common understanding upon which it is based. We should likewise oppose developments in our Commonwealth relations which might be inconsistent with our desire to participate fully in the task of building an effective international organization on a wider scale.

It is this dislike of rigid commitments and of emphasis upon consultative machinery[5] which brings Canada more in line with South Africa than Australia, although as the Canadian paper points out the people of the two countries differ in their interest in the republican idea. Except among small French groups Republicanism is, according to this paper, not an issue in Canadian life. There is consequently no distrust of the Crown or the Sovereign as a symbol, and in fact the existence of a King of Canada is regarded as a factor in stressing the identity of Canada in a hemisphere peopled by republics. The Canadian paper observes that in no important section of the population

[5] For that reason Canadian statesmen have preferred the informality of the Prime Ministers' Conferences to the carefully staged Imperial Conference. Thus the Secretary of State for External Affairs said after the meeting of April, 1949, "We can sit down to business in these talks without formality or preliminary palaver."

is the existence of the Crown regarded as a restriction on freedom. There is, however, a caution in defining what the ties of monarchy actually involve in the way of obligations. The Canadian position also differs from the South African in its greater emphasis upon the subordination of the Commonwealth to an international system in which the United States would also be a welcome partner. And finally it differs from the position of all other Commonwealth countries in the extent of its appreciation of the attitudes and psychology of the American people. Too much can be made, as the Canadian paper properly points out, of the role of Canada as an "interpreter" between the United States and the Commonwealth. The United Kingdom and the United States were dealing directly with each other long before Canada as a nation had come into existence. But in an uneasy world in which the Commonwealth is more dependent upon the United States than ever before in its history, the value of the Canadian appraisal of the American situation when expounded in Commonwealth meetings can be of real importance. As Dr. Brady puts it:

In this matter Canada is likely to exert her most notable influence in the Commonwealth deliberations, and in it her responsibility is great.

In the United Kingdom papers there is little direct comment and description of attitudes in Britain towards the Commonwealth. There is, however, in the analyses of foreign policy and strategy, a frank admission that Britain is more dependent than ever before in her history upon the United States and the Commonwealth countries. The economic aid which she has already received from them has not involved any loss of self-respect, one writer explains, because of " . . . the consciousness that her need is largely due to a war effort which benefited other peoples than herself and to the manner in which aid was extended. There is also an expectation that trade with the Commonwealth as a whole will continue to increase and by 1952 will account for 50 per cent of United Kingdom imports as compared to 29 per cent in 1929 and 40 per cent in 1938. Some concern is expressed as to how association with Western Union will be reconciled with Commonwealth co-operation.

Professor Mansergh's published volume of essays on *The Commonwealth and the Nations,* which is one of the United Kingdom submissions, has mainly to do with a lucid description of changes in the Commonwealth and particular problems such as the respective roles of Britain and Russia in Southeast Asia, the evolution of Anglo-Irish relations and the changed position of India. But he does let fall some observations upon the general nature of the Commonwealth which are most suggestive and have stood the test of developments since the book was published in 1948. He states flatly that, "The British Commonwealth of Nations is now the Commonwealth. . ." and for corroboration points to the British Nationality Act of 1948 in which it is stated that, ". . . the terms British subject and Commonwealth citizen are and will henceforth become interchangeable." On various occasions the author refers to the Commonwealth as "an international partnership" and "an international democracy." He points out that "The Commonwealth of Nations has no common foreign, economic or defence policy, nor indeed does it aspire to one." In his opinion its essence in the post-war years was "faith in discussion." This faith carries implications of a willingness to consider every problem that arises on its merits and a distrust for a rigidity of policy whether imposed from above or agreed upon in advance. In support of these views he can quote the Secretary of State for Burma when moving the bill providing for that country's independence:

The essence of the Commonwealth relationship is that it is a free association of nations, with a common purpose, who belong together because they have decided of their own volition to give and to take their fair share in a world wide partnership.

Dr. Mansergh also reminds the Commonwealth states that partnership in such an association strengthens the international position of each one of them as a member of a world-wide group of states.

In a world dominated by Great Powers ever becoming greater, there is no mean contribution to be made by a group of states, which, by the very fact of its existence enables individual member states to play a role in international affairs not otherwise possible for middle or smaller Powers.

In a closely reasoned essay on "The Implications of Eire's Relationship with the British Commonwealth of Nations," the author developed an argument about the greater advantages of external association rather than Dominion Status for countries "who share a wide community of interest but different political concepts." Such an association, which Irishmen were seeking in 1921 but without success, gets round the difficulty of grouping countries as "Dominions" which because of their age, their culture and their traditions look upon themselves as "mother countries," and reduces the danger of the Crown as a symbol of association and common allegiance being looked upon, as it was in Ireland, as "a symbol of subjection." Dr. Mansergh admits that in the light of the Irish experience it is easy "to put too much emphasis on the adjective, too little on the noun." On the other hand he writes,

an element of constitutional untidiness is a small price to pay for a flexibility in Commonwealth relations which enables peoples of many races and traditions to co-operate whole-heartedly in the common purposes which the Commonwealth serves the world.

Here is foreshadowed the United Kingdom attitude towards the acceptance of India as a republic within the Commonwealth. By making this concession to India the Commonwealth Prime Ministers may well have given greater vitality to the Commonwealth, as Professor Berriedale Keith suggested over a decade ago. Writing in 1938, he warned, "If no place can be found in a British Commonwealth for republics then the enduring character of the Commonwealth may well be doubted." Lastly Dr. Mansergh grapples with the problem of "two-level membership" that may arise from a lack of common allegiance to the Crown, which are discussed in the Australian paper. The problem of relationship between states that are Dominions with those that have been "more formally associated" may be solved in practice,

. . . by regarding all partners in the Commonwealth as having equal privileges and mutually agreed obligations, and using the defined relationship of the associate states as a statement of first principles to which appeal is made only on one of those rare and critical occasions for which it was designed to provide.

Commonwealth Foreign Policies

One of the interesting features of the delegation papers on foreign policy is the general agreement that there is a solid backing in each country for the foreign policy being pursued at present. Such a unity of feeling is indicated in the United Kingdom paper[6] when Sir Charles Webster states:

At no time in their history have the British people been more united in the furtherance of their foreign policy than at this moment, except during the war itself.

In a Canadian paper there is a similar emphasis. "For the first time," Professor Eric Harrison writes, "the Government is sure of itself on questions of external policy." He notes that the country is "virtually unanimously in favour of a policy of precise commitments designed to prevent war if prevention is possible." Three statements by French-Canadian members of parliament are cited as illustrations of the fact that "we need no longer distort our policies and cripple our influence through the inhibitions of a nationalist provincialism dead to the atomism of our time." In an Indian paper, where the views of Prime Minister Nehru are quoted several times, the author comments that "almost all the prominent publicists of our country are in agreement with him so far as the main objectives are concerned." The Australian paper is less clear on the degree of domestic unity in support of foreign policy but credits the Labour government with having produced "an independent foreign policy for the first time in the history of our country." It is also of the opinion that the Government's vigorous policy

has made impossible a return to the negative, derivative, somewhat casual attitudes to the development of international policies which were characteristic of Australian governments between wars.

The South African delegation did not contribute a paper on foreign policy in general but described South Africa's attitude

[6] Sir Charles Webster's paper on "British Foreign Policy since the Second World War," together with those by Major General Sir Ian Jacob on "United Kingdom Strategy," and by Mr. E. A. G. Robinson on "Economic Policy," have been published by Chatham House in a booklet entitled *United Kingdom Policy: Foreign, Strategic, Economic.* Appreciations by Sir Charles Webster, Major General Sir Ian Jacob, and E. A. G. Robinson 1950 (London: R. I. I. A. 101 pp. 4s).

towards the United Nations in which there appears a common resentment at the manner in which South Africa has been pilloried for its racial policies. There is also general agreement in South Africa on common resistance to the militant actions of "atheistic Communism."

It is clear from the data papers that it is the militant policies of Communism under the aegis of the U.S.S.R. which have provided in various countries the greatest bond of unity in foreign policy. As a Pakistan paper puts it bluntly, "the Commonwealth looks upon Russia as a common enemy." The main policy of the British people, says the United Kingdom paper, is "resistance to the Communistic attack made under the protection of the Soviet Union." In an Indian paper the writer frankly admits that an element in his country's change of attitude towards the Commonwealth is "the rapid spread of Communism in Asia and the position created in Malaya, Indonesia and Burma." That Canada's entry into the North Atlantic Pact was made possible only by ". . . a sense of profound uneasiness arising from Soviet political strategy," is the verdict of the Canadian writer on "Strategy and Policy in Defence of Canada." In a report of discussions in two Australian study groups in Victoria and New South Wales on "Strategic Problems" the major assumption is that "the only major military conflict possible in say the next twenty-five years would appear to be between Russia and the West." Three South African students of international affairs who contributed a paper on "The Position of South Africa in the Strategy of the Commonwealth and the World" make the shrewd observation that,

. . . the condemnation of Communism, however just in itself, has the advantage of imparting a superficial unity to countries that cannot frankly face their own domestic stresses.

In their own country, as is described in another South African paper on "The Union's Political Position,"

. . . it is tolerably clear that the perils of Communist aggression which are seen in very vivid colours . . . have actually drawn the Nationalist party closer to the Commonwealth than at one time would have seemed possible.

A logical sequel to this concern about the menace of Communism, which is also fortified by the recollections of wartime experience, is the general realization that the Commonwealth must more and more co-ordinate its policies with those of the United States in order to receive the necessary economic and military aid. Gone are the days when the natural dependence of Canada upon the friendly support of her mighty neighbour might have been regarded with a certain degree of self-satisfaction that such a dependence was not necessary elsewhere! Three extracts from the United Kingdom paper on foreign policy are illustrative of this current attitude. "Britain," says Sir Charles Webster, "is obviously more dependent on the decisions of others and especially on those of the United States." Speaking of European defence he comments:

All are conscious that Europe can only organise her defence against the present threat if she can obtain the assistance of the United States and the Dominions.

In discussing the balance of power in the Far East, the verdict is reached that:

It is clear that the responsibility for the security of this area no longer rests mainly on Britain, and the United States must take the major share in maintaining it.

An Australian paper is equally frank in discussing the problems of the same area and admits that "on grounds of sentiment Australia turns to Britain but from a sense of reality, looks increasingly towards the United States." In the absence of a general system of security in the Western Pacific, it would appear to be in Australia's interest to give "general support for American policies in this area." In a "Report from New Zealand" (*Pacific Affairs*, March, 1949), submitted by the New Zealand delegation, Professor F. L. Wood notes that in the Pacific the dualism between the United States and Russia is even sharper, and proceeds to describe the New Zealand attitude as follows:

New Zealanders are drawn towards the United States by a sense of affinity that has always underlain, and with surprising strength, the majority's more vocal insistence on their exclusive preoccupation with Britain. They realise that they owe their preservation in World War II to the United States and have good reasons, grounded in national experience, for believing that, if it comes to the point, American strength has the last word in the Pacific.

South Africa does not feel the need of American support quite so much because of her belief that at present she is blessed ". . . in having no enemies powerful enough to disturb her . . ." On the other hand she believes there would be powerful friends to ensure her survival "if assailed by revolutionaries" and for that reason will pursue a defence policy that will ". . . bring her into hearty co-operation with the Commonwealth and/or the United States." The Indian paper on "Aspects of India's Foreign Relations" includes an essay on "Indo-American Political Relations" in which considerable stress is placed upon similarities in the experiences of the two countries. The author comes to the conclusion that ". . the atmosphere is very favourable for the growth of friendliness and co-operation between the two countries." Throughout his paper he repeatedly stresses India's determination to pursue "an independent line of foreign policy," but suggests that this need not be a source of conflict with the United States. The two countries may differ in attitude or emphasis but this does not preclude friendly co-operation and the sharing of common objectives in foreign policy. Nor would it prevent ". . . any temporary alliance between the two countries if it is to the advantage of both."

At the preceding Conference on Commonwealth Relations in February, 1945, discussions were influenced by the fact announced just as the meetings got under way that there would soon be a conference of the United Nations in San Francisco to draft a constitution for world order. The section of the Conference report on World Organization recorded the view of the delegates that: "The security and welfare of the Commonwealth alike demand world organization, world co-operative institutions." The experience of the four years since the adoption of the Charter of the United Nations Organization have not lessened appreciation of the need for world order but have lessened the hopes that in the present climate of international affairs, security and co-operation can be assured under the Charter. This attitude is reflected in the comments of the various preparatory papers on national attitudes towards the UN. Thus the United Kingdom regards the United Nations as "a principal object of British foreign policy but not *the* principal object." Australia declares that "full support for the United Nations has been and still is a vital principle of the Australian Government," but the delegation paper admits that the vigorous policy followed by Dr. Evatt, then Australian Minister of External Affairs, in UN matters has been criticized by his political opponents for its "dangerously unrealistic infatuation." In the Canadian paper on "Strategy and Policy in the Defence of Canada" Mr. Harrison examines the assumptions which underlie defence policy, and suggests that Canadian adherence to the North Atlantic Pact was due to ". . . a sense of profound uneasiness arising from Soviet political strategy since the war." "We should prefer," he continues, "the United Nations as a vaguer, holier and less expensive way to universal peace." But even the most sentimental of us have learned to defer our hopes. Like Mr. Pearson (Secretary of State for External Affairs), "we believe that the maintenance of an overwhelming superiority of force on the side of peace is the best guarantee today of the maintenance of peace." The data paper on "South Africa and the United Nations" is chiefly concerned with explaining the prominence which South Africa has achieved in the UN debates during the last three years, a prominence, says the writer ". . . nearly always embarrassing and deeply resented by the majority of South Africa's white population." In describing South Africa's position he asserts that South Africa entered the UN "determined to surrender no title of its sovereignty" and warns that, "The day full sovereignty is denied its members, South Africa will leave the United Nations and it will not be alone." In the debates in the General Assembly on South Africa's policy in administering her mandate for South West Africa and her treatment of Indian residents in the Union, South Africa has consistently rejected assertions of authority on the part of the General Assembly as beyond its competence and denied ". . . the right to deal with the internal or domestic affairs of South Africa." The attempts of Field Marshal Smuts when Prime Minister to show some regard for world opinion as expressed in the UN have been criticised by his successor,

Dr. Malan, who believes that United Nations meetings have become to a large extent a platform for propaganda. But he has disclaimed any policy of isolationism, and took the position that the Union was, "in spite of these difficulties . . . in favour of throwing its weight in an attempt to get rid of the weakness of the Organization and make it one which would work for peace and co-operation for the world." The Asian countries are more positive in support of the UN. Although the Pakistan paper declares that in the handling of such difficult questions as Kashmir, Palestine and the future of the Italian colonies, Pakistan has "suffered a series of disappointments," she is still prepared to give ". . . full support to the purposes and organization of the United Nations." India believes that support of the Commonwealth must be subordinated to loyalty to the UN and the data papers quote the statement of Prime Minister Nehru, 1949:

We propose to function entirely in terms of the Charter and in order to help the United Nations see that peace is established and justice is done.

Describing New Zealand's position, Professor Wood writes that:

. . . there is no doubt of her willingness to honour her obligations to the United Nations, just as there was no question of the response when the call came in 1914 and 1939.

He believes that his country, which shrinks ". . . from the inevitability of a headlong clash between American and Russian power," will direct its policy ". . . towards finding some middle ground, seeking, maybe a little naïvely, to maintain the union among the United Nations that brought defeat to both Germany and Japan."

It is to be expected that the various Commonwealth countries, as independent states with widely different environments, economic interests and cultural traditions, should have distinct foreign policies. They do have certain ideals in common, and are very much alike in their attitude towards the United States, but there are bound to be marked divergencies of outlook and policy.

Of the eight states, the United Kingdom is the only one

which can be said to have a world outlook and to be concerned with developments in every quarter of the globe. That is the reward—and the penalty—for being a great power. Although British power has declined relatively to American and Russian this decline has had, as the United Kingdom paper argues, less influence on foreign policy than might be expected, except in the Far East where the process of limiting commitments had been under way before the second world war began. The advent of new weapons of destruction, such as guided missiles and atomic bombs, has made Western Europe even more important to British security than in the past. This concern has been heightened by the continued weakness of France and the defeat of Germany and Italy. When to this situation is added the westward thrust of the U.S.S.R. in Europe, it can be appreciated that the balance of power is completely upset. As a result, says Sir Charles Webster, the United Kingdom possesses ". . . a much greater interest than ever before in the creation of a powerful and friendly Western Europe." Such an interest is reflected in British leadership in negotiating the Treaty of Brussels, and in the growth of the concept of Western Union. It also affects the British attitude to Germany, which was described by the Foreign Secretary in December, 1948, as follows:

In the matter of European recovery, Germany is regarded as an equal partner in her production with the whole of Western Europe. In the matter of security the question of control is absolutely vital.

At present that is as far as the United Kingdom is prepared to go. She is reluctant to expand any further Germany's partnership in Western European policies until there has been adequate evidence of the German people being able to create and operate a genuinely democratic state. Meanwhile, on the continent there has been great interest in the idea of a United States of Europe which has led to the creation of the Council of Europe. Here again Britain has co-operated, though not as enthusiastically as some European states would wish, partly because of her doubts that such an agency might be in danger of becoming, as Mr. Bevin once said, "a mere talking shop for the passing of resolutions." In developing the Council of Europe, the British preference is described as being for:

. . . functional machinery to be set up for specific objects in which each state retains its own choice of whether to agree with the proposals of others. Anything more organic would not only embarrass Britain's relations with the Commonwealth but in the present state of the other countries of Europe might put upon her impossible burdens.

Since Britain is also aware that the defence of Europe against present threats of aggression cannot be assured by the European states themselves she has played an active part in negotiating the North Atlantic Pact which the United Kingdom paper says is generally regarded as "a great piece of constructive statesmanship." The next step is to co-ordinate the security system of Western Union with the defence of the new grouping of powers, a policy which the United Kingdom will do all in its power to further. By so doing Britain will be enabled ". . . to take its place in the defence of the liberties of Europe without loosening the even more powerful ties which bind her to the overseas world."

In the Middle East the United Kingdom has long been directly interested, because of its importance in the strategy of defending the most direct route to India and the Far East. British foreign policy upheld the integrity of the Turkish empire as long as that was feasible, and then developed treaty relations with the various Arab states that fell heir to much of the Ottoman empire, of which Egypt was the most important. Although the Middle East is less essential as a cover for sea routes with the change in the positions of India, Burma and Pakistan, it is of much greater importance as a key source of oil. Its security is probably more threatened by Russia than ever before. For these reasons the United Kingdom paper on foreign policy concluded that "the defence of the Middle East against aggression must therefore still be regarded as a major object of British policy." Agreement on this objective, however, is not paralleled by agreement upon means. As the U.K. paper admits, "there has been more difference of opinion . . . than on any other major point of foreign policy," a difference created chiefly by the emergence of Israel as an independent state which came in its final stages without British support or agreement.

British interests in Southeast Asia and the Pacific are based upon the location of three Commonwealth states there, the retention of valuable colonies in various stages of economic and political development, and considerable trading interests in China. But for some time Britain has not been able to play a major role there because of the "insistent problems of Europe." This helped to give Japan her opportunity. Her desire to dominate the Pacific was only checkmated by the United States with the assistance of the Commonwealth states most immediately concerned. It is unlikely that American predominance will disappear. As the U.K. paper frankly describes it:

It is clear that the responsibility for the security of this area no longer rests mainly on Britain and that the United States must take the major share in maintaining it.

On the other hand Britain will remain "a powerful factor" in any combination that may be organized by the United States to check the danger of aggression in that region.

Canada's foreign policy as described in three delegation papers dealing with the Commonwealth, Strategy and Policy, and the North Atlantic Treaty is that of a middle or secondary power "instinctively Atlantic" whose maturity has been immensely accelerated by the experiences of the second world war. Her political connection with the United Kingdom and her dependence for economic well-being upon international trade have never allowed her to be as isolationist in outlook as the United States has been but her North American location and lack of colonial possessions have encouraged a policy of detachment and a dislike of formal commitments. In recent years Canadian political leaders have consistently emphasized to their countrymen Canada's changed position. In April, 1948, when Secretary of State for External Affairs, Mr. St. Laurent warned that Canada was now "inevitably and inextricably involved in the full current of international events." His successor, Mr. Pearson, gave an additional reminder that "the world to-day is too small, too interdependent, for even regional isolation." Such an emphasis on greater participation in international affairs, which has resulted in Canadian representation abroad quadrupling between 1939 and 1948, cannot alter immediately and completely old habits of thought and long standing attitudes.[7] As Mr. Harrison, the author of the paper on "Strategy and Policy in the Defence of Canada", notes:

We dislike the detail of international affairs, as in the case of Trieste—though we fought in the Italian campaign. In thought we stop at the Rhine—though we crossed the river in battle. The Near and Middle East seem alien to our interests—though of great strategic importance to our allies. In a three ocean country we mistrust the Arctic and neglect the Pacific. In a collectivist world we abhor state trading. We fly easily to principle, leaving the ground far below our feet, so that discussion, usually not well informed, tends to become unreal.

But it should be noted that such attitudes of mind have not deterred the government from making rapid adaptations of policy to changed circumstances in a two power world. Support of the United Nations which in 1945 was genuine and widespread in Canada has been modified by the reluctant recognition that it cannot in present circumstances give to its members the degree of security once anticipated. Based upon that realisation and encouraged by a similar attitude on the part of the United States and the United Kingdom, the Canadian government therefore adopted what it admitted to be a policy of the "second best," and was from the outset an active partner in the negotiations that preceded the North Atlantic Pact. This shift of policy was generally approved in Canada which was the first of the signatories to deposit her ratification of the North Atlantic Pact. Yet the Pact is not hailed in the Canadian papers so much as a great triumph of statesmanship as ". . . an indication that its participants have a genuine desire to achieve a workable system of collective security however limited," and as ". . . a diplomatic move to checkmate the Soviet Union." Its value over the years will be strengthened in Canadian eyes by the manner in which its clauses dealing with closer economic and political co-operation

---

[7] In 1949 Canada was represented in thirty-three countries by fourteen Embassies, eight Legations, six High Commissioners' Offices, one Military Mission, one Liaison Mission, two U. N. offices, and twelve Consulates-General or Consulates.

are implemented. Nor is Canadian opinion interested in the Pact as the basis for a great military crusade against Communism. Such a notion, which might find support in some excitable sections of American public opinion, would be repugnant to the more stolid Canadians. They would heartily dislike the prospect of what a Winnipeg study group refers to as ". . . the dangers of being swept into imperialist adventures by American pressure."

The North Atlantic Pact was all the more palatable to Canadians because it brought them into a military alliance with countries well known to them as comrades, neighbours and customers. Canada has long felt herself a member of the Atlantic community. She does not as readily think of herself as an American state (as distinct from a "North American state") and has not therefore displayed the same readiness to sign the Treaty of Rio de Janeiro, a mutual assistance pact for the whole of the Western Hemisphere, as has been exhibited in her adherence to the North Atlantic Pact. Nor does she, despite her western coast, put much emphasis upon her position as a Pacific power. One Canadian paper quotes as an apt generalisation the comment of Professor Morton in an article in the *International Journal,* which he himself qualified as too sweeping, namely that ". . . while the United States has been isolationist with respect to Europe and interventionist with respect to Asia, Canada has been interventionist with respect to Europe and isolationist with respect to Asia." The small percentage of Canadian trade which flows across the Pacific, and the great distances that in the pre-aeroplane age separated Canada from the Far East led to a lack of interest in the developments in that region only partially modified by missionary and educational activities, and the presence of a considerable Oriental population in the province of British Co'umbia. Consequently it is as a North Pacific Power that Canada is still inclined to view Pacific problems. That leads her to work most closely with the United States in a joint approach to the prob'ems of strategy created by the position and po'icy of the U.S.S.R. It will be only occasionally that Canadians will look over their shoulders at the major Pacific problems emerging in the Far East and

Southeast Asia which are of such concern to six other Commonwealth states.

Like Canada Australia regards herself as a Midd'e Power, or as her former Minister of External Affairs, Dr. Evatt, has sometimes put it a "Security power." In spite of her great distance from Europe political, racial, and economic ties make it impossible for Australia to "contract out of Europe," as her government has publicly declared. But geography has made it equally impossible for Australia to contract out of Asia, a fact of great importance in view of the momentous changes now taking place in Southeast Asia. Faced by these conditions and mindful of the lessons of the second world war when Britain found her strength over-extended and was obliged to limit her aid to Australia against Japan, the Labour Government evolved a vigorous and independent foreign policy for the first time in Australia's history. This policy was not entirely the result of external factors but also reflects the preconceptions of the Australian Labour party before it assumed office and the greater authority which the federal government became accustomed to exercising in the war period.

With Dr. Evatt, a man of "vigorous and ambitious character", as Minister of External Affairs, the Labour government pursued an energetic policy which the Australian paper compared to Bismarck's in its complexity. The government, comments the paper:

is trying to juggle three, perhaps four, balls; cultivating Commonwealth ties and seeking to maintain the Commonwealth as one system of mutual advantage and security; seeking to build up the authority of the United Nations Organisation and proclaiming its views within U.N.O. as an independent sovereign state; more sketchily and tentatively, as a Pacific people trying to promote friendly relations and common interests with other Pacific peoples and peoples of South East Asia; and finally the establishing of close relations with the United States as the major Pacific power.

Such a policy did not prove completely successful, as the paper readily admits, and drew sharp criticism from the Opposition parties on the ground that it was overambitious,

. . . that these four balls cannot be kept in the air at once, and that Australia's interest requires that, whether the others fall or not, we should keep our eyes fixed on the first.

In particular the Opposition objected to "the unnecessary assertion of Australia's independence of Great Britain" and criticized Dr. Evatt, in Mr. Menzies' words, for having failed to realise

that whilst a new world charter may have a value that is as yet untried, our relationship with the British Empire has a value which has been proved in times of very great trial in every generation.

In developing this independent foreign policy the Labour government, while asserting its right to views of its own on European questions, as during the Paris Conference on the lesser peace treaties in 1946, did not differ with the United Kingdom on the main lines of policy. There is, says the Australian paper,

. . no reason to believe that development by Australia of an independent view regarding questions of European settlement has affected collaboration with Britain and within the Commonwealth, since the matters on which Britain and Australia have differed are of little weight in comparison with the interests they have in common.

In the Pacific the situation was slightly different. The Australian government firmly believed that:

. . . in the region to the north and east of the Australian mainland it must have a leading role, and that in the affairs of this area its voice must carry a weight second to none.

Consequently there was much less willingness to accept United Kingdom policies in this area as a matter of course and a far greater willingness than in the past to consider the views of the peoples in this region. Speaking of Southeast Asia in February, 1947, Dr. Evatt declared that:

just as far as the peoples of South East Asia cease to be dependent upon the decisions of European governments, so far does Australia's interest in the countries of South East Asia increase. We must work for a harmonious association of democratic states in the South East Asian area and see in the development of their political maturity opportunity for greatly increased political, cultural and commercial co-operation.

In keeping with this policy the government showed marked sympathy with nationalist and independence movements—at the cost of strained relations with the Dutch over Indonesia. It readily accepted an invitation to attend the New Delhi Conference on Indonesia early in 1949. It was greatly interested in any projects for furthering industrialization and easing the pressure of population on food resources in this region. Critics of the government's policy argued that there were dangerous possibilities arising from this championship of Asian nationalisms and warned, as the delegation papers put it, that,

. . . we are like the sorcerer's apprentice encouraging the growth of forces which we will not be able to control, and which may themselves develop as a grave threat to White Australia and to her cherished Australian interests.

Although Australia is convinced that one of the best means of furthering security in the Pacific is to further economic welfare and friendly relations among the Asian countries in that region, a policy which is described as "attempting to build a bridge between the European colonial powers and the nationalists of South East Asia," she has not concentrated upon such a policy to the exclusion of other methods. The recollections of Japanese aggression are much too vivid for that to be possible. The Chifley government believed that Australia in association with New Zealand must assume a considerable degree of initiative in helping to hammer out for this region a coherent Commonwealth security policy which took into account the reduced strength of the United Kingdom in that area and the vastly increased importance of the United States. As a result Australia played a vigorous part in the occupation of Japan and in acting as the British Commonwealth spokesman in the Allied Council in Tokyo. She repeatedly made clear her conviction that the peace treaty with Japan must be framed by the combined action of all countries vitally interested in the Pacific and not simply by the Great Powers. She also furthered regional Commonwealth co-operation in support of such a policy by her Anzac agreement with New Zealand in 1944. To date such policies have achieved only a limited success. Because of differences among the Great Powers they have not secured a peace treaty with

Japan. Nor have they influenced, as Australia would have wished, American policy in Japan. As the Australian paper admits:

One of the main sources of uneasiness in Australia is lest Japan, as a result of American-Russian antagonism, should achieve a position which makes it a threat to Australia.

The Opposition criticized the Chifley government for claiming too great a role in the Pacific and for running the risk of squandering American and British goodwill by over-assertiveness in statements on such questions as the disposition of Japanese territories and the control of wartime bases. There was also in Australia some concern at the current inclination of the United States "to contract her spheres of interest and to limit her commitments in the Pacific." As a consequence there have been proposals that the time was at hand for a Pacific Pact, a counterpart of the North Atlantic Pact, which might be in line with the proposals for a similar agreement that the Australian Prime Minister presented to the Imperial Conference of 1937. But these suggestions are still rather nebulous. The majority opinion recognizes the necessity for maintaining close co-operation with the United States. As the study groups in the Victoria and New South Wales branches, which presented a report on "Strategic Problems", summarize it:

In the absence of an effective international security system Australia's long and short term interests in the Western Pacific would appear to be in general support for American policies in this area.

Professor Wood's "Report From New Zealand" demonstrates that his country, like Australia, recognises that "as a Pacific country, she is in a new sense within the American political sphere." Realization of its changed position does not mean for New Zealand, any more than for its neighbour, a passive uncritical acceptance of American leadership. There is, the author reports, "a current of uneasiness about American 'imperialism'." He detects a "friendly scepticism" about General MacArthur's claims for the strength of Japanese democracy and grave doubts whether a re-armed Japan "as a military bastion against Communism" could be trusted to remain democratic in its attitude towards small powers. Like other Commonwealth countries, New Zealand "would shrink from accepting the inevitability of a headlong clash between American and Russian power." She would like to see on European questions a group emerging, organized in some such fashion as Western Union, to hold the balance between the two super-powers.

Some of the author's comments about New Zealand's attitude as a Pacific power have a familiar ring for Canadians. Although New Zealand is far more concerned with the Pacific than she was a decade ago, with the result that there is "a new note of reality in her approach," there is not yet a coherent vigorous policy. The truth is, the author explains, that for New Zealanders, "their knowledge and political experience are still primarily of Europe." Their concern with the Pacific is aptly described as "relatively speaking, a matter of intellectual calculation; [lacking] warmth and continuity." But participation in the occupation of Japan, from which New Zealand forces were recently withdrawn, membership in the South Pacific Commission, Trade Union interest in the Indonesian conflict have left their mark. They are cited to illustrate the assertion that:

More and more New Zealanders talk and write as if events in Asia were of serious concern to them and matters on which their country should have a policy.

What New Zealand carried over into the field of Pacific policies is her belief "in the value for peace of economic amelioration and liberal-minded social democracy" and a preference for

collective security, safeguarded by a strong, democratically managed international institution, which besides being an effective policeman would sponsor social progress in all its forms.

Because of these convictions, which were repeatedly voiced in the thirties at Geneva, New Zealand has displayed in the United Nations a frank dislike of Great Power dominance—particularly as exhibited in the use of veto—an interest in native welfare— which has led to New Zealanders serving more than once as Chairmen of the Committee of the General Assembly on Trusteeship questions—and a readiness to co-operate in freeing international trade from the hampering restrictions of wartime policies.

On European questions New Zealand's foreign policy also remains much as it was in the thirties, firm in rejection of appeasement as a policy. This dislike of surrendering to threats, whether the source be Germany or Russia, prompted the government to offer the help of the New Zealand air crew in the Berlin Air Lift. At the same time in the deadlock over Berlin, the New Zealand government also displayed "a vehement feeling that common sense could surely build a bridge." On such problems as Western Union and military commitments, Mr. Wood speculates that the New Zealand attitude would probably be "friendly, slightly apprehensive, but realistic." As a small country, "with a strong parochial pull," and isolated from the centres of power, New Zealand realises that she can do little in peacetime but lay emphasis on what she believes to be the right principles. This has been criticised as a policy of peace by exhortation, but, as the author pertinently comments, "it is ideologies rather than material weapons that seem to have got out of hand today."

The South African delegation did not present a paper on foreign policy, which is possible evidence of their country's sense of security from external aggression at the present time. It did present a lucid analysis of the debates in the United Nations affecting South Africa. In New York and Paris, the country has been at times alone in resistance to interference by the General Assembly with what South Africa regards as matters of domestic concern. It is their contention that according to the Charter, the UN has nothing to do with such questions since that document ". . . specifically excluded the right to intervene between a government and its subjects." In a paper on "The Position of South Africa in the Strategy of the Commonwealth and of the World" there are some brief references to foreign policy. The three authors argue that, in addition to "hearty co-operation on defence matters with the Commonwealth and/or the United States," their country is likely to negotiate with "the other great African powers," Portugal, Spain, Belgium and France, in an effort to secure understandings or alliances. The purpose of such arrangements would be, from South Africa's point of view, to see to it that "come what may her boundaries to the north will be secure." It is suggested that such friendships might better be secured "comprehensively" through Western Union, a solution which the authors regard with great favour. On this somewhat cryptic observation the paper does not enlarge.

The foreign policy of India, as described in the delegation paper, reflects her geographical position and the imprint of her struggle for complete freedom. Geographically, as Pandit Nehru has said, "she is so situated as to be the meeting point of Western and Northern and Eastern and South-Eastern Asia." Because of this fact, the author of the paper on "Indo-American Political Relations" describes his country as "The Pivot of Asia" and quotes the Indian Prime Minister in support of that claim. This key position should not be taken to mean that India will assert leadership in Asian affairs as a matter of right. In fact Pandit Nehru has said that he disliked "this business of leadership." Yet the fact remains that from the compelling logic of her geographic position to which should be added her size, her resources, and her population, India cannot help being vitally concerned with what happens in the Middle East or Southeast Asia. In the present state of world politics, with two power blocs seeking for support in all quarters of the earth, the position of India is of peculiar importance. Suspicion of Western imperialism and dislike of Soviet Communism, together with the fact of so recent an attainment of freedom, have combined to make the government insistent that India will not link herself with either bloc but must follow an independent policy based upon democratic principles and in no way tinged with isolationism. On this attitude Prime Minister Nehru has made his position clear time and again. As recently as March 8, 1949, he told the Constituent Assembly:

We have kept apart from joining rival blocs. Our policy is to be friendly to all countries and not to become entangled in any alliance which might drag us to possible consequences. . . . We very strictly follow the policy of not getting entangled in any kind of commitment, certainly not military, and any other kind of commitment with any other power or group of powers, and we propose to adhere to that policy because we are quite convinced that it is the only possible policy at present and in future as well. This does not involve any lack of close relationship with any other country.

With this attitude at the heart of her foreign policy India has refused to consider any possibility of the Commonwealth becoming a bloc in foreign policy. In the UN she has voted with the Soviet Union on some occasions, with the Western powers on others, or has differed with both groups, as in the case of Palestine. Thus the leader of the Indian delegation told the General Assembly of 1947 in her opening address:

We shall offer our support to, or withold it from, the proposals that come before us solely in the light of our judgement on the merits of the case in question.

In this independent policy India lays considerable emphasis upon loyalty to the principles of the United Nations. Such a loyalty must have precedence over allegiance to the Commonwealth. Similarly, Prime Minister Nehru has been careful to explain that regional conferences of Asian states, such as met in New Delhi to discuss the position of Indonesia, were in no way designed to weaken the authority of the United Nations. At the New Delhi conference of January, 1949, the Indian Prime Minister pointed out the Charter of the UN recognised regional arrangements, and added:

We propose to function entirely in terms of the Charter and in order to help the United Nations to see that peace is established and justice done.

Although bloc action by Asian countries in the UN or elsewhere is deprecated, the Government of India feels that Asian countries should receive adequate representation in UN meetings and in all those of the specialised agencies associated with it.

This emphasis upon the rights of Asia is in accordance with the first ideological objective of foreign policy enumerated in the Indian delegation paper, "The Recognition of the Continent of Asia and the Need for its Re-emergence." The long years of European expansion at the expense of other continents have ended. The countries of Asia, declares Nehru ". . . can no longer be used as pawns by others; they are bound to have their own policies in world affairs." Those Asian states which are already free should give their sympathy and whatever form of assistance is possible to complete the end of colonialism in

Asia. Again to quote Nehru's words from a speech delivered in December, 1948. "Our foreign policy is that no foreign power should rule over any Asian country." In keeping with this view Indian soldiers were withdrawn from Indonesia after India's independence had been conceded by the United Kingdom, and she took the initiative in calling a conference on Indonesia at New Delhi after the Dutch had broken the truce of 1947. India feels that this phase of her foreign policy has not received the sympathy it deserves in the United States and elsewhere in the West. This is a disappointment to her and reveals, in her view, a short-sighted attitude on the part of the West. Since "colonialism is one of the breeding grounds of Communism," it is clearly in the interests of the West to support the demand of Asian peoples for freedom. In aiding and encouraging them India feels that she is only acting in the same spirit as prompted the United States to help secure the freedom of the Spanish and Portugese colonies in the Western hemisphere. Also in conformity with this attack on colonialism is the desire of India to incorporate in her territory the small enclaves of Goa and Pondicherry belonging to Portugal and France respectively. "The new resurgent India would not willingly accept that bits of territory should belong to countries far away," Pandit Nehru warned the powers concerned; yet he made it clear that termination of sovereignty in these areas would be sought by peaceful means. A third aspect of India's anti-colonial policy is the keen desire for the disappearance throughout the world of racial discrimination and any policy based upon it. Acting on this principle India has brought to the attention of the UN the racial discrimination practised by South Africa at the expense of Indians resident in South Africa. (A well-documented Indian delegation paper was submitted on this subject.) Where discrimination may be on other than racial lines, India will be equally desirous to see that the legitimate interests of Indians abroad are protected in such countries as Burma, Ceylon and Malaya. Pride in the past of Asia and belief in its re-emergence as an important factor in the contemporary world do not prevent India from admitting the economic backwardness of the Asian peoples. On the contrary, it is the Indian contention that the aid which is being granted for the economic recovery of Western Europe "should be extended to the countries of Asia also." To extend such aid, as Nehru told the third session of the Economic Commission for Asia and the Far East, would not be simply a question of western powers doing so out of the generosity of their hearts, praiseworthy as such an action might be. It would also be on their part an act of "enlightened self-interest," based upon the realisation that the sovereignty of one part of the world has an adverse effect upon the economy of the rest. There too India feels that the United States "is not very enthusiastic and liberal" but takes comfort from the remarks of President Truman in his inaugural address in January, 1949, upon the need for a bold new programme for "making the benefits of our scientific advances and industrial progress available for the growth and improvement of under-developed areas." She is also aware of the fact that Secretary of State Acheson named India as one of the countries to which this aid might be applicable. Although the delegation paper is frank in admitting that the success of Indian democracy is "intimately bound up with American financial aid," it makes it clear that India will not accept aid on conditions which would result in foreign capital dominating her economic future. This declaration was supported by Pandit Nehru's statement: "We would rather delay our development, industrial or otherwise, than submit to any kind of economic domination by any foreign country." Later he told the Indian Parliament that foreign capital would be treated in precisely the same way as Indian capital, and would be permitted to earn profits "subject only to regulations common to all." Facilities would be provided for remitting profits abroad, and no restriction would be placed upon the withdrawal of investments. Although normally Indian capital and management would have the major interest and control in industrial enterprises, the Government would "not object to foreign capital having control of a concern for a limited period if it is found to be in the national interest." If a foreign enterprise is expropriated the state would give compensation "on a fair and equitable basis."

Although India still believes in "non-alignment with any power bloc," dislike of entangling alliances should not be interpreted as a proof that she is blind to the menace of Communism or indifferent to the gravity of the problems it raises. Prime

Minister Nehru is described in the delegation paper as regarding Communism as a "disruptive force" which has already challenged the success of nationalism in free countries like Burma, or retarded its progress in countries like Indonesia struggling to be free. He is much concerned with the implications of Communism winning control of China. A Communist victory there would be "a very heavy factor in future Asian problems" which might prove "of considerable psychological effect," especially in Southeastern Asia. The Prime Minister also believes that Communism threatens the security of Indian frontiers in both the north-east and north-west. The delegation paper recognises that there is a power vacuum in Eastern and Southeastern Asia which will have to be filled sooner or later, and that "the only Asian power that can fill this to-day is Soviet Russia." It likewise concedes that in the Middle East "India's interest lies in this region not falling completely into the hands of any power bloc which might upset the balance of Asia." The conclusion drawn from these facts does not seem as compelling as the facts themselves. It is that:

The maintenance therefore of a balance of power until the U.N.O. has the necessary resources becomes a matter of supreme interest both to India and to the United States which has so many commitments in the continent of Asia. But this ought to become the basis for friendship and co-operation between the two countries.

In discussing "Some External Interests of Pakistan" the delegation paper exhibits the same distrust and suspicion of Indian policy which have already been noted in describing Pakistan's attitude towards the Commonwealth. Thus the paper declares that all other external interests for the people of Pakistan are overshadowed by their constant and deep concern for the welfare of the thirty-five million Muslims of India. Any suggestion of Indian leadership in Southeast Asia is rejected as out of the question. As the writer of the paper bluntly puts it:

Those who imagine there is the remotest possibility of the people of Southern or South East Asia allowing India to be imposed as their "leader" have no first hand knowledge of the thought and feelings of those people.

From Pakistan's point of view, in this region India does not qualify for leadership, whose requirements are described as follows:

The country that seeks to lead, must at least be able to satisfy its neighbours that it has no designs against them and no expansionist ambition, that its internal and external policies are based upon tolerance and good neighbourliness and that at home it practises a form of democracy under which there is security, at least for the lives, liberties and cultures of vast majorities that are outside its traditional hierarchical systems.

Pakistan's interests in Southeast Asia are based upon geography, religion and trade. She has a common frontier with Burma which in turn is close to China and contiguous to Indo-China and Malaya. In the latter country there are a large number of Muslims, while to the South in the Indonesian islands almost all the people are of the Muslim faith. In this area there are not, in the view of the Pakistan paper, the prerequisites of stability and complete independence for all the peoples concerned to make possible a Southeast Asian regional organization at the present time. But if and when a Southeast Asian regional organization does come into being, Pakistan believes that she herself must be a full member of it.

The other region of particular interest to her is the Middle East. Here the links are "past associations, cultural affinities and physical contiguity." It is the aim of Pakistan's policy to further the closest co-operation among the various Arab nations of the Middle East which have so much in common. Because of that fact and in recognition of her sympathies with them the Arab states allowed Pakistan

to take the lead in the fight in the United Nations against the tortuous diplomacy of the Western powers whose aim was to create the state of Israel and to re-establish foreign imperialist rule in the ex-Italian colonies.

The subsequent emergence of the state of Israel, under the aegis of the United Nations and through "a series of transactions in which the United States played a prominent part," is described as having had an adverse effect upon the attitude of the Muslim peoples towards the West.

Because of the manner in which this Palestine problem, the future of the Italian colonies and the Hyderabad and Kashmir questions have been handled by the United Nations, it is the verdict of the delegation paper that ". . . Pakistan has suffered a series of disappointments in the United Nations." Nevertheless it states that Pakistan will continue to give full support to the United Nations "as the only hope of mankind."

In some respects India and Pakistan share a common approach towards the problem of Communism. They both believe that Communism thrives on frustrated national aspirations and depressed living conditions. They agree that the West has not been prompt enough in furthering the grant of self-government to Indonesia and Indo-China. They are prepared to see Western capital given "equitable profits" if the peoples of Asia are provided with the necessary capital and technical skill to raise their standards of living. Pakistan further believes that oppression of minority groups likewise helps to breed Communism. The delegation paper states that there is "a distinct likelihood" that the Muslim minority of India is in this plight, in which desperation may drive them into the Communist ranks. Pakistan is also more keenly aware of the immediate danger since she is in the uncomfortable position of being nearer to Russia than any other Commonwealth country, separated as she is from it by only "a narrow and negligible tongue of Afghan territory." The delegation paper is frank to admit that "Pakistan would be an easy prey if Russia chose to invade her," and adds the salutary reminder that the defence of Pakistan is important for the safety of India and the maintenance of Commonwealth communications. Against that danger is to be placed the view of the author of the paper that a war between the two power blocs is neither imminent nor inevitable and that ". . . Russia neither would nor could fight."

2
Strategy and Economic Problems

In the delegation papers that dealt directly or indirectly with strategic problems three main assumptions can be detected. These are that Soviet Russia is the greatest potential threat to the security of most Commonwealth states, that it is not possible to have centralized control of strategy, and that co-operation with the United States in concerting defence is imperative. On the first point Sir Ian Jacob frankly assumes in the paper on "The United Kingdom's Strategic Interests" that:

. . . the danger from Russia may develop either through Western Europe or southward towards India, or, if science can solve the long range rocket problem, across the Pole towards Canada. The spread of Communism, inspired by Russia, may cause in Asia a movement of races southward towards the open spaces of Australia. The Commonwealth must be prepared for action in several directions, and all its members, like the United Kingdom, must be prepared to fight for their lives. Russian aggression will be a mortal danger to all of them.

The Australian paper says equally definitely that "the only major military conflict possible in say the next twenty-five years would appear to be between Russia and the West." In commenting on the general acceptance in Canada of the North Atlantic Pact, the Canadian paper remarks that:

Only a sense of profound uneasiness arising from Soviet political strategy since the war has induced us, a people more addicted to opulence than defence, to go as far as we have done and enter an alliance.

Although the author of the Pakistan paper insists that the danger to Pakistan from India is "real, likely and immediate" and constitutes the country's major problem of defence, he agrees with the assumption that Soviet Russia is a potential enemy, a suggestion which he believes to underlie all plans, official or unofficial, for the defence of the Commonwealth.

In examining the nature of co-operation for defence, Sir Ian Jacob points out that although the United Kingdom is the most experienced, most heavily industrialized, and most powerful of the Commonwealth states, she needs the close support of other Commonwealth members as sources of manpower and supply and as essential terminals of lines of communications. On the other hand, she believes that it would be "inconceivable" for the United Kingdom to remain neutral if any Dominion were attacked by an external enemy. For effective reciprocal aid in time of war, preliminary planning and co-ordination are necessary in peacetime. But this should not be taken to mean that the United Kingdom advocates "a central organization in London or anywhere else that would direct or co-ordinate the defensive preparations and plans of the whole Commonwealth." What are required are bilateral discussions between the United Kingdom and each of the Dominions separately. From the United Kingdom point of view:

The whole conception, however, is one of enabling sovereign countries with a common allegiance and background to solve those problems which they have in common without being committed to the consideration of problems that they do not feel to be theirs and without any kind of regimentation or control.

Such a concept is in contrast to the older theory of "a mother gathering her children together in the ancestral home and laying down action for all of them," the conception which was represented in pre-war days by the Committee of Imperial Defence. Experience with joint staffs for specific purposes that proved so successful in the second world war has helped to further the development of plans for "co-operating organisms" in London and Ottawa or London and Canberra. For the South Pacific it is suggested Canberra might serve as a centre for planning by the United Kingdom, Australia and New Zealand. Later "another zonal organisation," based probably on Delhi, might deal with Commonwealth defence in the Indian Ocean. For additional practical reasons the Australian paper on "Strategic Problems" also supports decentralization of defence responsibility. It believes that this policy will be necessary for industrial reasons in view of the likelihood that in the event of war the United Kingdom, "the hard core of Empire defence," will suffer heavy initial damage to its industrial output. The paper recognises that, under such a policy of decentralization, Australia will have to assume greater responsibilities for security in the Pacific. It accepts this necessity and suggests that in such circumstances "Australia may be regarded as an aircraft platform, a shipping centre or as a source of undeveloped power." The Australians also believe that South Africa must be a pivotal area in any decentralized scheme because of her possession of the Simonstown naval base. But they are a little uneasy as to whether close military collaboration can be developed with South Africa because of the political uncertainty there and the technical reorganisation of her army along American rather than British lines. An interesting contrast is afforded by the three authors of the paper on South Africa's strategy who argue that South Africa has to "wait on the orientation of Australia's thought." They believe the latter should be considering linking up with Asia since alliances there would offer "infinitely more splendid prospects" for Australia than might be gained by rallying to "the upholders of white South Africa." They point out too that many South Africans firmly believe that

the Union is strong enough in isolation to prevent invasion, or to eject or destroy invaders or to withstand siege by invaders; and that, in vast empty spaces, there are refuges from bombs, guided missiles and what not else; including gas and bacteriological weapons.

Because of this widespread feeling and the old distrust of being committed to "Empire Defence," the paper warns that if the Commonwealth countries want South Africa's aid they must accept it "in accordance with South Africa's ideas, prejudices, hopes and fears."

The time has gone by when the Union could be lectured on its duty to the Commonwealth as if a particularly strong willed and stiffnecked people inhabited a colony that had no duty to itself but a duty only to an imperial master.

The Canadian paper makes no direct comment on the pros and cons of centralized defence but, in describing the provisions for joint defence concerted with the United States, the paper remarks that "co-operation with both the United States and the United Kingdom follows from our geography." It also quotes the statement of the Minister of National Defence on the role of Canada's armed forces in June, 1948, which he summarized as follows:

What we want are forces which can defend Canada and enable such part as Parliament and the People may support in any efforts at common defence with other countries.

The Canadian belief that defence collaboration is necessary with the United States for the protection of Canada's interests in the North Pacific, the North Atlantic and on this continent finds parallels elsewhere in the Commonwealth. In describing the need for "well-developed machinery for consultation in defence matters and plans for collaboration prepared in peacetime" with each Dominion the United Kingdom paper inserts the significant clause "as indeed with the United States." South Africa talks of defence policy in hearty co-operation with "the Commonwealth and/or the United States." Pakistan notes ". . . the tendency of the Dominions to re-insure themselves in the United States," and believes that preventing Soviet Russia from penetrating the Middle East is "a high American interest." Australia agrees that the Commonwealth is less qualified to function as an effective security organisation than in the past and admits that "the South Pacific cannot be defended on a purely Commonwealth basis." She draws the logical inference that:

Collaboration with the British Commonwealth must be accompanied by the closest liaison with America who will be for the next twenty years the most powerful of the Pacific nations.

The paper argues that Australia's general role "may be akin to that of Canada, of endeavouring to build a bridge between the United States and the Commonwealth, in this case in the Pacific and the Middle East." New Zealand thinking is on similar lines in suggesting that in the Pacific, the relative power of the United Kingdom and of Western Europe is far less and that consequently "the dualism of the United States and Russia is even sharper." Professor Wood writes that his countrymen have good reason for believing from their recent experience that

". . . if it comes to the point the United States has the last word in the Pacific."

It is interesting to note the variations in national attitudes to the problems of regional defence which the different delegation papers display. The United Kingdom paper begins with the assumption that a "conventional all-out war" must always be guarded against and that in such a conflict the mortal danger, as in the past, would spring from Europe. The new element in the situation is the absence of any continental power which can hope to stand up to Soviet Russia and remain in being so as to provide "the base of resistance and the stone of attrition." Russia herself has twice played that part in 1812 and 1941-42, while France offered such a base in the first world war. In the absence of such a country and in view of the manner in which the weapons of war have been "fearfully improved", Sir Ian Jacob gloomily remarks that:

We are bound to conclude that if Russia could in the next few years overrun rapidly Western Europe the sequel might be disastrous for this country.

That is the reason for attempting to establish a Western European coalition which might prevent Russia by force, if necessary, from controlling all Europe and gaining the Atlantic seaboard. Here too, however, the diagnosis is pessimistic since Sir Ian agrees that for at least several years to come

. . . the nations now composing or likely to compose Western Union cannot stand on their own as a balance-weight to Russia, or prevent the occupation of Western Europe.

Although the North Atlantic Treaty gives Western Union "an immense addition of strength" which would prove decisive in the long run, it is still not safe to assume that the combined forces it could invoke could, at the outset, hold a line down the centre of Europe. The probabilities are that they would be forced to retire to the Alps, the Pyrenees and the English Channel and hold on there until a counter-offensive could be mobilised. Such a development, which would give Russia a chance to create a Fortress Europe by gaining support from the occupied countries in a fashion Hitler never equalled, and which might expose the

United Kingdom to such a pounding as might destroy her use-fulness as a base for counter attack, would create a grim situa-tion. The way out appears to be either a world-wide coalition that would deter Russia on every front—a difficult achievement that, even if successful, might drive Russia to desperation—or a particular deterrent in Europe, linked with anti-Communist groups of states in other areas. If such a deterrent is to be achieved it is frankly recognized that:

We must gather Germany into Western Europe, identify her interests entirely with those of the Western European powers, in-tegrate her military potential with our own, and thus build an almost unassailable strength just where it is most necessary.

In United Kingdom strategy the Middle East still exerts a powerful influence. Although it is not quite as important for sea and air communications to Australia, India and the Far East as in the past, it does constitute a barrier to Russia's entering the Indian Ocean, contains substantial oil deposits on which the United Kingdom is "heavily dependent" and is linked up with Africa which is "beginning to emerge as one of the great strategic factors of the modern age." The Middle East also offers one of the few areas where, if war broke out, bases for offensive operations against the Soviet Union would be most useful. In the past the United Kingdom through its Suez bases was able to ensure the Middle Eastern states a stability which they could not provide for themselves. Today their weakness has been heightened by the Palestine dispute. They need to be revitalized, so that they will not fall victims to peaceful Soviet penetration, and to be encouraged to settle quickly their diffi-culties over Palestine so that a regional security agreement may be established that will be a counterpart to the North Atlantic Treaty. To be effective such a system must ensure full support for Turkey, and be underwritten by the presence of enough American and Commonwealth troops "to back up the combined strength of the Middle East states and to put up a strong offensive and defensive deterrent to any forward move by Russia." These forces would require bases, both administrative and operational, which could only be secured with the willing co-operation of the Arab states and by "a strategically sound disposition of the ex-Italian colonies."

Beyond the Middle East the United Kingdom begins to contract its military responsibilities. Although desirous of ensuring a tranquil Indian Ocean which, like the Middle East, requires for its stability a strong regional arrangement, General Jacob does not suggest anything more than a willingness on the part of the United Kingdom to "play its part in this." In the Pacific he warns that the United Kingdom must be careful "not to attempt to play a part there which is beyond its powers." Accordingly the limits recommended for her active participation should be the Southwest Pacific and the Southeast Asian areas.

Finally his paper attempts to assess the nature of the military contribution which the United Kingdom can make. It is here that the economic factor becomes of great importance. The reduction of her overseas wealth and the increased demands upon industry to provide the immensely complicated weapons for war point to the conclusion that "unless a fresh and larger system of lend-lease is instituted, the war potential of the United Kingdom would be gravely weakened." If planning on a thorough scale is not developed in peacetime with her associates, the United Kingdom will not be able to exercise as great a war power as in the past. Whether the British Isles can constitute as useful a base for counter-attack and invasion of Europe as in 1944 is also doubtful. For another war the parallel of Malta's experience in 1939-45 is regarded as the most apt. That island endured the worst furies of the enemy's attack to remain a thorn in the enemy's side and to play its proper part in the offensive against the Continent.

With this realistic assessment of the possible role of the British Isles in wartime the Australian paper is entirely in agreement. It believes that the new weapons have made the United Kingdom "peculiarly vulnerable" to attack and that in the event of a European war Britain may well "become initially a beseiged fortress, incapable of acting as a Commonwealth arsenal." It also accepts as inevitable "a steady contraction of British forces outside the European and Mediterranean zones" which, in its opinion, may continue until the range of United Kingdom power is confined to Western Europe and North Africa. Under these conditions the Australian paper examines the problem of protecting the sea and air approaches to the continent. Since Australia is a two-ocean country her "primary strategic interests" must lie in both the Indian Ocean and the Pacific Ocean. In the former the withdrawal of Britain from India and Burma "has removed the shield of British protection from the northern top of the Indian Ocean." For that reason Australia is directly and vitally interested in the close collaboration of India, Pakistan and Ceylon for the defence of this area. The position of Ceylon is clear because of its military arrangements with the United Kingdom. But Ceylon, though an important base, depends for its security upon close collaboration or at least "a very benevolent neutrality" on the part of India and Pakistan. These facts explain Australia's eager desire to see an end to the persistent friction between India and Pakistan and for their continued partnership in the Commonwealth.

The Australian diagnosis of the Middle East as "a major sensitive area for the Commonwealth as a whole" is almost identical with the United Kingdom's but places rather more in the foreground the increasing interest of both the United States and Russia in the oil resources of that region. The Australian formula for remedying the political and social weaknesses of the states there is ". . . to foster some form of Arab unity, to locate and foster stable leadership within the Arab league, and to try and ease internal social tensions." To do so the Commonwealth countries will be obliged to formulate "progressive diplomatic policies" with all the Middle Eastern states including Israel. If war should come, Russia would probably strike quickly there in an effort to drive through to the Persian Gulf so as to immobilize oil production and protect her own oil areas. Under such conditions Australia's role is described as being one "of collaboration with India and Pakistan to recover control." This collaboration might take the form of "a small expeditionary force" operating under a general Commonwealth plan for defensive or offensive operations in the Middle East. While recognising the increasing importance of the United States in the Middle East, the paper argues that Australia should "aim at strengthening the British rather than the American position."

In the Pacific area Australia has to contend with three problems. There is the fact that the predominant interests of the United States, the U.S.S.R., the United Kingdom, France and the Netherlands are elsewhere. With the emergence of a Communist China which could exert "a disrupting influence" on Southeast Asia there must be examined the ". . . vital strategic problem as to whether western sea-based air power could successfully challenge a land-based Chinese air power." The appearance of the Soviet Union as the major Asian land power may also create new difficulties. Other significant strategic factors are the scanty number of centres of military power in the Pacific possessing considerable industrial power, the predominant position of the United States which is partly offset by her greater interest in other regions, and the post-war position of Japan which, in the tension between the United States and the U.S.S.R. has become regarded more and more as "a strategic area in a possible American-Russian conflict." Since the entry of Japan into the Russian orbit would place Australia in the same critical position as she experienced in 1941-2, it is believed to be in Australia's interest to give "general support" for American policies in the Pacific.

A further complication for Australia in formulating her Pacific strategy is the rapid growth of Asian nationalism in Southeast Asia. This development is necessarily paralleled by a corresponding decline of Western European power, and by the spread of Communist influence in this region. Because of her dependence upon this region for strategic materials such as oil, rubber and tin, Australia realises she will have to collaborate closely for the defence of the various friendly states between New Guinea and Malaya and will seek to develop friendly relations with the new nationalist regimes, especially in Indonesia. In other words the security problem in the Pacific is for Australia "partly a politico-economic one, partly a military one." It is not easy for "a white outpost in a predominantly Asiatic area," "a small middle power with limited resources and geographically isolated, relatively immune from immediate attack" to evolve a sound policy but Australia is not blind to the dangers and to her responsibilities. She realises that she must do what she can not only to establish friendly relations with the Asian states but to ease social tensions in order to prevent the spread of Communism.

The Australian paper recognises that it will be necessary for Australia to plan her strategy with the United States and the United Kingdom since ". . . the real danger lies in Europe or possibly North America and only much later in South East Asia." In conjunction with them she must plan her maximum contribution "in the form of a balanced expeditionary force to a major theatre of operations." She must be prepared to make available "a minimum security force in South East Asia and the Pacific," to play her part in protecting by sea and air vital communications in the Pacific and Indian Oceans, and so expand her economy as to be in a position to produce more munitions, ships and aircraft. Because of her large unoccupied central area, Australia could be converted into a technological base for developing atomic weapons. Finally, in furthering the closest liaison with the United States, it will be to Australia's interest to support the standardization of basic weapons between the United States and the Commonwealth as a whole.

Like Australia, South Africa is vitally interested in the security of her immediate sea communications. Only by them can she receive the cereals necessary to feed her population, and supplies of such strategic commodities as oil. For that reason South Africa must combine with the United Kingdom to keep the seas open and safe, a fact recognised in making facilities available for the Royal Navy at the South African base of Simonstown. In the Indian Ocean the delegation paper argues that South Africa must reckon with the attitudes of India, with whom an alliance is "manifest destiny," and of Australia, Arabia and Pakistan. In the last three countries "clarifications of thought and sentiment" are necessary. But the authors point out that in the north the Union could be outflanked by an invasion of Mozambique on the east coast or of Angola on the west. Such an attack, they believe, would probably be followed by the construction from either side of a road across the continent. This possibility underlines the importance of co-operation with Portugal whch holds "great keys to the safety of Africa," the need for an adequate air force to guard the northern frontier, and for a substantial army. Faced by these needs the paper argues that South Africa must attempt "a realistic comprehension of what is called the Native problem." The writers admit that at present there seems to be little hope that a majority of the white people will "come to see the patent stupidity of ignoring the Bantu in the defence of the Union." They point out that to forbid the natives the use of arms is not only depriving the Union of a large reservoir of manpower, but leaves them "with the easy alternative of assisting the enemy and with the hard alternative of forcing their aid upon us." The delegation paper believes that "rabid seventeenth century Calvinism" is another unusual domestic factor which complicates strategy. Calvinism of that type is an element in South African nationalism and repugnant to Catholic countries like Belgium and Portugal.

Neither of the delegations from India and Pakistan presented a paper specifically devoted to strategy. In their observations on foreign policy and Commonwealth relations the Indian authors point out, however, that their country's interest lies in preserving the balance of power in Asia, and express concern at the power vacuum created by war and post-war developments. They recognise that danger might come from the north west from an expanding Russia which under Czar or Commissar has been interested in "a thrust towards the Indian Ocean," or from the north east from China. A Communist China might repeat Kuomintang China's claims to parts of Burma and aid Communist movements in Southeast Asia. Hence the necessity for a strong Indian government to combat the rapid spread in Asia of Communism, which has already had its effects in such parts of India as West Bengal and Madras. As one writer comments, "The example of Burma appears to have served as a grave warning." Since Pakistan acts as a cover for the North West frontier it might have been thought that some comment on the value of developing friendly relations with her might have occurred. No such comment is made; in its stead is a sharply critical analysis of Pakistan's role in the Kashmir dispute. There are few references to India's attitude towards the Middle East. To offset control of that area by a power bloc India regards the preservation of the independence of Arab and other states as "of prime necessity." No details are given about India's armed forces but one writer bluntly says that:

Every realist recognises India's weakness in the matter of defence—

particularly sea and air defence—as well as the fact that it will take India considerable time to be able to manufacture heavy and mechanized defence equipment.

For that reason the paper lays stress on "the key position that Britain still occupies in the defence system of South-East Asia from Aden to Singapore with Ceylon in the middle and the reliance that is placed by countries of the Commonwealth on the British Navy." Reasons of defence as well as other considerations make the retention of membership in the Commonwealth of distinct value. One writer points out that, in view of the belief that Pakistan is likely to continue in the Commonwealth,

. . . if India were to decide to leave the Commonwealth it is likely to affect prejudicially her defence position and her relations with the countries of the North-West and of the South-East.

Like India, Pakistan feels keenly the lack of adequate defence equipment and recognises that the bulk of her munitions and war stores must come from abroad. In manpower she feels that she can rank with India in providing soldiers and sailors and possesses potential strength for the air force. In view of the fact that her two divisions, Western Pakistan and Eastern Pakistan, are barriers against penetration into the Indian subcontinent from Soviet Russia or from China by way of Burma respectively, the author of the paper on "Pakistan and the Commonwealth" argues that his country should have been considered as of equal importance with India in Commonwealth plans for mutual defence. He believes it has not been so considered, and the result has been that ". . . far more of war equipment relatively and absolutely is being supplied to India than Pakistan." He does not concede that war with Soviet Russia is either imminent or inevitable but admits that by herself Pakistan would be "an easy prey" to Soviet aggression.

But the need of strengthening Pakistan's defence both industrially and militarily is a matter of concern to others besides herself. Pakistan's strategic position makes it so as does the recognition by the Commonwealth that Russia must be checked, "not only from establishing herself in Western Europe but also from penetrating into the Middle East and Africa." It is likewise to the American interest that the Middle East and its communications be protected from Russia. These facts point, the paper argues, to the importance of a prompt settlement of the Kashmir dispute by "an early and impartial plebiscite." It is also suggested that a military guarantee of the Indo-Pakistan frontiers is in order so that there shall not be dissension and bitterness in "an area of vital strategic importance."

In discussing economic problems the delegation papers brought out very clearly the importance of the Commonwealth in international trade. After a careful analysis of the figures an Indian paper stated that "as a whole the Commonwealth countries are the most important suppliers of both raw materials and manufactured goods to the world." In 1938 they supplied more than 23 per cent of the total world exports and absorbed more than 28 per cent of the total imports. A decade later they accounted for almost 30 per cent of total world trade.[1] The figures submitted also demonstrate the continuing and increasing importance of the United Kingdom as market for the other Commonwealth countries. Of her imports, 48 per cent came from Commonwealth countries as against 29 per cent in 1939. For Australia, New Zealand, South Africa, India, Ceylon and the Republic of Ireland, the United Kingdom is the best customer accounting for over three-quarters of their exports in the case of New Zealand, South Africa and Ireland. For Canada and Pakistan, the United Kingdom is the second best customer, India naturally being the chief outlet for Pakistan and the United States having passed the United Kingdom for the position of Canada's best customer in 1939 and held it ever since the end of the war.[2] For the first group of countries, the United Kingdom is also the chief supplier, and again ranks in second place for Pakistan and Canada.

Although the United States has replaced Europe as the second-best outlet for Commonwealth produce, from the pulp and

[1] The Commonwealth Economic Committee's recent publication, *A Review of Commonwealth Trade* (London, 1949) gives an excellent analysis of economic developments between 1938 and 1948.

[2] In the first half of 1949 the United States took 49 per cent of Canada's exports as against the United Kingdom's 24 per cent. In the same period 72 per cent of Canada's imports came from the United States and only 12 per cent from the United Kingdom.

newsprint of Canada and the diamonds of South Africa to the wool of Australia and the jute of India, all Commonwealth countries are faced by the problem of lack of U.S. dollars. This has been true of Canada as well as of the sterling area. Thus Canada, after a surplus of American imports over exports to the United States of $488 millions in the first half of 1947, was obliged to impose strict limitations towards the end of that year which, combined with a considerable increase in exports, helped to narrow the gap for the first half of the next year to $228 millions. A marked increase of Canadian exports to the United States and off-shore purchases by the United Kingdom with Marshall Plan funds permitted some relaxation of import controls during 1949. During this period the dollar gap of the sterling bloc which, after narrowing in 1948, began to widen in the spring of the following year, led to the conference of Commonwealth Finance Ministers in July, 1949, and to the programme of further cuts in purchases from the United States. Then followed the Washington talks among the United States, the United Kingdom and Canada that opened just as the Bigwin Conference began.

The analyses offered in the different papers of the reasons for this increased dependence of the Commonwealth upon the United States as a source of supply describe the situation produced by the remarkable expansion in North America's productivity under the stimulus of war, and the almost complete disappearance from international trade of such countries as Germany and Japan. As the author of the United Kingdom paper, E. A. G. Robinson, remarks in commenting on the British problems of economic adjustment;

When the historians of a hundred years hence come to sum up the great changes of the twentieth century, their emphasis will probably be on the emergence of the Western Hemisphere as a great economic force as well as a great political power.

With the United States Canada felt the full effects of this economic expansion. Her increase in industrial production over pre-war levels was greater than that recorded for any other country. She became the third largest trading country in the world, and doubled her exports to the United Kingdom. The importance of Canadian supplies to the latter, particularly in foodstuffs and raw materials, led the writer of the United Kingdom paper to say that "the discovery of a solution of the problem of paying Canada was more important than any other single aspect of the United Kingdom's economic difficulties."

One of the problems which has harassed many of the Commonwealth countries has been the shift of the terms of trade to their disadvantage. In the depression years, when prices of primary products dropped so calamitously while those for manufactured goods dropped less acutely, the United Kingdom was in a relatively satisfactory position despite the depreciation in the value of the pound that occurred in 1931. But in the period after the war the continuance of high prices for foodstuffs and raw materials created a situation where the terms of trade turned against her about 20 per cent between 1938 and 1948. This situation was rendered still more difficult by the fall in money income through the decrease in overseas investments. As a result, if the United Kingdom had maintained the same volume of imports as in 1938, it would have required an estimated 30 per cent increase over the 1938 volume of exports to cover the reduced real purchasing power of British foreign investments and a further 30 per cent increase to cover the worsened terms at which British exports exchange for British imports. This dilemma prompts the following observation in the United Kingdom paper.

At present the emphasis of criticism outside the United Kingdom is naturally on the high price of British exports. But to a British observer the mounting prices of foodstuffs and materials and the progressively worsening terms of trade have been more evident.

Ireland has experienced similar difficulties, which have been complicated by a decrease in the volume of her exports. The cost of her imports trebled between 1938 and 1947 while the value of her exports rose only about 50 per cent. As a result the gap in her balance of payments in 1947 was about £30 millions. Since imports from the United States and Canada that year were more than £35 millions, and exports to those countries were less than £300,000, Ireland needed American aid to overcome her dollar shortage. Consequently she readily participated in the European Recovery Programme established by the Marshall Plan.[3] For South Africa the shift in the terms of trade which has caused her the most trouble was the rise of over 100 per cent in the cost of her imports and the lack of any considerable change in the price of gold (from 148s. per fine ounce in 1939 to 175s. in 1948). Since gold accounts for about 50 per cent of her exports the disparity was serious. In his "Report from New Zealand" Professor Wood notes that the difference in price levels remains "a major problem" and sums up the position by saying:

The economic framework within which New Zealand lives remains the same in general, but its practical working is less friendly to New Zealand's standards and freedom of action than at any time since the great depression.

The appreciation of the New Zealand pound to parity with the United Kingdom pound in 1948 was an attempt to meet the situation, but has proved to date only a partial remedy. Not all of the Commonwealth countries, however, have had the terms of trade work against them. Both India and Australia have benefited by conditions; in the latter's delegation paper, the writer reports that "the real terms of trade appear to have turned slightly in Australia's favour."

One of the sharpest contrasts in the relative positions of the different Commonwealth countries is afforded by the changes in their financial positions. The greatest sufferer has been the United Kingdom. Between 1939 and June 1945, under the inexorable demands of war, she found it necessary to liquidate about one-third of her pre-war overseas investments, which yielded about £1,100 millions. She incurred debts totalling about £2,900 millions and reduced her gold and dollar reserves by about £150 millions. Since that time she has borrowed $5 billions from the United States and Canada, which have been largely used up for essential purchases, and has also incurred some further debt under the Marshall Plan. Despite this assistance her dollar and gold reserves continued to decline and were below the danger point by the summer of 1949. Included

[3] Cf. "Working with Europe; Ireland's Part in European Co-Operation" (Dublin, 1949), a pamphlet produced by the Department of External Affairs.

in the wartime debts were the so-called sterling balances which were incurred for goods and services provided by a number of countries. In 1945 the United Kingdom estimated their total as follows:

DISTRIBUTION OF THE STERLING BALANCES, JUNE 30, 1945.

	£ millions
Dominions	384
India, Burma, Middle East	1732
Other Sterling Areas	607
	2723
North and South America	303
Europe	267
Rest of World	62
Total	3355

The problem of gradually reducing these balances, which had been partially blocked by mutual agreement, has led to a series of financial negotiations with the countries concerned. The allocation as a charge on the sterling balances of a considerable portion of United Kingdom exports has been described not very appropriately as unrequited exports.

For India the accumulation of her large balance during the war resulted in an increase in her sterling holdings valued in rupees from Rs. 70 crores in 1939 to Rs. 1,688 crores at the end of 1945. By May, 1949, the reserves had declined almost 50 per cent to Rs. 877 crores largely as a result of the liquidation of some British assets, acquisition of Defence Stores in India, purchases of supplies and other financial adjustments arising from the attainment of independence. India's sterling debt was liquidated through the repatriation of about £329 millions in the decade ending March, 1948.

Since Pakistan was a part of India until August, 1947, she also shared in the sterling balances released to India in 1947 of approximately £65 millions. In a subsequent separate agreement she was to receive £15 millions between July 1, 1948, and June 30, 1949, while the latest arrangement increased the amount to be released by £2 millions for the period ending June 30, 1950. Pakistan has also been able, by arrangement with India, to convert part of the favourable balances owed to her by that country into sterling.

South Africa did not accumulate as much sterling during the war from sales to the United Kingdom as did other sterling area countries. But she did experience a substantial influx of sterling capital after 1945 so that her holdings of sterling reached a peak of £83 millions in May, 1948. South Africa was able to make a short term gold loan of £80 millions to the United Kingdom which could be called before it came due in 1950. Necessarily delayed demands for goods during the war led to a sharp rise in imports afterwards so that the imports for 1948 were about three times the figures for 1945. As a result the adverse balance of payments steadily increased from £64 millions in 1946 to an estimated £160 millions in 1948. Gold reserves, which had reached a total of £110 millions in February, 1948, dropped to about £45 millions a year later and the government imposed exchange controls affecting purchases in the dollar area in November, 1948. Sterling balances also declined rapidly, partly from the volume of imports and especially from the sharp decline in the influx of capital after the elections in 1948. In the first two months of 1949 alone they dropped £19 millions and were as low as £10 millions by the spring of the year. It is these difficulties which have sharpened the demand in South Africa for an increase in the price of gold and compelled sharp restrictions in imports.

Australia's experience has been much less disconcerting and as the delegation paper demonstrates her external financial position is "considerably stronger than it was a decade ago." During the war the sterling balances accumulated to £118 millions. The continuance of high export prices has led to Australia's short term balances in London building up to almost £400 millions, over seven times the pre-war figures. Overseas indebtedness has been reduced about £73 millions in the past decade. This reduction has been chiefly in sterling debt, which declined to £397.6 millions in June, 1948. Dollar debt payable in New

York has decreased by less than £4 millions, standing at £40.7 millions in June, 1948. In addition to reducing her overseas debt Australia has been able to invest funds abroad. In 1943-44 for example with a surplus of £125 millions of exports over imports, she was able to lend £84 millions. As this surplus decreased in the post-war period her volume of lending also fell off, but was still estimated at £16 millions in 1947-48.

About New Zealand's experience there is less detailed information but sufficient is available to indicate that it has been not as spectacular as that of her sister nation. During the war her accumulation of sterling was a little more than half that of Australia. She is described as having paid off "a considerable amount of public debt owed in London" but still owes a substantial amount there. As Professor Wood points out:

Unlike Canada and India, New Zealand is still very much a debtor country, drawing most of her imports from her creditor and selling almost all of her exports in the same market.

He believes that New Zealand is becoming disturbed at this dangerous amount of dependence on a single country and would like to secure more varied markets.

All these changes in the mutual indebtedness of the United Kingdom and the other Sterling Area countries have had profound, and possibly permanent, effects upon the economic relations of the Commonwealth. The United Kingdom is still, in an important sense, the banker of the Sterling Area. But few of the Commonwealth countries are now in her debt. Her former power to enforce conformity with an economic policy has now largely disappeared. In its place, as far as the Sterling Area needs a co-ordinated economic policy, it must be evolved by consultation and agreement. And because they are large holders of sterling balances, the Sterling Area countries are conscious of their interest in the policies of the United Kingdom, so far as they affect the value of Sterling. There is thus emerging (as could be seen from the discussions at Bigwin) a new watchfulness over the operations of the banker.

Under the stimulus of war orders the Canadian economy grew rapidly between 1939 and 1945 and made possible the considerable role which Canada played in international finance in the immediate post-war period. During the war Canada had repatriated a substantial amount of Canadian securities held in the United Kingdom and had made available to that country an interest-free loan of $700 millions, and a gift of $1,000 millions in 1942. Between 1943 and 1945 Canada provided Mutual Aid amounting to $2,211 millions to the Allies, approximately 90 per cent of which went to Commonwealth countries. In the war period Canada also sold large amounts of raw materials, foodstuffs, and some types of munitions (totalling over $1,000 millions from 1942-45) to the United States under the Hyde Park Agreement of 1941. Such sales, when combined with the substantial inflow of American capital, totalling about $870 millions, and with substantial U.S. Government military expenditures in Canada, were the main factors increasing Canadian reserves of gold and U.S. dollars to over $1,500 millions by December 1945 as compared with about $400 millions at the end of 1939. As the war ended Canada established a programme of Export Credits for a number of her Allies, under which drawing rights to a total of over $500 millions had been approved by June, 1948. A special agreement was negotiated with the United Kingdom extending to that country in May, 1946, a loan of $1,250 millions on terms and conditions similar to those granted by the United States, and wiping out some items of war indebtedness. The delay in ratifying the United States loan to the United Kingdom resulted in early and substantial drawings upon the Canadian loan. Continued economic difficulties in Britain then led to the loan being used up much more rapidly than had been expected. By the end of 1947, $963 millions had been advanced and the Canadian government was obliged to place restrictions upon the amounts which were still to be drawn.[4] These restrictions came partly as a consequence of the drain upon Canadian reserves from the huge purchases in the United States, a large part of which were for capital equipment, and from the decline in the net influx of American capital to Canada after the Canadian dollar was placed on a par with the American dollar in July, 1946. As the figures show, Canada was still lending far more than she was borrowing

[4] By March 31, 1948, U.K. drawing had reached $1,008 millions. Over the next twelve months only $37 millions were released.

but her loans were to countries still in difficulties and unable to make prompt repayment, while it was necessary for her to meet promptly her obligations to American creditors. When U.S. dollar reserves had fallen in November, 1947, to less than a third of their total at the end of the war, the government was obliged to restrict imports from the United States quite severely and to limit the amount of dollars Canadians could purchase for tourist travel in the United States. In a year's time the recovery of reserves had been quite substantial[5] and with the marked growth of Canadian exports to the United States and the prospect of Marshall Plan dollars it was possible to relax some of the restrictions. But the experience of these years impelled students of Canadian economics, like J. D. Gibson, the editor of *Canada's Economy in a Changing World,* to argue in retrospect that:

Given the upset state of the world Canadians as a people have tried to do too much too quickly. In addition to the aid which we provided as a nation to overseas friends and customers, we attempted to maintain a higher level of consumption than ever before and embarked on a tremendous program of capital replacement and expansion . . . . Something had to give.

It is clear from the delegation papers that no Commonwealth country has experienced since the war any real lack of employment for its labour force. In some of them full employment was probably as near realization as they were ever likely to experience. Of this situation Australia presented an excellent example. There, the acceleration in the rate of industrialization during the war had created a situation where "the proportion of wage and salary earners employed in factories is one of the highest in the world." Since the outbreak of war total employment had increased by 38 per cent, with the factories showing a dramatic increase in workers from 540,000 to 824,000. In contrast rural employment was still below its pre-war level and the mining and quarrying industries and the building trades had not maintained their proportion of total employment. The shortages in these key industries disturbed the writers of the

[5] By December 31, 1948, they had risen to $998 millions and were only slightly below that figure when the Canadian dollar was devalued 10 per cent in September, 1949.

delegation paper, who pointed out that the lack of fuel and electric power was limiting further industrial expansion and that houses, factories and public works were still urgently needed. The demand for labour, especially in the heavy and primary industries, was reflected in the increase in wage rates, which in 1947-48 were about 48 per cent above pre-war figures. This in turn influenced the price of Australian exports which, with the additional stimulus of keen demand, rose to about three and one-half times their pre-war level. One of the reasons for labour shortages in Australia was the decline in the annual rate of population increase, which fell from 2.01 per cent between 1911 and 1921 to .96 per cent between 1933 and 1947—the date of the last census. An analysis of the census figures indicates, as the delegation paper puts it, that

children, the younger workers and women in the child-bearing ages are losing ground to the older workers and to that section of the population which is no longer working.

These facts confirm the opinion expressed in the Australian delegation paper that the birth-rate, which has shown a temporary rise, must tend to decline, while the death-rate, with the increase in the proportion of people over 65, is rising. Efforts are being made to offset this prospect by a vigorous immigration policy. But it was not until 1948 that net arrivals exceeded the average net annual intake for the twenties of about 31,000. Shipping and housing shortages have been factors in producing this disappointing result. The delegation paper warns that:

In view of the demographic problems of the countries from which Australia is most anxious to accept immigrants the long-run prospects for a substantial flow of immigrants are not promising.

Although New Zealand did not undergo any marked increase in industrialization, the chief expansion being in the textile industries, she too has experienced full employment. The contributing factor in her case has been the keen demand for her primary products. As a result the annual report of the Department of Labour and Employment for 1948 listed only 18 persons of employable age not placed on March 31, 1948. The same story of work for all comes from South Africa, where with a gain of 53 per cent in employment since 1935 the labour force is at a peak level.

India offers the sharpest contrast to Australia in her approach to problems of population. For the latter, further advance in industrialization is retarded by lack of effective manpower in key industries. For India the pressure of manpower upon her economy makes an expansion of both agriculture and industry absolutely imperative. The opening sentence of a delegation paper advocating scientific crop planning strikes this gloomy note:

At a time when starvation, malnutrition and dwindling foreign exchange resources for buying food confront the country it will perhaps be unrealistic to talk of a plan which has not the production of food alone as its objective . . . . An agricultural plan for the country must of course in a very large measure be directed at food production: it cannot but do that. In any plan for this country one must start with the problem of feeding 347 million human beings who are increasing at the rate of four million or so every year.

The present gap in cereals alone for the country is estimated at 7.1 million tons a year, to which must be added another 0.6 million tons per year for the increase in population. The paper points out that on the basis of producing 18 oz. of food per day per adult, it has been calculated that India will have to increase her production of cereals by 10 per cent, pulses by 20 per cent, fats and oils by 250 per cent, fruits by 50 per cent, vegetables by 100 per cent, milk by 300 per cent and fish and eggs by 300 per cent. Such large targets are difficult ones for a country whose crop yields are described as ". . . perhaps the lowest in the world" and which, while possessing the greatest cattle population of any country in the world, has to admit a "disappointing record of performance whether in milk yields or draught power." After carefully examining the problems involved in increasing production of non-food crops as well, the paper sums up as follows:

This, then, is the pattern of our requirements. We have to find enough food for our people, enough fodder and concentrates for our cattle, enough of commercial crops to be able to buy capital goods from abroad and finally to have enough land under forest to meet our timber and fuel requirements as well as to preserve the physical and climatic conditions of our country.

The author has no difficulty in demonstrating that such an ambitious but essential programme can only be achieved by "conservation farming, based on land capability, in other words on scientific crop-planning." But it is also clear that the modernization of agriculture envisaged in this far-seeing prospectus cannot be achieved without an acceleration of industrialization which another Indian paper described as "an inescapable necessity." The expansion of industry during the war and the improvement in India's financial position during the same period point to the possibility of India being on the verge of such a large-scale development. To the writer of another delegation paper, however, there is a complicating factor which he regards as a problem entailing Commonwealth co-operation. It arises from the nature of Indian economic development before the achievement of political independence, and the deep-seated conviction that

. . . continued (foreign) control of key positions of Indian industrial economy is not compatible with India's economic liberation which has necessarily to be a basis of her political freedom. . . . British interests still control shipping, exports, foreign trade, banking, oil, copper, jute, tea, coffee and heavy industries, and hold a semi-monopolistic position in regard to those industries.

On the basis of statistics which the writer has compiled of about 761 important firms in India nearly 56 per cent are controlled by foreigners. He states that his country is in no position to buy out these firms in the near future and has no intention of doing so. She is aware of the value of the technical experience and business acumen of British firms in helping her to readjust herself to changed conditions. On the other hand the existing situation can be maintained only ". . . on the assumption that no foreign interest can and should remain indefinitely in a semi-monopolistic position with regard to Indian industries in general and key industries in particular." His contention is that the British government and other Commonwealth governments must prompt and guide firms of their nationality operating in

India ". . . to change their role and participate fully and whole-heartedly in India's effort to place her economy on a sound and progressive basis." The Commonwealth countries should also be prepared "to evolve schemes of co-operative effort" through which the industrialization not only of India but of Pakistan and Ceylon can be furthered. Such assistance might take the form of investment and loans, technical missions and the loan of technicians as consultants, technical training of Indians abroad and a supply of capital goods "on a carefully planned basis with due regard for the needs of the countries concerned, arranged in a proper order of priorities." It would involve as the author admits, a Commonwealth plan corresponding to Point Four of President Truman's programme.

In working out this programme the paper concedes that the United Kingdom is not, as in the past, in a position to extend loans or undertake investment on a large scale. Her contribution can best be made by accelerating the "pace of repayment of sterling debt," which in turn must be linked up with any programme of domestic investment or commitments in such areas as Greece, the Middle East and Hong Kong. Canada is singled out as the only country which is in a position to render financial aid and it is thought she might do so ". . . given the right purpose." Britain, Australia and Canada are all in a position (the omission of any reference to South Africa probably reflects the resentment of racial discrimination) to render technical advice, train Indians and provide consultants. It might be possible for them to set up "a permanent pool of technical experts, special technical missions or technical consultants in particular cases." The paper regards the supply of capital goods as the most important form of immediate assistance for India in view of the fact that so much capital equipment is old and worn out. During the past three years India secured over two-thirds of her capital goods from the United Kingdom. Although the quantity imported from that country rose by nearly 80 per cent in 1948 when compared to 1938, India's proportion of the total United Kingdom exports of capital goods remained about the same. The Indian delegation paper argues that still more could be allocated to India in view of the United Kingdom's production of machinery, vehicles, electrical goods and chemicals having been increased. For this to be done inter-governmental consultation will be essential, after India has drawn up a plan for industrial development, and after priorities for capital goods most urgently required for its execution have been carefully worked out. As the paper states the case:

India is entitled to special assistance. She has—as already stated, old memories to work off but what is more, she has pressing needs to provide for and it is up to the U.K. to show that she is more than willing to meet India's needs.

In addition to the United Kingdom three other Commonwealth countries, Canada, Australia and South Africa, have been supplying capital goods to India and, because of their war-time industrial expansion, in considerably increased amounts when compared to pre-war days.[6] Her capacity to manufacture equipment for hydro-electric and diesel electric plants, power stations and gas plants, for coal mining, cement factories and the chemical industry, caused Canada to be ranked next in importance to the United Kingdom as a Commonwealth source of supply.[7] Australia's war record in building ships and aeroplanes and in producing electrical goods, farm machinery and steel on a much larger scale makes her also "a potential source of supply of heavy capital goods for India which can and should be utilised to the greatest possible advantage." Although the United States has increased and is increasing her supply of capital goods for India, it is significant that even now American supplies account for less than one-quarter of the total Indian imports. The delegation paper ends on an urgent appeal to the other Commonwealth countries for what it calls "a working principle of new partnership":

What is needed is organized effort on the part of the Commonwealth countries to make the industrialization of undeveloped countries of the Commonwealth their special concern and duty in the matter . . . not only the pace of industrialization in India can be accelerated, but new bonds of friendship and fellowship

[6] In Canada's case exports of capital goods to India were among the chief reasons for the volume of Canadian overseas exports to that country remaining so high in 1949.

[7] It should be remembered that in a good many of these items there was a substantial American content.

can be forged which will make the Commonwealth also a really beneficent factor in the working of world economy.

As described in her delegation paper Pakistan is essentially an agricultural country in which over 90 per cent of the population is employed on the land, but is determined to broaden her economy and to further industrialization. Despite primitive methods of cultivation the country is able to feed its population of 80,000,000 and export foodstuffs abroad, especially to India. In addition, Pakistan ranks as the world's largest source of jute of which India alone normally takes 4 million bales a year, produces over 1.25 million bales of high quality cotton a year, and exports annually 27 million pounds of wool. But Pakistan does not wish to have her country remain so rural that raw materials constitute 90 per cent of her exports. At the time of partition she had about forty factories producing textiles, glass, cement and sugar, and employing less than 30,000 workers. To have ample supplies of cotton yet produce on'y 10 per cent of the cotton goods required for her people, to grow 75 per cent of the world's supply of jute and yet be without a single jute mill while there are over one hundred in Calcutta, to have large flocks of sheep yet only one woollen spinning mill, to grow sugar cane yet import 90 per cent of the country's requirements of sugar, is an exasperating situation which the government is bent on correcting. As the delegation paper puts the case:

The industrial development of Pakistan is a matter of first importance to her government and her people. The standard of living of the country is appallingly low. The vast majority of the people derive their livelihood from the land. The per capita cultivated area is less than an acre. There is thus a considerable number of people living on the land, whose withdrawal will not affect agricultural productivity. Because of the meagre income from land, the purchasing power of the people is low . . . . The only way to raise the standard of living of the people is through rapid industrialization. Industrialization will help to solve the problem of concealed unemployment on the land. By diversifying the economy it will be possible to make it more balanced. Besides widening the scope for employment, industrialization will make the economy less sensitive to external pressures.

What the government plans to do is to "develop those industries for which the country possesses abundant raw materials and for which markets exist either at home or abroad." Except for the manufacture of arms and munitions, railroad waggons, telephones, telegraphs and wireless apparatus, and the generation of hydro-electric power, the government is prepared to leave industry to private enterprise. It has made various concessions to manufacturers on import duties and taxation, besides setting up an Industrial Finance Corporation to provide long term credits. It promises to treat foreign capital in the same way as domestic capital. Like India, it is chary of exploitation by foreign countries. In the words of the government's Statement of Industrial Policy:

Pakistan would welcome foreign capital seeking investment from a purely industrial and economic objective and not claiming any special privilege.

What it would like to encourage is a partnership between foreign and indigenous capital. Like India also, the country expects foreign firms to provide opportunities for training and employment for its nationals. The delegation paper does not comment on the prospects of assistance from Commonwealth countries except the United Kingdom. While Pakistan has had enquiries concerning industrial opportunities from such countries as Belgium, Sweden and the United States, the delegation paper reports that the response has been "very poor" from British capital. The Prime Minister expressed his disappointment at this lack of interest in an interview with a B.B.C. correspondent in May, 1949, and added: "Pakistan cannot afford to wait. She must take her friends where she can find them." Another complaint voiced against the United Kingdom is the fact that the Indo-British trade agreement, which still governs Pakistan's trade with Britain, affords preferences only on less important exports from Pakistan, while preferred articles make up almost 50 per cent of British exports to Pakistan. The writer of the delegation paper on "Pakistan's Foreign Trade" believes that the abolition of this preference for the United Kingdom would make it possible for the people in his country to get their consumer goods at more competitive prices, and that under such a policy the country as a whole would be likely to gain. He also suggests that such a policy would reduce abroad the criticism of the preferential system, a consideration of some importance since those countries which are critical must be taken into account as sources for both the capital goods and technical skill "which Pakistan so sorely needs." As he puts it:

Taking into consideration that Pakistan must secure her requirements of industrialization at a rapid pace it seems necessary that Pakistan must revise the previous trade agreement in the interests of the country.

The post-war experiences of the United Kingdom and Canada offer striking illustrations of the persistent strength of long-term economic factors. The United Kingdom's problems, as the concise and illuminating delegation paper demonstrates, are characteristic of the changed position of Western Europe as industrialization has spread across the world and has, in particular, so powerfully affected the Western Hemisphere. To some extent the altered situation was masked by shattering effects of two world wars. But in any event the basic factors would have exerted their influence. As Mr. Robinson observes, "A clearer recognition of their existence and of their nature would have prevented many errors in the thirties." In the export of manufactures, for example, a field of economic development in which the United Kingdom reigned unchallenged seventy-five years ago, increasing competition from the United States and the declining position of the United Kingdom have been developing since the turn of the century. The table on page 69, included in the U.K. delegation paper, demonstrates this fact. Similarly the task of overcoming her adverse balance of payments had already emerged as a major one for the United Kingdom before the coming of the second world war. In 1913, about 92 per cent of total visible imports were covered by visible exports and re-exports. By 1937-38 less than 65 per cent of these imports were so covered. During this same period it was gradually becoming more difficult to pay for imports from the Western Hemisphere. Down to 1929 visible trade with Canada almost balanced, but in the thirties, "Canada became a relatively much more important source of imports, but not as yet a substantially larger market for exports." Exports paid for nearly half the imports from the United States in 1913, while with the rest of the Western Hemisphere there was a small visible deficit. Even at the peak of prosperity in the twenties the visible deficit with the Western Hemisphere as a whole had risen from about a third of the imports in 1913 to about one-half in 1929. This gap continued to widen in the thirties with the result that by 1937-38 direct exports covered less than two-fifths of the U.K. imports. Other countries were in much the same position, and

THE SHARES OF DIFFERENT COUNTRIES IN THE
INTERNATIONAL TRADE IN MANUFACTURES

	U. K.	U.S.A.	Germany	France	Japan	Rest
	per cent	per cent	per cent	per cent	per cent	per cent
1876-1880	37.7	4.0	. . .	16.2	. . .	. . .
1896-1900	30.7	7.0	19.4	13.4	0.7	28.8
1906-1910	28.8	8.2	20.6	12.5	1.1	28.8
1913	27.2	9.7	21.7	11.7	1.4	28.3
1926-1930	21.0	16.2	16.9	10.8	3.6	31.5
1936-1938	18.6	16.3	19.8	6.0	7.0	32.3
1947 (provisional)	20.2	44.6	0.5	4.5	0.6	29.4
1948 (provisional)	25.2	32.9	4.3	4.8	1.3	31.5

the gap in trade with the United States was largely covered by transfers of gold. Between 1934 and 1938 the United States was importing on average $1.4 billions of gold a year. With the gap between exports and imports widening, in spite of the low prices for foodstuffs and raw materials in the depression years,[8] the United Kingdom had reached the position by 1938 where the income from her invisible exports, such as interest on investments, insurance and shipping earnings failed to balance her international accounts. The deficit for 1938 was approximately $335 millions which necessarily meant a drain upon existing reserves.

The general problem is described by Mr. Robinson as follows:

[8] Between 1931 and 1938, the terms of trade were far more favourable to the United Kingdom than at any time in the previous century.

The position of the United Kingdom in the 1930's was thus in several respects unstable. The declining share in a relatively constant or declining world trade in manufactures was making the purchase of the existing volume of imports increasingly difficult. The payment of the Western Hemisphere was emerging as a problem and had already contributed to the difficulties of the 1930's and had been a factor, conscious or unconscious, in stimulating the closer relations with the Commonwealth countries which had been formulated in the Ottawa agreements. The temporary bridging of the gap in the balance of payments by gold sales was on a scale that could not continue indefinitely. Thus a mere reconstruction of the situation in 1938 would not provide a solution of the world's difficulties. It is necessary to find a solution also of these more fundamental underlying problems.

Elsewhere in this chapter references have been made to the effects of the war upon the position of the United Kingdom. Disinvestment abroad, the accumulation of huge sterling debts, a decline in gold and dollar reserves and a sharp alteration in the terms of trade, have been paralleled by loss of a little less than one-eighth of the nation's internal capital through war damage, decline of reserves of stocks and plant depreciation. The U.K. paper estimates that about one-half of this destruction and internal disinvestment has since been made good, but points out that it has involved keen competition for capital equipment between domestic producers and overseas countries, of which the comments in the Indian delegation paper are indicative. The war also inevitably reduced U.K. exports to a marked degree, to less than one-third of the 1938 volume and affected the markets for these goods. Although the United Kingdom share of international trade in manufactures had by 1947 passed the pre-war figures, the United States had more than doubled her share and the enforced absence of Germany and Japan was obviously drawing to a close. A further complication had been the increased dependence upon the United States and Canada for imports, with the result that they provided 30 per cent of the U.K. imports in 1947 as against 21 per cent in 1938. Finally the rise in the price of imports greatly decreased the real purchasing power of gold, a commodity which had been so useful a factor in balancing accounts before 1939. Since the decrease in purchasing power came at a time when the United Kingdom's reserves of gold and foreign currencies were virtually exhausted, the need arose for the country to try and secure a balance independent of gold movements.

In grappling with these difficulties it is realized that the most important problem is to finance the imports from the western hemisphere. It is in that area, especially in the United States and South America, that the terms of trade have turned most heavily against the United Kingdom. By 1947 it had been possible to achieve a surplus on account with the rest of the world outside the western hemisphere so that the strains on the balance of payments came wholly from that area. What had eased the situation in the post-war years had been the loans and gifts from the United States and Canada without which the United Kingdom could not possibly "have supported any reasonable standard of life or have made anything like the progress that has been made towards a balance."

Obviously such devices cannot be permanent, and it remains to work out a long term solution for achieving a proper balance that will satisfy all concerned. In the figures submitted to the Organization for European Economic Co-operation in October 1948, for British trade and production after the Marshall Plan has ended (1952), there are positive indications of how the United Kingdom hopes to meet the situation. The estimates call for an increase in the share of exports going to the western hemisphere from 17 per cent in 1938 to 20 per cent in 1952-53. This increase would require a doubling of the 1947 volume of exports to Canada and a gain of 120 per cent in exports over the 1947 figures to the whole area. A balance would also involve a reduction of about 17 per cent in the total of western hemisphere imports in 1948, this reduction being valued at about $400 millions, a decrease which would bring the proportion of western hemisphere imports to about 24 per cent of the whole. It would also be necessary to keep the volume of retained imports from all sources close to the level of 1948. To do so would require a decrease in volume of about 19 per cent from the pre-war figures.

The United Kingdom paper, which Mr. Robinson had of course written before devaluation, did not minimise the extent of the achievement which such a programme entailed. With Germany and Japan becoming increasingly effective competitors again in international trade, and with other European countries also striving to expand their exports, it would be no easy task to hold U.K. exports at their present high level. It was also recognised that the volume of world trade in manufactures could not be expected to record any further "vast and spectacular increase." It had already risen about 15 per cent above the level of 1938 and it was "dangerously optimistic" to expect in 1952 a gain of more than 5-10 per cent above the present figure. With this in view, and in the face of American competition, the U.K. target of 150-160 per cent of the volume of 1938 exports in 1952 would "necessarily require very great energy and initiative." It would involve an increase in the competitive power of exports which must, in the main, be achieved by cheapening them. How this could be achieved was the heart of the matter. Official policy at the time of writing (mid-July) was described as follows:

to strive to get the necessary adjustments by technical efficiency and reduction of profit margins without revision of exchange rates, and to restore, so rapidly as may be possible, a large measure of multilateral freedom in the external trade of the United Kingdom.

It was Mr. Robinson's view that the "more solid fears" which should be taken into account in cheapening exports, and an important consideration—selling them in the right market—were:

that, with the existing levels of activity rising wages and rising money costs will make price reduction increasingly difficult and that wage advances cannot be sufficiently halted without some measure of unemployment; that rising government expenditures will continue to absorb too much of the positive increases of productivity.

On the wages question, he warns that bargaining must be conducted "with some sense of reticence and responsibility." Otherwise the government's efforts to achieve a standstill on wage claims will fail and the existing high level of activity will be imperilled, particularly in view of the situation produced in 1949 by the recession in the United States. Statistics show that real wages have increased about 9 per cent over 1938 while other incomes have decreased about 7 per cent. This development has created a vigorous debate in Britain as to whether the policy of so redistributing income by taxation has not destroyed valuable incentives to produce and to take risks. Not only opponents, but some supporters of the government are fearful of the prospect of rising government expenditures. Should this take place it would necessarily be in conflict with the demand for an increased consumption of goods at home which is the twin brother of wage increases.

It is significant that Mr. Robinson was cautious in his estimate of what might be gained in cheapening exports by devaluation. He believed the immediate result would be "to increase quickly the cost of imports while increasing more slowly the volume of exports." On a short term run devaluation would be likely to diminish the real purchasing power of exports but over a longer period of time it might tend ". . . to put the whole trade on a more stable basis and to develop a greater volume of it." But this increase in volume would depend upon curbing demands for wage increases aimed to keep real wages at their pre-devaluation level. Otherwise devaluation might be largely ineffective. It was suggested that "devaluation as against certain very hard currencies only would be substantially more likely to produce the required results." There were also doubts reported in some circles that devaluation would create sufficient increases in demand for U.K. exports to make it worth while. But whether devaluation took place or not the only solution for the present difficulties lay in making U.K. goods more competitive, through increased efficiency, greater productivity and lowered costs, in the North American market[9] and in a position to compete with American goods in other markets. On this possibility depends ". . . the balance of payments, the possibilities of a high level of employment and the whole standard of life of the British people."

As may be inferred from the U.K. analysis of the economic position, the Canadian problem arises to a large degree from

[9] The necessity of making the North American market more accessible is not overlooked in the U. K. delegation paper. It is described as a problem which involves "a fundamental change in the present attitude to imports in the United States."

the difficulties of Britain and Western Europe. Mr. Gibson, who edited the volume on "Canada's Economy in a Changing World," comments that "the relative decline of the economic position of Western Europe is the centre of our political and economic problems." Like the United Kingdom, Canada has also had to contend with the same dilemma of selling much of her products abroad for a considerable period of her history. Exports are vital to her prosperity. As a country with great resources and small population (even with an increase of about one-third since 1929 it only stands at 13.5 millions) she must export a large proportion of her production. Moreover the type of production characteristic of some of her provinces is essentially designed for sale in external markets. If the Prairie Provinces and British Columbia cannot dispose of most of their wheat, base metals, lumber and apples in export markets they are very soon in trouble. The application of North American technology has greatly increased Canadian capacity to produce with the result that exports have increased in value from $418 millions in 1913 to $2,759 in 1947, and imports in the same period from $618 millions to $2,570 millions. But the markets for exports and sources of imports have changed very little. Canada relies upon the United States as her chief source of imports of fuel, some raw materials, capital goods and manufactures. To meet her unfavourable balance of trade with that country, she has counted upon a surplus of exports with overseas countries and, to a lesser degree, with other countries. Thus in 1913 Canada sold 51 per cent of her exports to the United Kingdom and 36 per cent to the United States. She purchased only 21 per cent of her imports from the United Kingdom and 64 per cent from the United States. Although Canadian exports have increased considerably to the United States, especially in recent years, sales elsewhere remain of great importance. The table on page 75 illustrates that position.

The fact that in 1947 Canadian sales to other areas than the United States had declined only two per cent from their proportion of total exports in 1937-39 is not as encouraging as it might appear. Such an achievement had only been made possible through the programme of underwriting exports to the United Kingdom and Western Europe by the loan and exports

credits which have already been described. Exports were also
bolstered by a Wheat Agreement with the United Kingdom for a
five year period commencing in 1946 at a price below that in
other markets. To hold as much as possible of the U.K. market for
other agricultural products which had been in great demand
during the war[10] other food contracts were made which involved

CANADIAN MERCHANDISE TRADE
Percentage distribution by Main Areas.

DESTINATION OF EXPORTS

	1928-29	1937-39	1947	1st half 1949
United States	40%	36%	38%	49%
United Kingdom	21	38	28	24
Other Empire	7	10	13	11
Western Europe and Dependencies	23	9	11	9
Others	9	7	10	7

SOURCES OF IMPORTS

	1928-29	1937-39	1947	1st half 1949
United States	68%	64%	77%	72%
United Kingdom	15	17	7	12
Other Empire	5	10	6	6
Western Europe and Dependencies	7	5	3	3
Others	5	4	7	7

embargos on sales of beef and other foods to the United States
in order to meet the volume required. These devices were
generally approved in Canada although critics complained that
too much of the burden was p'aced on the prairie wheat grower.
As the author of the chapter on "Canadian Agricultural Policy"
in the delegation paper remarked:

They (the critics) have never objected to selling to Britain at a
special cut price as part of national policy paid for by all Canadians. What's objected to however is that the policy as it has
actually worked out has compelled the Western farmer to help
Britain out of his own pocket.

[10] The Canadian delegation paper points out that: "At different periods
in the war we sent two and a half times as much cheese to Britain as in
1935, four times as much bacon and ham and greater quantities of wheat
than since the 1920's."

Because of such arrangements, because of Britain's need for wheat, and because of the sharp curtailment in her purchases of many other Canadian products, exports of wheat and flour to the United Kingdom constituted nearly half of Canadian sales in that market during the first six months of 1949—about twice the pre-war proportion.

Since 1947, because of Britain's acute shortage of dollars, the reduction in Canadian financial aid, and the greater availability of goods from non-dollar sources, the United Kingdom's purchases of many Canadian products (including lumber, newsprint, canned salmon, apples and tobacco) have been sharply reduced and some (such as processed milk, fresh and frozen fish and coarse grains) have been virtually eliminated. The curtailment of Canadian sales would have been even more severe had it not been for the off-shore purchases under the Marshall Plan. Such dollar-saving restrictions against purchases from Canada have been paralleled in Western Europe, the sterling area, and in some of the countries of Latin America. However the total quantity of Canadian exports was fairly well maintained up to mid-1949, because of a substantial increase in sales to the United States and of a quite large export of manufactures and capital goods to South Africa, India and Pakistan. South Africa was Canada's third best customer in 1948 and India replaced her in that position during the first half of 1949. But as compared to the fifty year old trend of selling one-third of her exports to the United States and the rest overseas, about one-half of Canada's exports are going to the United States and the balance elsewhere.

Exports of capital goods and manufactures are particularly welcome to Canada since it is obvious that the United States cannot be expected to replace overseas markets for finished goods. Nearly half of Canadian exports to the United States consists of wood, pulp and paper while another third is made up of asbestos, base metals, some agricultural products and fish. But Canada has greatly expanded her industrial capacity under the stimulus of war, and her exports should naturally reflect that trend. The Indian paper made an interesting comment on this Canadian development:

In 1914, for example, primary goods accounted for 63.2 per cent of total exports, partially manufactured goods 10.1 per cent and fully manufactured products 26.7 per cent. Since then the relative importance of the raw material group declined steadily and by 1945 the position had been almost reversed with primary products accounting for 26.7 per cent of total trade, semi-manufactured 16.6 per cent and fully manufactured products 56.7 per cent.

Although the dependence upon the United States for imports reached its peak in 1947, when it was aggravated by the heavy demand for capital goods for plant expansion, it is still true that over 70 per cent of Canadian imports are from the United States. Canada would like to see imports from overseas regain some of their lost ground. She is well aware that if the sterling area countries can provide only 18 per cent of Canadian imports, a drop of one-third from the pre-war total, their purchases from Canada are bound to be affected. She shares the United Kingdom's keen desire to see British goods return to the Canadian market in much larger quantity. There has already been an improvement and, indeed, Canada was consistently purchasing more than the United States from Britain during 1949. But it is felt that more still would have been bought from Britain if prices had been more competitive, if delivery had been more assured, and if, in some instances, there had been more sales effort by U.K. firms. Canada is also anxious to see international trade free itself from the mesh of restrictions that still hamper it, and become less bilateral in character. As the delegation paper says, it is Canadian policy "to hasten and return to full multilateral trade throughout the world." This policy has been steadily pursued by Canada in the negotiations that preceded the formulation of the Charter of the International Trade Organization and in the trade talks that have taken place in Geneva and Annecy. As a country whose exports have been almost 50 per cent greater in volume over the pre-war totals, Canada is as eager as the United Kingdom to see international trade remain at a high level. She is equally concerned at any prospect of the sterling and dollar areas becoming sharply separated by various restrictions. Her general interest is well described by Mr. Gibson in an additional memorandum on "The Changing Pattern of External Trade":

Because economic conditions are still favourable in Canada and the demand for imports thus remains high, the trading problem appears as one of obtaining sufficient U.S. dollars to pay for imports from the United States and to meet other obligations to that country. But behind the U.S. dollar problem, and of more fundamental concern, is the problem of markets for our existing industrial and agricultural capacity on which the future level of economic activity depends. The severe exchange and import restrictions in most of the overseas world and the reduction in ERP funds available for "off-shore" purchases are reducing Canada's earnings of U.S. dollars at a time when direct dollar earnings from exports to the United States are levelling off. More than that, they are threatening the level of activity in a variety of Canadian industries, more particularly because the backlogs of domestic demand accumulated during and before the war are filling up and because the period of general shortages is past . . . . It may well be that the core of Canada's trading problem is to maintain adequate markets for the grain economy of the western plains and for a number of the much expanded machinery and metal products industries of central Canada. This country needs a market for grains a little larger than pre-war, but a substantially larger market for manufactured goods if efficient production in the industries concerned is to be continued.

To retain these needed overseas markets on a lasting basis, it is perfectly clear that North American imports from the rest of the world will have to be much larger. Indeed, the recent aggravation of the world dollar shortage largely reflects the increasing difficulty experienced by overseas countries in selling to the United States. A large increase in shipments from the sterling area and the other ERP countries to North America is basic to the bridging of the dollar gap. Hope of restoring multilateral trade depends on making the price, exchange-rate, and tariff adjustments needed to promote such an increase. The alternative is growing trade discrimination and more and more regional and bilateral arrangements. And Canada would clearly have great difficulty in maintaining her needed overseas markets in such an environment. Hence, the profound Canadian interest in bridging the gap which is still widening between the sterling and U.S. dollar trading areas.

Few of the delegation papers drew direct attention to the relation of economics to strategy. The United Kingdom paper on strategy puts it most bluntly when, after posing the question,

"Can the United Kingdom still put forward so great a contribution to the strength of a coalition as heretofore?", it replied that, "Our conclusion . . . is that everything turns on the solution of the economic problem." Elsewhere it is pointed out that countries of low living standards are breeding grounds for Communism and that steps must be taken to raise quickly the lot of the people of Asia. Unstable economic conditions also lower morale in Western Europe and increase accordingly the difficulties for the defence planners. It is obvious from the various papers that the appearance of "a wealthier and more powerful United States, a more industrialized Commonwealth and a relatively poorer Europe" offers a challenge to statesmanship in the United States and the Commonwealth which cannot be evaded.

PART II

THE WORK OF THE CONFERENCE

3

The Position of the Member Nations in the Post-war World

After the official opening of the Conference[1] and a summary of the main features of the delegation papers by the Conference Recorder the delegates examined Part One of the Agenda.[2] For most of them it was their first experience of a conference of this unusual type in which no resolutions were passed, no votes taken, and no attempt made to secure unanimity of opinion. Part One of the Agenda had been deliberately planned to make possible a "warming up" process so that the engine of discussion might soon turn over smoothly and steadily. The arrangement was that a spokesman from each delegation should comment briefly on the particular aspects of his country's position which merited special attention and invite questions or observations from others. The plan worked admirably. By the time the discussion on this phase of the Agenda had ended the initial feelings of reserve and restraint among the delegates had vanished.

For Ceylon, Ireland and New Zealand, who had not been able to circulate delegation papers in advance, the opening statements were particularly useful. In the case of Ceylon, it was interesting to note how in many respects the problems which the newest Dominion faced were comparable to those of India and Pakistan. Although British traditions of parliamentary government and justice were firmly rooted in Ceylon and the attachment to Britain was described as "very firm and very genuine," a descriptive phrase which would not have been used by either of the other Asian states, the speaker was proud of his country's

[1] See Appendix A.
[2] See Appendix B.

independence and observed that "foreign domination weakens a nation and develops unstable characteristics." Although his country was concerned at the decline in British strength, she was still inclined "to follow where Britain leads." He also added that Ceylon shared the cultural heritage of India and referred approvingly to the attempts of Gandhi to make "the first modern application of the spirit of Christ." He explained that Ceylon was faced by the problem of low living standards, since three-quarters of the population earned less than £2 a month. There were "many hungry stomachs." Efforts were being made to diversify the economy so as to make it less dependent on exports and to expand social services. But the cost of living had risen two and one-half times since 1938, the terms of trade were heavily against Ceylon, and the rubber industry was in a depressed condition. These economic hardships had resulted in suspicions that American interests were using the scheme of stockpiling rubber to force the price of rubber down, and contributed to the strong attraction Communism exerted on the underprivileged. Nearly a quarter of the members of Parliament were communists, but fortunately they were divided by doctrinal differences. Ceylon had won her freedom peacefully but there was a marked sympathy with the armed struggles of other Asian people to do the same. Such sympathy was reflected in the prevalent view in Ceylon that a Communist Indonesia was preferable to a Dutch-controlled non-communist state.

At Bigwin as at Strasbourg the Irish delegation used the opportunity to present the case against the partition of their country.[3] Although their delegation did not include a supporter of Mr. De Valera, through no fault of its own, it provided an impressive reflection of public opinion. A former colleague of John Redmond, a leading figure in the Irish Labour Party who was also a junior minister in the Costello administration, a veteran Senator who had once been "on the run" with Michael Collins, and a prominent businessman in Dublin, could and did speak up for Ireland. By the time they had stated their case with fire and conviction other Commonwealth delegates were

[3] H. E. Sean MacBride, the Minister for External Affairs, has described the Irish attitude in his address on "Anglo-Irish Relations" in a pamphlet reprinted from *International Affairs*, Vol. XXV, No. 3, July, 1949.

uneasily aware that if Ireland had had too much history the rest of the Commonwealth had read too little of it. The Irish spokesman began by pointing out that Ireland shared other sterling countries' difficulties, in being short of dollars at a time when it was compelled to import feed stuffs, fertilizers and some machinery from the dollar countries to develop its agriculture, and therefore readily participated in the European Recovery Programme. He stressed the fact that, unlike most Commonwealth countries, Ireland had almost nothing to fear from the internal activities of atheistic Communism. (The adjective was invariably employed when Communism was mentioned.) Then he turned to the subject nearest his heart and declared that "special attention" should be given to the division of his country into the Republic of Ireland and the six northern counties. He denied the existence of two nations in Ireland and described the existing border as having no roots in geography, economics or history, but as having arisen from decisions taken in Great Britain which were harmful to both countries. Had the Home Rule Bill been implemented before 1914 Ireland would have been a constructive rather than a disruptive force within the Commonwealth. As it was, the artificiality of the border was demonstrated in sports, ecclesiastical organization, and in police co-operation. Was it not, he asked, sounder strategically to have a single government for Ireland with its people friendly to Britain than to have a divided country? What was needed was the end of blind negation in discussing partition and the working out of a gradual solution in which "partitionists" would make some sacrifice not only for Ireland but for Great Britain and indeed the Commonwealth. Such a solution would win the active goodwill of the Irish people and would put an end to the sole remaining problem standing in the way of friendship with Great Britain. Other Irish speakers, then and subsequently, supported the spokesman in his argument. In defence of the decision to establish a Republic it was pointed out that the insistence upon the oath of allegiance and other symbols in the twenties had caused Ireland to regard the Crown quite differently from the way it was looked upon elsewhere in the Commonwealth. For her it was "a symbol of servitude and persecution." But it was perceptible that, as such formal links were severed

with Great Britain, relations between the two countries noticeably improved. The delegates assured the Conference that all
parties in Ireland regarded partition as "an unjust situation
forced upon their country by Britain." One of them expressed
the hope that another great Englishman might find a formula
as Peel had done for Catholic emancipation. Although Ireland
had been neutral in the second world war because of the danger
of civil war which active belligerency would have entailed, and
of her differences with Britain, many thousands of Irish men
and women had served with distinction in the British forces,
receiving seven Victoria Crosses, and had worked in English
factories during the "blitz." As a Christian democratic country
that wished to oppose atheistic Communism, Ireland was in
complete accord with the aims of the North Atlantic Pact. But
she could uphold it only as a single national unit and could not,
if unity were denied her, enter into a military agreement with
a state which acted in a manner contrary to her ideals. It was
necessary to undo the British statutes of 1920 and 1949 which
confirmed partition, before Ireland could co-operate.

The point of view of Northern Ireland, which was not expounded at the preliminary discussions, was later clearly described by a United Kingdom delegate who especially qualified
for that purpose. He welcomed the examination at the Conference of the partition issue which, he claimed, had only recently
been revived as a political issue becaue of the nature of party
controversies during the Irish election of 1948. In his view
the repeal of the External Relations Act and the proclamation
of the Republic of Ireland had been undertaken by Prime
Minister Costello to spike Mr. De Valera's guns. The arguments employed had inflamed the Irish peasant, "the only
person ready to crusade over an abstract constitutional issue,"
but had not really made republicans in a country which had
"more kings to the acre than any other country in Europe."
The speaker described Irish objections to joining the North
Atlantic Pact as "incomprehensible and indefensible," and said
that the people of Ulster were ready to put at the disposal of
the United Kingdom their naval bases and "great resources of
Field Marshals."[4] To the argument that Britain enforced

---

[4] In the second world war six Field Marshals were of Ulster origin.

partition his reply was that the chief parties in the United Kingdom had made it plain that they would not force Ulster into political union with Ireland against its will. Belfast had avowed that it would never be governed from Dublin and that was a reasonable view. The people of Ulster had found peace through partition and were content with it as was shown in the recent election, when only two of thirteen constituencies had voted Nationalist. They did not live in a police state as had been charged, and found their country attractive to other Irishmen "owing, no doubt, to the lack of social services in the South." The speaker closed his defence of Ulster by suggesting that Irishmen stop worrying international conferences with partition and turn to improving their own domestic government.

Although all the speakers from other parts of the Commonwealth expressed genuine sympathy with the Irish plea for unity, they were unanimous in deprecating any effort to solve the situation by exerting pressure upon Ulster. A United Kingdom delegate said that his country respected the ideal of unity and realised the advantage of having a unified Ireland adhering to the Atlantic Pact. But it was the policy of both main parties to preserve the principle of self-determination within the Commonwealth, and he did not see how the United Kingdom could force the people of Ulster to enter the Republic of Ireland. A Canadian said it was a question "solely between the two peoples of Ireland" and that the Republic would have to convince Ulster "not merely by pledges for the future but by such present domestic policies and external affiliations as Ulster would become anxious to share."

Other speakers from Australia and New Zealand who referred to the views of those of Irish origin in their countries expressed sympathy with the Irish delegation's case, but in each instance felt that the wider problem of security should take precedence over partition. Their comments were partly in response to the argument that the Irishmen in the Dominions were in support of the Republic's position. In summing up the situation the chairman of the Irish delegation assured the Conference that no one advocated using force to end partition, insisted that Great Britain had a continuing responsibility for the intransigent attitude of Ulster, a position which had been strengthened by the "wrong and unnecessary" assurances given her in the Act of 1949, and reiterated that Ireland could not adhere to the North Atlantic Pact until she was united. On a subsequent occasion an Irish delegate who stressed the fact that he spoke "very personally," offered an ingenious solution. He suggested that the Prime Ministers of Ireland and Ulster should issue a joint declaration of adherence to the North Atlantic Pact in order to demonstrate the solidarity of all Irishmen with the West in combating Communism.

The picture given of New Zealand's position in the post-war world was that of a country which was more conscious than ever before of its problems as a Pacific power, and which must, in future, look to its neighbours and to the United States rather than to the United Kingdom for effective measures of mutual defence. That lesson had been learned in the second world war, when, for the first time in its history, New Zealand had to contemplate a threat of invasion. Although New Zealand forces had not been withdrawn from the Middle East and Europe for service in the Pacific, the country had been obliged to put into uniform a higher proportion of its men and women than any other country, and had placed its forces under the command of General MacArthur. In spite of the apparent withdrawal of the United States which was causing concern, it was the hope of New Zealand that "the spirit which was displayed from 1941 to 1945 was not altogether lost and that the United States could be interested again in the affairs in the South Pacific." Meanwhile New Zealand and Australia had drawn closer together for mutual defence in the Canberra Pact of 1944, and in a recent referendum the country had voted three to one in favour of compulsory training. Although disappointed with the progress of UN, where the stultifying effects of the voting provisions of the Charter against which her delegates had vainly protested in San Francisco were obvious, New Zealand still hoped it could be made to function efficiently and continued to give it full support. She was reluctant to accept the division of the world into two opposing camps. Further proof of the country's wide interest in international affairs was the fact that New Zealand had established her External Affairs Department in 1943 and had opened missions, during and since the war, in

Canada, Australia, India, the United States, the U.S.S.R. and France. In the South Pacific and South Asia, New Zealand was a member of the South Pacific Commission, the South Pacific Air Transport Council, and the Economic Commission for Asia and the Far East. She was trustee for Western Samoa, and a joint trustee with Australia and the United Kingdom for Nauru Island. As a consequence she was also a member of the Trusteeship Council of the United Nations.

In the economic sphere New Zealand's trade had retained its pre-war pattern, with 60 to 70 per cent of her exports going to the United Kingdom and between 40 and 50 per cent of her imports coming from that country. Like Australia and Canada the Dominion had contributed to the United Kingdom's recovery by negotiating bulk purchase agreements in which New Zealand had accepted a price sometimes substantially less than the world one. The dollar shortage was a serious problem for her, since she had an adverse balance of trade with both the United States and Canada in spite of severe restrictions against dollar imports. Yet in spite of such difficulties and the allied one of attempting to hold the line against wages and costs, New Zealand was a land of full employment with no evidence of poverty. Such facts explain the absence of a powerful Communist party in the country.

In general the remarks of speakers from the other Commonwealth countries were in keeping with their delegation papers. There was noticeably more emphasis on nationalism in the Asian statements than in those from the older Dominions except South Africa. Their attitude was illustrated by the remark of a Pakistani delegate that, "since 1939 the one great event for Pakistan" had been the acquisition of Dominion status in 1947. In contrast the Australian spokesman observed that in his country some Australians feel "that insistence on nationalism in an atomic age is rather irrelevant." The Asian dominions were likewise agreed in expressing concern about the future evolution of the Commonwealth. They were faced with the problem of making the Commonwealth a reality to millions of their non-English speaking citizens. They wondered if an association which had become less homogeneous in racial composition and cultural traditions could retain the intimacy of pre-war days.

Would the Commonwealth, with the existing tensions over racial discrimination and colonies, be able to retain internal cohesion when danger threatened it? It was certainly a question for the Conference, said a delegate from Pakistan, how far the Commonwealth could become an association or a family of nations. How could the United Kingdom continue to give her traditional leadership in the Commonwealth now that she was becoming more and more associated with European political and economic groupings? To this question a United Kingdom speaker replied that Europe was most important in the fight against Communism, and that the recovery of Western Europe was essential to all Commonwealth members. The United Kingdom would not go "beyond certain limits" in Western Union because Commonwealth links were the fundamental ones and therefore Customs Union and political federation with Western Europe were barred. The new states were also obviously uneasy about the nature of the impact of the United States upon the Commonwealth, an impact which might limit the latter's freedom of action; and yet they recognised that co-operation with such a colossus was essential and unavoidable. With their common dislike of colonialism and imperialism they appeared suspicious of the United States, as the champion of the anti-Communist front, on the score that she might be too willing to purchase support against Russia by watering down her own anti-imperialist policies. An Indian speaker was uneasy about the possibility of the association of the United States with the Western Union powers resulting in "a new imperialist alliance with the United States for the maintenance of colonial empires." This concern about the nature of American leadership was widespread. A Canadian remarked that power had passed to a country which has not as yet "found the means of playing the vitalizing role so long sustained by the United Kingdom." On the other hand a United Kingdom speaker pointed out that the new position of the United States as a world power had resulted in the disappearance of differences between the United States and Britain over policy and strategy which had formerly acted as a brake on Commonwealth action. Closer association with the United States was now urging the Commonwealth forward. The same delegate was encouraged by the absence at the Conference of major differences over constitutional issues. This feature also impressed an Australian, who remarked that since no Commonwealth country displayed to-day a curious inferiority complex about its status, centripetal factors ought to make themselves felt in Commonwealth affairs. As he said: "The extent to which Commonwealth ties should be loosened has been settled; it now remains to decide how close these ties should be."

The remark of one speaker that, in his opinion, the issue of Communism furnished a new background for the discussions and was perhaps the most fundamental one, epitomized the view of almost all who had spoken in the preliminary debate. In commenting on this concern a South African made the interesting point that the marked increase in educational facilities for natives in his country, an increase which, he claimed, could be paralleled in only a few other countries, might lead to an increase in their vulnerability to Communist propaganda. It was quite clear, he said, that a little education as opposed to none or much provided a good seed plot for Communism. This plot, he admitted, was being fertilized and watered by the petty irritations due to racial friction, and by the way the present South African government was enforcing its *Apartheid* policy. His plea for thoughtful consideration of the difficulties which two and one-third million white people experienced in the presence of nine million non-Europeans, of whom the great majority were still in the tribal stage of their development, paved the way for the earnest discussion that later developed on racial discrimination.

4

The Member Nations and the United Nations

One of the few debates where the United Kingdom point of view, as expounded by most of its speakers, was not shared by any of the other delegations took place on the working of the United Nations. It was here that the United Kingdom speakers seemed to reflect the attitude of a Great Power as, of course, no others present could. When an Australian urged that the delegates give some attention to what the Commonwealth as a whole could do for the United Nations in order "to see with some vision, and perhaps passion, how the Commonwealth could lead the world towards a unitary conception of itself and be a sort of cementing agent for a wider world organization," a United Kingdom speaker followed with a speech of ruthless realism. He did not see how the United Nations could organise any real collective system. It was true that, by providing the possibility of discussion, it had dragged issues into the open, which had helped to slow down the rate at which crises developed and lowered the temperature of argument. But the lack of a pre-existing confluence of interests meant that the United Nations could not provide a substitute for national or regional policies, and at most could only reconcile them. Soviet sabotage in UN meetings had obscured real defects which were present in the handling of such problems as Palestine, Kashmir and Indonesia. Since security through the UN was to be based on the Great Powers imposing peace on the smaller ones, and since a rift had quickly developed among the Great Powers, it was impossible to regard UN as an instrument of security. For the U.S.S.R. it was useful as a megaphone for her propaganda and a means of inhibiting the reactions of other states to her own aggressive policies. The U.K. delegate suggested there had been too much "sloppy talk" about the achievements of the Specialized Agencies. He thought the Economic and Social Council had so far produced only disappointing results, that the Refugee Organization had got to work only after individual nations, Britain in particular, had made possible some solution, and that the Trusteeship Council had worked in an unrealistic fashion with South American delegates advocating for such regions as Tanganyika native policies which were not practised in South America itself. He did not see how UN could initiate policies on the great issues at present dividing the world. He himself regarded it as being useful only as a buffer or a refrigerator. Other United Kingdom delegates were less severe in their criticism of the achievements of the United Nations, but were plainly dissatisfied with its progress. They stated that public opinion in Britain was very disappointed and even cynical about the United Nations. They were exasperated at the way in which the Security Council had been "hobbled and hamstrung" by the operation of the veto. The Security Council was "a sand-pile for burying heads," just as Collective Security had been for the League of Nations. They deplored the failure to make any beginning at a solution of the control of atomic energy. They did not see how UN, "merely a collection of nations meeting under its charter to discuss common problems," could deal with such urgent questions as Communism or the dollar-sterling relationship. They saw no point in putting every emphasis on UN and not exploring other methods of attaining security, such as the North Atlantic Pact. They quoted approvingly the remark of the British Foreign Secretary, Mr. Bevin, that the United Kingdom did not intend to be prevented by stalemate in the United Nations from taking vital action with those who would work with her.

Whether because of less direct experience with the frustrations of the UN, or from "dewy-eyed idealism," as a Canadian described it—whatever the reason—the other Commonwealth delegates were far less prepared to discount so markedly the performance and prospects of UN. Thus a South African conceded that UN stock was not very high in his country but added that membership in it would bring an "educative experience" to the citizens of South Africa and teach them that they must share in the moral valuations of other groups including a number of non-white nations. He thought the United Nations would create a climate of moral opinion. In similar vein a delegate from Pakistan, who said that his country had suffered a series of disappointments in UN because issues of interest to her had been influenced by power politics, still believed that the United Nations should, as "the only hope of the world" be given "all possible support." An Indian speaker felt that UN provided a forum and an opportunity for solving dangerous problems. This had been clearly demonstrated in the Indonesian dispute. If UN were to fail, he was fearful of the attraction Communism might exercise in Asia. A delegate from Ceylon, the only Commonwealth country represented at the Conference which was not a member of UN, thanks to the Soviet veto, admitted that initial enthusiasm for UN in his country had quickly been followed by disillusionment, but readily conceded that we were better off with it than without. It was his view that the two dangers to be guarded against in supporting it were excessive expectations that the UN could "deliver the goods," and too little realization that the UN lacked the community of interest upon which political institutions must rest. Canadian delegates inquired whether it was "worldly wisdom or world weariness" that affected the attitude of the United Kingdom, pointing out that Canada had not been blind to UN weaknesses, as was evident in her early advocacy of the North Atlantic Pact, but that she still valued the ideal which UN represented, and did not regard it as a nuisance. UN had also had a useful effect in enabling the Canadian government "to have a policy to which no racial or religious group in Canada could have any serious objections," and in increasing Canada's prestige abroad. They were persuaded that belief in UN and active participation in its work have helped to bring Canada out of her shell of isolation and to appraise more realistically power politics. For Australians the UN possessed a certain psychiatric value in facilitating the airing of disputes, and still remained "a shrine of belief in one world" which the Commonwealth should support for that very reason. A New Zealander made the interesting point that, if it had done nothing else, UN had given smaller nations a chance to see at close range the policy of the U.S.S.R. in action, and had thereby contributed to the hardening of their opinion against that country. His colleague also felt that UN was important for countries like Canada and New Zealand, which were not in immediate danger of attack and in which there were racial differences or sharp differences between Right and Left on colonial policies. In them unity of opinion for effective action could be obtained only where foreign policy was related to principle. The two best ties for the Commonwealth were external danger and emphasis on principle. The latter was most easily expressed in the United Nations. In response to the New Zealand proposal that the role of UN should also be examined in social and economic questions as well as in politics, an Indian delegate maintained that assistance to under-developed countries was necessary if these were to be in a position to meet the Communist threat, and that such assistance must come from UN. Others pointed out that basically the aid must come from creditor countries rather than from UN—the United States and

Canada were particularly mentioned—but that UN could be used for the co-ordination and assessment of claims on such funds as were available. The discussions on the atomic bomb, described by one delegate as "only conventional warfare carried to an extreme", presented a bleak prospect. A United Kingdom speaker was convinced that there was not the slightest chance of Russia accepting any method of control involving international inspection or operations in Russian territory. The only practical solution appeared to be the prospect of overwhelming punishment for the use of atomic bombs, retribution which depended upon the free nations becoming so strong that no aggressor would have a chance of succeeding. It was thought inadvisable to carry the analogy between atomic bombs as weapons and poison gas too far. Although the latter had not been used in the last war, since neither side regarded it as being an advantage to do so, there was the danger that an aggressor might be tempted to use atomic bombs as likely "match winners." One feeble ray of hope was afforded by the reminder that atomic bombs were so costly to construct that widespread competition among the nations in their manufacture was unlikely.

The general reaction of the United Kingdom speakers to criticisms of the other delegates was expressed in the comment that differences of opinion at the Conference arose from the fact that "the older and more experienced powers" tended to see UN as impeding their policies without substituting any effective policies of its own. It was true that for newer powers such as Canada UN had provided a stimulating experience which had helped them to understand and deal with world problems. This was so because UN had redressed the balance in favour of the small and middle powers to a much greater degree than the League of Nations had ever done. The United Kingdom delegates were also disinclined to accept the validity of the argument that once the German and Japanese peace settlements had been negotiated UN might be less hampered by the manoevring going on at present for advantage in the beaten countries. In their view the return of Germany and Japan to the status of Great Powers, as must happen eventually, would introduce new political and economic strains that would only render more difficult the solution of what were already complicated problems. Before the discussion had ended, it was encouraging, however, that despite variations in national attitudes, the differences of opinion had tended to narrow and had become those of emphasis rather than of principle.

5

Policy and Strategy in a Divided World

If the debate on the United Nations found the views expressed by most of the United Kingdom delegation in contrast with those held by the other delegates, the discussions on the politics of power resulted in an equally clear division of opinion between the Asian dominions and the other Commonwealth countries. A Canadian who introduced the topic took as his premise the thesis that "the secularised religion of Russian Communism" is central in modern international frictions. He did not deny the existence of clashes of material interest among the Great Powers but thought the main cause of instability was the ideological cleavage. In his view it was essential to recognise the fact that the men in Moscow "who thought in broad terms of shaping history throughout the world" accepted the fact of two worlds as inevitable and regarded all contemporary institutions, including the United Nations, as instruments for their grand design. Co-operation with non-Communist states might be pursued on occasion, but as a tactic for furthering policies and not as a principle of action. With their Messianic belief in the righteousness of their cause the little group in the Kremlin demanded complete and unquestioning obedience from Communists in every part of the globe. As a U.K. speaker pointed out, they did not regard war as the only method of achieving world domination as Hitler had done but were equally fanatical in their determination to win their objective. To meet the Communist challenge the free world must close its ranks and achieve a strength which would be sufficient to deter aggression. In so doing they could buy time, during which there might be a chance to build bridges between the two worlds, bearing in mind that ideologies come and go and it was unnecessary to assume that revolutionary Russian Communism was immortal. The strength of the free peoples was, of course, more than a matter of arms and bases, essential though they were. It involved, he suggested, social and economic policies designed to further social morale by narrowing internal social cleavages. It also involved the necessity for close collaboration between the United States and the Commonwealth in support of what they shared in common, ideals as well as economic resources. Such collaboration would entail unlimited patience before it could be achieved, in view of the suspicions of British or Australian socialists of American imperialism and the American distrust of British socialism, or even in some quarters of anything British. But unless this collaboration could be secured the free nations would not possess adequate strength.

To this forthright argument, which accepted power as neither good nor bad but a fact in world politics, an Indian replied with equal conviction that his country had never accepted the two world theory of international politics because ". . . it meant naming an aggressor and regimenting affairs in such a way that smaller countries could not have room to consider other policies or opinions." It also meant the subordination of other policies to military considerations. This in turn might result in big powers being tempted to support reactionary elements in weak or newly established democracies in order to have an ally against Communism. Such elements could be "an even worse enemy than Communism." The speaker agreed that the national policy of the U.S.S.R. must be resisted but wished to draw distinction between it and socialism as a policy or political belief. He preferred to emphasize the values of democracy and to look to ideals and institutions rather than merely to military potential. In his own words, "if a division into two worlds were accepted, India would not be able to build up a democracy."

Although not going as far as his colleague in playing down the value of military strength a speaker from Ceylon argued that if in point of *time* strategic considerations came first, in point of *importance* economic and social considerations ranked ahead of them. He doubted whether Russia intended to fight militarily as much as ideologically. In his own country the young people were not satisfied that democracy could solve contemporary problems, and the "have nots" were being won over by

Communism. He warned that "unless democracy is revitalized, the peaceful conquest of Ceylon by Russia will be effected within measurable time." The delegate from Ceylon favoured less emphasis on the preponderance of power, which he feared would bring war, and greater efforts to deal with ideological and economic problems. The teeming masses of Asia, he said, must be made to feel that they are being helped to raise their own standard of living. Since they could not do this "under their own steam," it would be necessary to invest public and private capital in the underdeveloped countries "in an almost benevolent way."

A delegate from Pakistan was less concerned about the infiltration of Communism into his country than the speakers from India and Ceylon. Communism was ideologically opposed to the Muslim religion and had so far made little progress in the Islamic world. He recognised that Pakistan, which firmly believed in the democratic ideal, must be kept strong to prevent the U.S.S.R. from getting through to the Indian Ocean, and expressed some concern about the possibility of Indian Communists affecting the security of Eastern Pakistan, but asked for help from the Commonwealth and the United States to raise the standards of his people. It might, he knew, seem tiresome for Asian countries to stress so much economic considerations but these were of immediate urgency. The speaker made the significant point that in countries like his own the ruling class, which constituted only one or two per cent of the population and was the only class familiar with democratic ideals, must give tangible proofs of the benefits which the rest of the people would derive from their policies. Unless they could do so, power would pass into the hands of those less sympathetic with the West.

The Pakistan stress upon religion as an effective barrier to Communism appealed to an Irish delegate, who declared that the only way to oppose the Communist religion was by a belief in God. He pointed out that all Communists regarded organized religion as their greatest enemy. The speaker doubted whether the emphasis on material welfare was enough and suggested that over-concentration on social improvements and other materialistic developments might create conditions in the Western world quite undistinguishable from those now found in Soviet Russia.

In his view, to take military or social measures in a spiritual vacuum would not defeat Communism. This argument did not carry much weight with an Indian speaker who said he was convinced that, if it would serve the purpose of the Kremlin, every Communist outside Russia would profess a firm belief in God. His country had found that one of the most effective means of discrediting Communism was to expose the proofs of direct interference by the Kremlin in Indian questions. Constant vigilance was required, and they had learned that what appears in *Pravda* to-day will be "whispered in Bombay to-morrow and heard in Delhi the day after." To stress military measures as others proposed was to lay yourself open to the charge, such as was made by Indian Communists, that the democracies were preparing for an aggressive war against the Soviet Union.

Speakers from Australia, Canada and the United Kingdom readily conceded the difficulties of deciding which should have greater priority, the necessity for national security or the urgency of improving economic conditions. They admitted the possibility that Russia might prefer to continue the infiltrating methods to which we had become accustomed in the past two years. But they did not see how one could avoid taking sides in the struggle. The Communist menace was there and could not be wished away. An Australian delegate, who expressed deep sympathy with the Indian dilemma and who conceded that Australia was "not facing her responsibilities fully," felt that a "complete change of front" was necessary on the part of India, Pakistan and Ceylon. He believed that the strategic position of the Commonwealth in the Indian Ocean was the weakest that it had been in the past three hundred years. The "cruel, crude and dreadful facts" of defence had to be faced. He made the same appeal to the Irish delegation because of the possibility the danger from submarine activities in the next war would be even more serious and crippling than it was in the last one. Irish bases were missed in 1939-45 and might be even more necessary next time. In the face of the immediate danger "a realistic attitude and a complete change of heart" was necessary.

Not all the critics of what might be described as the Asian point of view were as outspoken as the Australian. Some of them indicated other useful approaches to the problem of how best to meet the Communist threat to security. One delegate, who felt that the element of power had been understressed by the speaker from Ceylon, agreed with him that the intellectual world should not be overlooked in the strengthening of defence against Communism. It was her opinion that the building of morale to withstand Communist aggression must "come through intellectual training and the development of a belief in democratic institutions." She thought that the intellectual climate of the Commonwealth was not favourable to the growth of Communism—less so than in France and Italy, where there was real concern about the infiltration of Communism into intellectual circles. Generally speaking it was her belief that intellectual leaders soon became disillusioned with the over-simple ideology of Communism. In furthering common attitudes she favoured interchange of teachers and students among the Commonwealth universities and encouragement of the German universities in their efforts to train future leaders for a democratic Germany. Another United Kingdom speaker suggested that by viewing world conditions through Soviet eyes the measures required to offset Communist strategy might be better appreciated. He thought that the Soviet leaders hoped to profit from the following "inherent weaknesses" in the capitalistic system:

1. A division between social classes.
2. A division on inter-imperialist lines between States (sterling and dollar, victor and vanquished).
3. The inevitable economic breakdown in the non-Communist world.
4. The struggle for freedom by oppressed peoples.

If the Russians could exploit the racial, economic and social divisions arising from these difficulties they might risk aggression, but they would not act unless they were certain of victory. It was our duty to prevent the balance from tipping in favour of the Soviet group, and to eradicate by democratic methods the divisions which the Russians would try to exploit. He believed that the problems arising from the West's seeking to aid the underdeveloped areas were greater than those resulting from the current dollar-sterling difficulties. Tremendous energy and initiative would be required to develop functional guarantees of security and stability. Geographically the Commonwealth, which was "a skeleton of the new world system," was ideally situated to do the job. In addition to its links with all parts of the world it had special links with the United States, whose economic power was vital for the development of backward countries. If Western democracy succeeded in developing such a world system, which economic forces made imperative, he thought that Russia might become a state like Franco's Spain in Europe—"an unpleasant but harmless anomaly."

By their contributions to the debate three Canadian speakers reminded the delegates that the agenda called for a discussion of Commonwealth relations with the United States as well as with Soviet Russia. The tendency to take friendly relations with the United States for granted did reflect the fact that since the "cold war" co-operation between the Commonwealth countries and the United States had become closer than ever. But co-operation also raised new problems, such as the right of the United States to take strategic action on Commonwealth territory. This question was of even greater concern to Canada than it had been in the war, when the Bases Agreement of 1941 had given the United States long-term military rights on Newfoundland and of a very sweeping character. Canada had inherited these concessions now that Newfoundland had entered Confederation, and they were much greater than any concessions which Canada had made to the United States since 1940 in working out common defence problems. One of the Canadians who had attended the Unofficial Conference of 1945 thought that the intervening years had strengthened the force of the contention, which was then less generally admitted, that close co-operation with the United States was "essential to Commonwealth security." In his view it was the Commonwealth, rather than the United States, which should make the greater part of the major adjustments required in working out defence policies. On the question of standardization of equipment, in which to date little progress had been made, he thought it unsound to expect the United States to accept Commonwealth standards when the United States was the main supplier of equipment and funds. He urged consideration of what effective steps and adjustments were necessary. His argument was supported by the third Canadian speaker who emphasized the importance of the correct psychological approach to Americans when seeking their assistance. If approached in the right spirit they were a generous people, but they were also hard traders. He believed that it was also important to realise that American financial resources were not limitless, and that if the United States were relied upon for aid in strategy and defence, it would be a limiting factor upon the extent to which it could also contribute to economic rehabilitation.

The debates on the problems presented by Germany and Japan in the field of strategy were influenced by unhappy recollections of past experiences in dealing with defeated nations. To curb the economic power of either nation too drastically would lead to further uncertainty as to their future and resulting discontent which Communism could exploit. It was hard to distinguish clearly between war potential and non-war potential industries, and difficult to dismantle factories without prejudicing economic recovery. The risk of German and Japanese recovery was not as great as that of continued economic instability, argued one delegate. To exclude them from the United Nations indefinitely might lead to difficulties in the future. In the case of Japan there was the additional complication of Communist success in China which might have a general unsettling effect on the neighbouring states, as the experience of Malaya had already indicated. Two United Kingdom delegates were agreed upon the vital importance of incorporating Germany in the group of Western European states if Russia was not to absorb in peace or conquer in war the peoples of that region. It was obvious that sixty million energetic and industrious Germans in the heart of Europe were bound to be attracted to one side or the other. Strategically it was essential that they should not fight on the other side. Otherwise there would be a repetition of the last war, aggravated by the alliance of the Germans with the Russians. It was suggested that, in a war between Russia and the West, the Russians as "land animals" would want to overrun and organise countries in their path and might therefore refrain from indiscriminate use of the most terrible modern weapons of man. They would "want to conquer going concerns and not merely ruins." The West could control the sea, as in the past, but would have difficulty in bringing pressure to bear on land, where the bulk of the land forces would probably have to be supplied by the United States. In such a war bombing alone would not secure victory; the contested territories would have to be occupied by ground forces and large armies would again be needed. How were these problems and probabilities to be faced?

The pros and cons of rearming Germany for the defence of the West, of allowing her to enter into Western Union or be associated in some way with the North Atlantic countries, were weighed with great care. The military argument as it emerged during the discussion for ensuring that a rearmed Germany should be on our side was based on the contention that it was vital to have the aid of such skilled and virile people to avert the dangers to Western Europe from any war with Russia. These were "firstly, the over-running of Western Europe by the Russian armies; secondly the disruption of British overseas communications; thirdly the breakdown of the United Kingdom as a main arsenal and base for the Western world." Strategically there was a case for the immediate rearmament of Germany, for it was impossible to keep Germany permanently disarmed when Russia was rearming the eastern zone. Admittedly there were dangers in any co-ordinated plan for rearming Germany and getting her "firmly into the Western European camp," but what was the alternative? Against this there were presented certain political considerations. It was true that, at the present time, anti-Soviet feeling was strong in all parts of Germany, including the eastern zone. In Western Germany—the industrial area—there were eleven million refugees from the eastern zone who were bitterly anti-Russian. It was also true that there was a power vacuum in Central Europe which a rearmed Germany, if she were freed from all restrictions, could and would fill very quickly. Moreover, as a United Kingdom speaker pointed out, it was dangerous to assume that the German army would be so anti-Russian that we could safely rely upon its constant support. Under the Weimar Republic and for a time under Hitler there had been contacts between the Russian and German General Staffs. Even today some right-wing German politicians, such as Nadolny, had had contacts with the Russian authorities. A rearmed Germany would be a remili-

tarized Germany in which the temptation for the army to ally
itself with Big Business would be great and would have serious
deleterious effects on the growth of German democracy, whose
strongest supporters were the Trade Unions and the Social
Democratic party. Other disastrous consequences of an alliance
with Germany that were suggested were the probable effects it
would have upon opinion in Western Europe, especially in
France, which would not easily consent to such a policy, and
upon the peoples of Eastern Europe who disliked their domination by the Soviet Union. If we allied ourselves with a Germany
whom they had had so much cause to fear in the past, it would
"almost certainly turn these people against us and rally them to
the cause of Russia." Thus the political disadvantages outweigh-
ed the military arguments for allowing Germany to rearm. It
might be possible to incorporate German forces into a Western
military system, but it was first necessary to establish such a
system. Meanwhile, both the occupation of Germany and the
control of the Ruhr should continue indefinitely. A Canadian
agreed with this diagnosis by a United Kingdom speaker and
maintained that there were only three countries which possessed
the manpower and reserves to sustain a major, modern war.
These three were the United States, the Soviet Union and
Germany. To associate the last named with the Atlantic countries "would build up a third force that would inevitably claim
full control of its resources." The speaker expressed a "profound
distrust" of the German temperament, and feared that the
Germans, if given this opportunity, would use their regained
power to play off one side against the other for their own benefit.

Although these arguments against rearming Germany at present or admitting her to membership in the North Atlantic
Organization were generally approved, there was less agreement
on what steps might be taken politically to associate Germany
with the Western powers. One speaker warmly supported Mr.
Churchill's proposal for a federal solution of the problem by
associating the German states as partners in a Western Europe
federation. Since the federal state would have sole control of
arms and armies, except for the police forces required to
maintain law and order, Germany could not then be a source
of danger. She would be guarded in the Western European

state "like a wild elephant between two tame ones." The speaker said that he had advocated such a policy at the Hague conference expecting that it would not be regarded sympathetically by Germans. To his surprise German observers had told him that they felt such a plan would give German people hope for the future, something which they needed even more than bread. In reply it was pointed out that the Bonn Constitution was now in effect and was much less federal in form than that of the United States. Its existence would make difficult the entry of individual German states into a Western European federation. It was also claimed that in Germany there was strong tendency to oppose increasing federalization and to take a neutral attitude between East and West. From another angle the case for federalism was attacked by speakers who argued that a viable federal state, able to stand up to Russia, must have ample powers for defence, foreign policy and control of the economy of the whole federation. If it acquired these powers it would accordingly fatally weaken the loyalty of Europeans to their national governments before it had won their loyalty to itself. In discussing the effect of a European federation on the Commonwealth, it was pointed out that the United Kingdom membership would necessarily reduce her to a status comparable to that of the state of Virginia in the United States. Such an association would be incompatible with Commonwealth relations. To suggest that the Commonwealth should enter the European federation was to overlook the trend of discussion at the conference. This point of view was shared by Australian and Canadian speakers. The former said that with all the advantages of common origin and geographic unity it had taken Australia thirty years to achieve federation. In the light of their country's experience, Australians thought that the movement for Western European federation was proceeding too rapidly. They feared that a federated Europe would underwrite a colonial system which Australia felt was "completely outmoded in the present world." The Canadian suggested that the logical policy required for setting up a viable Western Europe was to include not only the Commonwealth but also the United States. However, in the present state of American public opinion, as illustrated in the debates on the North Atlantic Pact, it was unthinkable that the United States would consent to enter such a group. An Indian delegate supported the Australian view on colonies and feared the adverse effect of federation with reactionary powers upon the United Kingdom which he felt had been following, on the whole, an enlightened colonial policy and had always represented "a progressive liberal force." If this federation with powers which held reactionary colonial views were established, it would make more difficult the liberation of the colonial peoples at present under the rule of such member governments. If Germany were included in the federation, she would inevitably dominate, and in view of her racial theories would use her dominance for reactionary purposes. A delegate from Pakistan pointed to the strength of the Communist parties in Europe and wondered if, in the light of that fact, there was enough public support for federal ideals. When comment on the attitude of public opinion in the United Kingdom was called for, a United Kingdom delegate, who expressed belief in Western Union, said that she thought the electorate would certainly not contemplate voting for Britain's entry into such a federation. The typical British distrust of blueprints and paper constitutions and that of the Commonwealth which, to judge from the conference discussions, "shied like a frightened horse from proposals for new machinery of Commonwealth co-operation" were contrasted with the attitude of Europeans, who "snatched at any suggestion that more machinery for co-operation should be provided." She returned to the German problem to stress the "terrible spiritual vacuum" we had utterly failed to fill and the bad effect of our dismantling policy. To get Germany on our side would, she recognized, take a good deal of psychological wisdom and would require us to face certain dangers. But these might be minimised if German forces were part of a larger European force and if we maintained "our real safeguard," the international control of the Ruhr. Other speakers then drove home the argument that rearmament was not a practical policy for the next few years. They were uneasy about the possibility of the numerous brilliant German generals, now holding menial jobs, jumping at the prospect of regaining their lost glory. These delegates believed, however, that the likelihood of war in Europe in the next few years was not great, and that this period should be employed by a democratic Western Germany in gaining the confidence of her Western neighbours. They admitted that a price must be paid for this policy of postponement—a price which could be found in the economic and political spheres by permitting an increase in the levels of German production and by allowing Western Germany to enter the Council of Europe. If she were admitted it was suggested that contacts with German politicians there might dispel some of our "comfortable illusions," while at the same time they might learn more of the arts of self-government in which Germany had never been proficient. As Germany soaked up these ideals and practices, the risks of permitting progressive rearmament might be correspondingly lessened.

In the light of these considerations the delegates proceeded to an examination of the North Atlantic Pact as a guarantee of regional security. Since the second phase in the evolution of the Pact—the period of organization—was just being inaugurated, with the meeting of the North Atlantic Council in Washington, the discussions were more concerned with possibilities than realities. It was suggested that, whereas the Brussels Treaty had been designed to create a counterpoise to Soviet power in Europe, the Atlantic Pact was intended to organize such a preponderance of power as would be a deterrent to Soviet aggression. For Europeans the possible implications of the removal by the Atlantic Pact of the centre of gravity further West were of great significance. Another question which greatly concerned them was the degree of economic and political integration which was necessary or desirable for successful defence. In commenting on the strategic aspects of the problem a United Kingdom delegate listed seven dangers which must be overcome. They were economic collapse, "obviously of the first importance from the military viewpoint," Communist infiltration in peacetime which was not as menacing as it was a year ago, the German problem which had just been discussed, the over-running of Western Europe in wartime, the co-ordination and standardization of war production, the possibility of a breakdown of communication in wartime, and the danger of the breakdown of the United Kingdom as a centre of production and a base for operations. He thought the Atlantic powers would have to recognise their corporate responsibility to meet these dangers, and to establish adequate machinery, a task which should not be too difficult. They would have to work out how best to distribute the load of war production and equipment, as for example in the manufacture of fighters and bombers, and how much standardization was necessary. Standardization in the Commonwealth was practically complete, and the main question was "matching up" with the United States, a policy which was essential for Canada. The startling improvement in the performance of the latest submarine made the problem of a breakdown of communications a "very large question" and would necessitate a great deal of effort to find the answer. But as long as Western Europe could be held, the Battle of the Atlantic could be won. The position of the United Kingdom in the event of war depended on the defence of Western Europe and on the proper organization of its own defence. Here was to be found the parallel with the position of Malta in the second world war which had been mentioned in the United Kingdom paper on strategy. The Atlantic powers would also have to make proper provision for economic strategy in the event of war. So far as the Commonwealth was concerned the main part in the Atlantic Pact must be played by the United States and Canada. There was not the slightest doubt of the closeness of co-operation between the United States and Canada, and all that was wanted was "that this closeness be matched by the closeness of United Kingdom co-operation with both."

In comments by Canadians on the Atlantic Pact it was clear that their country regarded the Pact as an instrument but not as an end in itself. It should be not only a weapon against Russian military power but also a defence against the threat of militant Communism. That was why Mr. St. Laurent, the Prime Minister, had said we should confront the Soviets with an immense moral force. It was hoped that behind the retaining wall of the Atlantic Pact Western Europe might become rehabilitated both economically and spiritually. Therefore, it was important that the use and allocation of our resources in order to obtain military security "should not endanger this rehabilitation." It was also believed in Canada that success in stopping Russia by the Atlantic Pact was not enough. We could not rest content with the existence of two worlds standing in irreconcilable conflict, but must get back to some common ground and "find some bridge or common purpose" on which we could act together. A Canadian also drew attention to the importance of Canada's securing an arrangement with the United States by which there could be an interchange of munitions. Without such a provision it would be extremely difficult to tool up Canadian plants solely for her own service requirements and, possibly, for those of the United Kingdom. Without it the Canadian aircraft industry, for example, would be in a very serious situation. It should also be remembered that practically all Canadian production had a large U.S. component. If arrangements could be made with the United States for the manufacture and sale of certain types of equipment, it would be of significance to the Commonwealth as well as to Canada. Other Canadians endeavoured to answer questions about the strategic role of Canada under the North Atlantic Pact but had to admit the paucity of public information. They felt that Canada would have an auxiliary position in the general framework and might make a special contribution in the form of a preparatory reserve for production. They did not anticipate that the R.C.A.F. would serve as a strategic air force but rather that it would focus on an air cover in coastal command, on fighter defence, and on medium bombers which might be utilised for offensive operations. The Canadian data paper had indicated that Canada would be expected to concentrate first on North America and then on the North Atlantic, where the Canadian navy could play an important part in helping to provide sea cover for convoys to Western Europe and the United Kingdom. Action in a wider field would depend upon the decisions of the Council in Washington.

A United Kingdom speaker asked for comment from the other Commonwealth delegations upon the duplication of machinery which was developing through the establishment of Western Union, the North Atlantic Organization and other regional understandings. In reply an Australian said that his countrymen were fully in accord with the necessary steps taken by the United Kingdom to secure co-operation, since they recognized that the

Atlantic Pact was basically "a military alliance to meet desperate possibilities." They were not, however, in favour of a federal scheme unless the United States was prepared to substitute such a plan for the United Nations. A South African speaker thought that South Africa was not "very concerned" with the North Atlantic Pact and regarded federal union as a "remote conception." On the other hand, the government had made it clear in no uncertain terms that in a war against Communism South Africans would "for the first time in their history come in as a united people within the Commonwealth." A delegate from Pakistan said he believed he expressed the view of the people of the three Asian countries in stating that Western Union was "the business of the Western people." His government had not yet found it necessary to consider any commitment but would be happy to see any developments for peace and stability in any part of the globe. A United Kingdom speaker emphasized the point previously made by another speaker, that economic stability was the first necessity from the military point of view. He pointed out that the United Kingdom had been participating fully in European organization in all three fields, military, political and economic, and that there were, in the last mentioned, aspects peculiar to Western Europe. There were, for instance, "many working organizations for economic co-operation . . . overlapping both in their purposes and membership." This statement prompted another United Kingdom speaker to point out some of the difficulties involved in working out the proper political and economic ties for Britain with Europe. The United Kingdom was a maritime nation, a situation reflected in the fact that she did the bulk of her trade overseas. Europe was a continental area whose trade was mostly overland. It was too simple to suggest that if a customs union were achieved for Europe, all would be well. Europe was a deficiency area in foodstuffs and raw materials. The various countries spent from 15 to 30 per cent of their national income on imports, as compared to only three per cent in the United States. To tighten the bonds between Europe and the United Kingdom would not solve the problem of dependence upon outside sources. Nor was it true to argue that because North America had single customs and currency Europe could have the same. The United States production was not due exclusively to her huge markets but was also due to the high degree of mechanization and the extent of natural resources. Small countries might develop remarkable productive capacity in specialized industries, as had been demonstrated by Canada, Sweden and Switzerland. In the United Kingdom there were many industries in which the firms were on the average as large as those in the United States. It should also be remembered in discussing Britain's part in a European customs union that her trade with Commonwealth countries was 50 per cent of her total trade as against 22 per cent with the OEEC countries. His conclusion was that:

The United Kingdom has to get trade with the outside world, and it makes better sense to develop her overseas trade than to tie herself more closely to the continental trade of Europe.

In reply to a question the same speaker stated that a complete customs union with Europe was not a necessity. He pointed out that:

An effective customs union cannot do without a central economic organization, involving for example a greater merger of fiscal policies and a single currency issuing body.

It would require a sacrifice by the participating nations of some degree of control over their economic policies and would lead to stronger pressure to ensure a uniform type of economy for all European countries. It was the view of this speaker that there was no need for closer political integration in order to achieve economic co-operation for strategic purposes. In commenting on these observations Canadians drew attention to the fact that the North Atlantic Treaty had purposely avoided closer political integration and was intentionally vaguer than the Treaty of Brussels. Its broad terms made the Atlantic Treaty a more effective instrument for the wide scale of operations it envisaged. On the other hand, Canadians were somewhat disappointed at the vagueness of the economic provisions in Article Two of the Pact. It was also suggested that the Continuing Committee which might arise as a result of the financial talks in Washington among the United States, the United Kingdom and Canada could be used for developing closer economic integration.

Further examination of the existing economic machinery created by the OEEC, the Economic Committee for Europe under the United Nations, the Council of Europe, the Continuing Committee, and what was envisaged under the Brussels Treaty provoked the warning that, if Commonwealth governments were considering further Commonwealth machinery they should take note of the difficulties that were emerging from what was already in existence. As a United Kingdom speaker declared, it was even now "a hideous problem to find sufficient manpower of the right calibre to keep in touch with all economic developments and sing the same song." Simplification of machinery for economic co-operation would be advantageous in furthering the concentration of highly trained manpower when only a limited number was available in the world.[1] It was pointed out, however, that there was no machinery in existence for settling the question of the balance of payments with North America. This problem was complicated for the United Kingdom by the fact that she was very short of the "hard" currencies of the United States and Canada but had a surplus of other "very soft" currencies. It was then suggested that if the North American balance of payments problem could be solved most of the machinery would then disappear. In this connection a United Kingdom delegate said that the OEEC had been handicapped by the absence of official United States representation from its discussions, and that, although unity had been achieved in the wording of reports, interpretations of them had varied with individual ideas. This admission evoked from a warm advocate of federalism the remark that in other words the deliberations in OEEC were "chartered impotence." Another comment on the proliferation of machinery came from an Australian who said that his country could not spare any more manpower for new economic committees. That was one reason why it had refused to participate in a proposed Commonwealth Council to exchange information on the European Recovery Programme. One speaker asked if, "in this bewildered and bureaucratized world," the

---

[1] Cf. "Europe's Committees," *The Economist,* January 14, 1950, pp. 65-66. *The Economist* estimates ". . . it will take some 100 committees of varying size and degrees of importance to plan and execute the military, financial, economic and political policies in Europe to which this country is committed under its various treaties with neighbours and allies."

Conference could suggest some way of simplifying both the aims and the machinery of the Commonwealth. If that could be done it would result in one area of the world not becoming involved in too numerous consultative bodies.

As a result of the discussion, the delegates generally realised that overdevelopment in the European sphere might affect regional organizations in other parts of the world. It was also appreciated that, in the field of strategic co-operation, plans which had been originally based upon the assumption of a unity of command and high degree of planning for producing war material in Europe, had been altered by the centring of these basic features in the United States. Once again this change underlined the need for close links between the Commonwealth and the United States which might guarantee to Europe the security that she needed. It was further realised that the development of effective regional defence measures in Western Europe might render more possible Soviet expansion in other less protected areas.

The appreciation of this difficulty resulted in the Conference turning to the study of defence arrangements for the Middle East. In this area, which was of immediate concern to all the Commonwealth countries but Canada, there were, as the delegation papers had demonstrated, grounds for serious concern. One United Kingdom speaker argued that, in the event of another war, there would be an "enormous advantage" in the Middle East remaining neutral. At the present time all the states in that area were extremely weak, politically, economically, and socially. In the past they had been threatened with danger from Europe. Now the threat, which was much more difficult to meet, was from the Caucasus. Oil, which the Russians needed, was right in the front line in Iraq and Iran, and there were no military forces worth talking about closer than the Caucasus and Egypt. Consequently, the Middle East was a complete military vacuum in which a Russian aggressor would possess the advantage of having great opportunities for deploying his forces and the United States would be faced with great difficulties in mobilising hers. The attraction of oil and the temptation to break through to the Indian Ocean would exert a powerful influence upon the Russians. For these reasons neutrality for the Middle East—however desirable—was unlikely

in another war. The speaker suggested that one alternative
policy was to try to improve the general conditions of the Middle
Eastern states and to make them realise that they must agree to
such steps "with the help of powerful friends." It would be
necessary to overcome very real suspicions that the dangers
which confronted them were bogeys, and that the Western
states wanted only to dominate them. Somehow "we" must
get a sufficient degree of confidence in the motives of the
United States and the United Kingdom in order to obtain
wholehearted co-operation in the development of bases so that
our forces could be more rapidly deployed than at present. The
new Dominions, particularly India and Pakistan, should pay
the utmost attention to this area and the United Kingdom
would of course co-operate.

This diagnosis of the situation in the Middle East was endorsed
and expanded by another United Kingdom delegate who thought
that the consequences of recent developments there were
". . . more far reaching than anything that had happened since
Allenby's victory and the collapse of the Ottoman Empire." He
pointed out that of the six Middle East states, Lebanon, Syria,
Iraq, the Hashemite Kingdom of the Jordan, Israel and Egypt,
all but Egypt were of comparatively recent origin. Four of them
had been "artificial creations of the 1914-1918 war" established
on a feudal basis. Thus Iraq had been handed over to Feisal
and Trans-Jordan to his brother and others to the French. These
Arab states had remained feudal in outlook and in government,
with political power and wealth concentrated in the hands of
a few families. In Egypt, for example, a country of seventeen
millions, four-fifths of the total wealth was in the hands of
eight hundred pashas. In such a group of states, "ripe for
internal combustion," a new dynamic state had emerged in the
shape of Israel. Its overwhelming victory in Palestine had been
a defeat of the Arabs not only militarily but politically and
spiritually as well. They were now "a disillusioned people realizing the worthlessness of their leaders and institutions." This
created a very dangerous situation and would lead to profound
changes in the Middle East, once peace was signed with Israel,
as must eventually happen. The speaker believed it would be
a great mistake "ever again to bolster up the old feudal states,"

and that alignment would be necessary with forces which would make for a complete change of leadership.

In commenting on the new state of Israel, the speaker pointed out that it was based upon a "communal" system which should not be confused with Communism. Political power was in the hands of a virile trade union movement, whose party held the majority of seats in the Israeli parliament. He argued that in any defence of the Middle East, co-operation would be necessary with Israel as well as with the Arab states, which would have to be reorganized on a more sure and sound democratic basis. He conceded that Israel was bound to show expansionist tendencies in view of the present political vacuum in the Middle East which held "too many temptations even for a politically moral state." He did not accept a common belief that Israel would side with Russia in the event of a war. The Jews remembered too vividly the Russian pogroms; and the existence of their state was based upon the flow of American dollars. Israel was likely to play off East against West, and would seek the highest possible price for an alliance with the West. On the other hand, if Israel did come in on our side in war, it would be hard to get the Arabs to take an active part. We could only hope that new democratic forces might get control of them and eventually "make a deal with the Jewish state."

This emphasis upon Israel as "the keystone of resistance to Communism in the Middle East" did not pass unchallenged. It was pointed out that from the standpoint of strategy, Egypt was the only base worthy of the name in that area, since it possessed both a "back door" and a "front door," and harbours of the size necessary for handling military traffic. It was true that negotiations for revising the existing treaty with Egypt had broken down, but there were grounds for hope that they might be resumed in a more favourable atmosphere later. Egypt was becoming more favourably disposed to the West because of the considerable gains which Communism was making there. The Egyptians' great problem was to "choose between their hatred of Israel and their hatred of Communism." To make an arrangement with Israel, before being assured of the Suez canal zone as a strategic base, might mean that we had backed the wrong horse. Another United Kingdom speaker reminded the delegates that the Foreign Office had always stressed close friendship with the Arab states, and that recent events in Palestine would make it hard to convince the British public that it was necessary to have an immediate link with the new state. It was also well to remember that geography, religion and pan-Islamic policies gave the Arab states a community of interest which was of wider significance in the Muslim world. To depart from the old association with the Arab states would be a mistake, although it was advisable to remember the changing social conditions to which reference had been made. The wisest course would be not to put all our money on one side or the other, but to see what United Kingdom and Commonwealth diplomacy could do to bring Arabs and Jews together and to further "some kind of economic federation in the Middle East."

A South African delegate, who had recently visited Israel, agreed with a previous speaker that Communism was without any considerable political significance there. The overriding need was for United States dollars and also, to some extent, for South African pounds, as South Africa ranked next to the United States in contributions per capita to the new state. The West held the key to Israeli development, and in serious trouble with Russia, after first neutrality and then hard bargaining, Israel would "come down heavily on our side." The speaker thought that conciliatory gestures by the United Kingdom would pay handsomely, and pointed out that the president of the new state, Dr. Weizmann, had been a distinguished British scientist and had always believed firmly in promoting a wider association with the Commonwealth. With much that had been said about the feudal nature, backward condition and weak military position of the Arab states a Pakistan speaker agreed. He thought that they might get used in time to the situation but that any talk of a Jewish-Arab federation was "out of the question for some years to come." The backing of Israel by the United States was an important factor in the security of this region. Although Pakistan did not consider herself a part of the Middle East, she had always been profoundly interested in developments there and shared the Arabs' spiritual and cultural heritage. The Arab states might be written off as a military factor but not the Arab people. Nor could Arab feeling, from the borders of Persia to the shores of the Atlantic, be neglected. The speaker made the significant comment:

It often happens in war that a country wishes to make use of the territory of another state in order to implement its strategy effectively, and it is perhaps worth while considering if the government is weak, whether it would not be the best course to befriend beforehand the people whose territory one wishes to use.

One of his colleagues added that public opinion in Pakistan was greatly exercised over the Palestine dispute, and to date the government had not recognized the new state of Israel. If Israel did join the West in a war, it would be hard to control public opinion, and the Pakistan government would be on the horns of a dilemma as to what course of action it should take. It was also stated that although her Foreign Minister was held in high esteem by the Arabs and had acted on occasion as their spokesman in the United Nations, Pakistan did not wish to be regarded as a leader of the Middle East. If encouraged to do so, she might use her influence to foster the growth of democracy there, but could not do more than that.

In view of the Anglo-Egyptian Treaty, the United Kingdom guarantees to Iraq and the Hashemite Kingdom of the Jordon, and the importance of the Arab states as possessors of oil, harbours and important communications, there was general agreement that, from the military point of view, the Arab states must be won over to the West. But much would depend upon the passing of the feudal regime in those countries since, as one speaker remarked, "the trouble was that whenever the Western democracies put money into the coffers of these states it did not go to irrigation but to Monte Carlo." It was believed that Israel, which was about 40 per cent self-supporting, would continue to receive contributions towards its support from all over the world, particularly from South Africa and the United States, and would accordingly be, in the long run, on the Western side in a clash with Russia.

The Conference then turned to an examination of the general problems of defence in the Indian Ocean. As the delegation papers had already indicated, it was necessary to take into due account the bearing on it of the acrimonious dispute between

India and Pakistan over Kashmir, of Asian hostility to Colonialism, and of the attitude of the Asian countries generally to aid,
whether military or economic, from the Western world.

In examining the plans for defence of the Indian Ocean and
South Asia against possible Soviet aggression it was clear that
the Commonwealth countries were faced with a difficult situation. A United Kingdom speaker pointed out that in the past
British power had had such effective control of the orifices of
the Indian Ocean that its security and stability had been largely
taken for granted. In the second world war the Japanese had
made some penetration of that region, sufficient at least to demonstrate the grave damage that could be done to Commonwealth strategy if control of that region were lost. To-day the
United Kingdom did not have the same capacity to defend the
Indian Ocean which she had possessed in the past and the burden
of its defence must fall more upon those countries which bordered
it. At present none of them was ready to contribute to what
might be called extra-territorial defence, and there were no
multilateral defence arrangements with the United Kingdom.
There were, it was true, bilateral arrangements between the
United Kingdom and India, and the United Kingdom and
Pakistan, but the dispute between India and Pakistan over
Kashmir precluded any joint contribution by them to peripheral
defence or to the maintenance of such vital points as Singapore.
Until all Commonwealth countries could accept as axiomatic
that war between them was unthinkable there could not be
a sound strategy for the Indian Ocean.

Closely related to the strategic question were economic and
social problems. The transition from imperialism in South Asia
had not solved problems of strategy, and had not necessarily
improved social and communal relations. In Malaya, for instance, the mere use of democratic forms had offered no solution,
and in Indonesia there had clearly been grave stresses and
strains. These complex problems were for the Asian peoples themselves to work out. Simple formulae such as denunciation of
imperialism or opposition to Communism were not enough. But
the Commonwealth could afford an opportunity for frank discussion, without misunderstanding and recrimination, and for a
recognition of differences, in their respective positions. In their

comments on this thoughtful analysis of the situation the "Western" members of the Conference were torn between a concern for the urgency of improving the defences of this region, and an appreciation of the importance of the economic factor in Asian policies. If one South African warned all three Asian states of the danger of a thrust to the Indian Ocean from the north through Persia which might out-flank India and Pakistan, another argued that it would be prudent for other Commonwealth countries "to assume that defence considerations would not alone be sufficient in view of the present relations with the new Asian dominions." As might be expected, Canadians drew attention to the importance of the possible role of the United States, now that that country had washed her hands of China. They felt that India and Pakistan might be materially assisted by the United States but, if assistance were offered, that country would naturally expect some co-operation in barring the door to Communism in Asia. United Kingdom speakers speculated whether Indians would like the receipt of American military and economic aid, which would necessarily involve supervision by United States missions in their country. One of them suggested that it might be better for India to secure financial assistance from private agencies, if that were possible, as they would not be in the same position to influence Indian policy as the American Congress. Another addressed three questions to the Indian delegation. Would India take an interest in Burma even to the extent of intervention in order to prevent Burma from becoming a Communist outpost? He feared that Burma might become a "trouble spot" which Communists could exploit and thus make a source of difficulty for all Southeast Asia. Secondly, was a plebiscite acceptable to India as a solution for the Kashmir dispute? Could a Southeast Asian pact, on the lines of the Atlantic Pact, and including France and Holland, be arranged before the problems of Indo-China and Indonesia had been solved? If so, how should the United Kingdom guide itself in working for such a pact? The speaker himself thought that the suggestion of such a pact was based on a "too simple outlook."

An Indian speaker, who was not connected with any political party or the press, and who made it plain that he could reply only as an individual, answered these questions as follows. He believed that Indian public opinion was opposed to forcible intervention in Burma because of "the fundamental belief of India that each country should decide its own fate for itself." He admitted that some unwise speeches had been made by Indian delegates at the Asian Conference of 1947, which had led people to believe that India was seeking a sphere of influence in Southeast Asia. If intervention were necessary in Burma, it would have to be made in conjunction with Pakistan, which was Burma's immediate neighbour, and which had already experienced difficulties from the fighting on her borders and from refugees. He did not think that Pakistan would be willing to intervene militarily, but suggested that any intervention should be rather along the line of assistance through the committee of British, Indian and Pakistani ambassadors in Rangoon. The speaker added slyly that if the policy of intervention produced a bad odour India would "want to share it with countries more accustomed to bearing the responsibilities of such an odour." On the Kashmir question he agreed that it should be settled by a plebiscite, and thought it was unfortunate that the Indian undertaking to accept the will of the people as expressed in a plebiscite had been obscured for a time by "other considerations." He felt that eventually the problems could be settled to the satisfaction of both India and Pakistan, and expressed appreciation for the value of the present conference in permitting contacts between Indian and Pakistani delegations which were most difficult elsewhere. The speaker ruled out a possible Southeast Asian pact as impossible at present "because of the absence of a solution of the Indonesian problem to the satisfaction of the Indonesians and the absence of a solution in Indo-China." The same questions were also answered by a delegate from Pakistan, who said that his government had very cordial relations with the present Burmese government. If this government failed in its fight with the Communist rebels, it would then be necessary to re-examine the question of intervention in the light of the circumstances prevailing at the time. He argued that, in any event, the burden of intervention should fall on India because Pakistan already had its hands full with its own problems of security. Pakistan also thought that a plebiscite should be held in Kashmir and wanted to get on with it. In spite of the Indian speaker's "clever and eloquent speech" about reaching a solution the Pakistan delegate added that he was extremely sorry to say that there had not been "the slightest effort on the part of India to bring this about." He also charged that India had taken over Indian States "which had declared either in favour of Pakistan or in favour of independence." He urged that there should be investigation of the refugee and communal problems which India had not been willing to concede. As the speaker summed up his views: in short India was determined to have its own way in all problems at issue. On the third question the Pakistan delegate agreed with his predecessor in opposing a Southeast Asian pact at the present time. Without popular support the governments in this area would be useless in war. An atomic bomb would not change that fact. How could it be used in Singapore, Batavia, Bagdad, Damascus or Cairo? A war must be followed by police action. It was only by giving independence to colonial peoples that we could "bring them on the side of democracy and the Commonwealth." This sharp attack on India's policy evoked equally frank remarks from an Indian delegate in defence of his country's position. He did point out, however, that partition had been accepted by both peoples in India and that to that extent, the situation was more satisfactory than in Ireland. He believed that leading people in India and Pakistan were getting "tired and alarmed at the defence expenditures and the stultifying of the influence of their countries in the world." In his opinion there would emerge in time a bilateral defence agreement which would still allow the countries to remain independent of the two world blocs. ". . . The influences of geography, economics and strategy, the emergence of a Communist China, and the link between influential people in both countries" would eventually lead to a solution.

A delegate from Ceylon, who said that his country, like India, regarded with apprehension the division of the world, frankly admitted that Ceylon must come down to earth and realize that any hopes it nevertheless had for security in the Indian Ocean "must be greater than its contribution." He believed that geography must inevitably bring the three Asian dominions together in shaping a common defence policy, but did not think the time was ripe for any cohesive defence system in Southern Asia. He

welcomed the agreement for a naval base at Trincomalee for
the United Kingdom, since it afforded defence that Ceylon could
not provide for herself, and favoured Ceylon's looking for security
in the Commonwealth. Apart from their sharp differences over
the Kashmir question, refugees, communal problems and other
related matters, the delegates from India and Pakistan had much
in common in their attitude on colonial and economic matters.
Both would agree, as an Indian put it, that military strategy,
in order to be fully effective, must be based upon a clear understanding of the objectives of the Western powers by the peoples
of North Africa, the Middle East and Asian countries. Both
asked for definite indications that "the realization of the ideals
of democracy is not only the ultimate but also the immediate
aim, and that the strategy of the democratic powers is based on
the strengthening of the progressive forces within each country."
An Indian speaker said that any impression that the defence of
democracy might become confused with the advancement of
other interests, such as building an economic empire in Asia or
Africa, must be removed. He maintained that the attitude of
both the United Kingdom and the United States on racial
discrimination at the United Nations had been very different
in 1948 from what it was the previous year and said it seemed
that the change was "mainly due to pressure from some
colonial powers that had signed the Atlantic Pact and were
members of the Western Union." If democratic strategy was to
be sound, it had to bear in mind that Nationalist movements
in Southeast Asia were anti-Western in content and directed
against the dominant social groups in the new states. As far as
his country was concerned, India did not want to join any
division of the world into two opposing blocs, and would do
nothing to worsen relations between them. She preferred to
work through the United Nations, to do all that she could to
strengthen it, and not to create spheres of influence. India would
also join heartily in all measures for common security based on
UN principles. At the same time Indian delegates were aware
that the advance of Communism in Southeast Asia was continuing, and that the shift of emphasis in Communist strategy to that
region might affect the policies of the Western powers who had
checked Russian aggression in Western Europe by the Atlantic

Pact and Western Union. The emergence of a Communist China, working closely with Soviet Russia, would create serious military problems for the Indian sub-continent. As one of the Indians stated, they were beginning to see that there was "virtually no chance for Pakistan or India to maintain their integrity against Russia" unless there was mutual co-operation. He thought there would have to be a solution of their differences "on U.S.-Canadian lines, and not on Franco-German ones." Such a solution could not come from the United Kingdom, since memories of past differences between India and the United Kingdom could not be wiped out in a few years, nor from the Commonwealth since its members, unlike the United States and Ireland, had shown little interest in India's fight for freedom. India had still to find out what the Commonwealth meant to it and what it meant to the Commonwealth.

In answer to a question as to the reaction of Indians to the United States' assuming direct responsibilities in the Indian Ocean area for both military and economic aid, an Indian delegate admitted that this matter was of "extraordinary difficulty." If the world had not been divided into two blocs, an answer would have been simple. He thought economic aid would be welcomed but aid in defence "would perhaps be less welcome." Although there was a strong conservative element in India which would find itself very much at home with certain American opinions, there were others, like himself, who were alarmed at the implications of American aid. They were not sure of the American position in the anti-Communist front, since it was known that in the United States all sorts of reactionary movements concealed themselves under the cloak of anti-Communism. In this respect the situation was different in the United Kingdom where the Conservative party was a conservative wing of a people that now believed in social democracy, the real enemy of Communism. Unlike the United Kingdom, the United States had also a record of racial discrimination. The other reason for their attitude was that most educated Indians had been brought up in a British tradition and had formed close ties with the United Kingdom. Neither educationally nor otherwise were there as close ties with the United States. Nevertheless, India would have to rely considerably upon the United States for aid. With that fact in mind the Indian delegate asked: Could India find a new unity in the Commonwealth that would make Indians feel there was a group of powers that stood, in the long run, for values that India cherished?

When an Indian speaker said the role of the Commonwealth countries as mediators was limited because India did not know them well enough yet, a delegate from Pakistan interjected "You can speak for us as well." In discussing strategy, another Pakistan speaker also agreed with the Indians that regional defence schemes for South Asia were necessarily directed against attempts by Soviet Russia to reach the Indian Ocean, and that neither Pakistan nor India could long hold out without aid from the United Kingdom and the United States. He was sure that if Russia decided to invade the Indian sub-continent "the Russian army would have to pass over the dead bodies of my countrymen." In reply to an earlier comment from an Australian delegate, he pointed out that nearly 60 per cent of Pakistan's revenues was already being spent on defence arrangements, and did not see what more could be expected. He complained that a considerable quantity of military stores due to Pakistan after partition had not been delivered. On the Northwest frontier, where Pakistan had inherited its defence from British India, the frontier tribes had been integrated and created little danger. On the Burmese frontier, the only other route for Communism to enter the sub-continent, East Pakistan provided a bulwark for security. But Pakistan must first think of her own security before regional security. The speaker gave details of aggressive actions by India since partition in Junagadh, Hyderabad and Kashmir. In contrast to India's position he deplored the lack of help from other Commonwealth countries and accused them of displaying a tendency ". . . to flirt with India at the expense of my own country." He believed that the Commonwealth countries should set Pakistan's fears at rest ". . . in order to prevent the people of Pakistan from seeking help elsewhere." Meanwhile, as long as India maintained "its bellicose attitude" and kept forces in Kashmir which threatened the borders of Pakistan, it was unreasonable for others to expect Pakistan to join India in any defence arrangement.

In this attitude of negativism the debate ended, a debate which had emitted both heat and light. The delegates were left with the uneasy realization that there was no immediate possibility of concerted military measures being taken in Southeast Asia to deter Communism. They were also again forcibly reminded of the fundamental importance of raising the standard of living of the Asian peoples and of satisfying their demands for self-determination and democratic government. Lastly they were confronted with the inadequacy of the Commonwealth as an agency for mediation between two of its Asian members, where deep-seated differences existed, and where either ignorance or indifference largely governed the attitudes of the other Commonwealth states.

The examination of security problems in the Pacific and the Far East presented another set of perplexing difficulties. The co-operation of Australia and New Zealand on defence and related questions was in refreshing contrast to the position of India and Pakistan in the Indian Ocean. But differences of emphasis on control and economic policy between them and the United States over Japan, the consequences of the possible re-emergence of Japan as a military power both in Asia and the Pacific, the baffling spectre of a communist China, and the problem of Hong Kong furnished ample grounds for controversy.

An Australian speaker who opened the discussions began by emphasizing the great changes which had been brought about in that area by long range air craft. Sydney, for instance, was only thirty-five hours' flying time from San Francisco, twenty-four hours' from Singapore and twenty-six hours' from Hong Kong. The development of long range aircraft had profoundly modified strategy in the Pacific, as was illustrated in the Battle of the Coral Sea, in which surface vessels did not come within range of each other. What seemed like "undue self-assertion" by Australia on Pacific problems arose partially from her realization that the centre of gravity was shifting eastwards. The speaker suggested that some of the basic factors in the Pacific were that the metropolitan powers of Europe "all had a finger in the Pacific pie," that the European concept of nationalism had taken root in the East, and that the more successful the counterpoise to Communism was in Europe the more likely its pressure would be felt in the East. For Australians the "cardinal date" in recent

Pacific history was February 13, 1942, when Singapore fell and Australia's "traditional reliance for security on the Royal Navy" was ended. It was realized that Britain was over-committed in the Pacific and had become essentially a European Power. This realization explained Prime Minister Curtin's famous New Year's message in which he appealed to the United States for help and later impelled Australia and New Zealand to take the initiative in grappling with Pacific problems. The result had been the Anzac Pact of 1944. Since that time Australian policy had followed four main lines; to develop Commonwealth ties (on this question there were differences of emphasis in Australia); to acquire what measures of security could be obtained through the United Nations, and to use that organization as a forum for a middle power; to promote regional stability and common interests in the Pacific; and to maintain and further good relations with the United States. These were all essential policies and apparent conflicts between them arose over questions of attitude and timing. What immediately interested Australia was a peace treaty with Japan, the appeal of Communism to the peoples of Asia, the measures necessary to secure stability in the Pacific, and the realization of a Pacific Pact which, in an area that was not highly industrialized, must be underwritten by the United States. Intermeshed with these problems were such basic questions as the standard of living in Asia, the different cultural values, the impact of capitalistic culture on pre-capitalistic culture, and the difficult transition from imperialism which was endemic in the whole area. The speaker summarized Australia's position as "of the West but not in it, in the East but not of it." He thought that Australia saw her opportunity to act as an interpreter of Western culture in Asia and of Eastern culture in the West, or, to vary the metaphor, as a bridge on the Pacific between the Commonwealth and the United States.

A New Zealand delegate followed with a detailed description of the Canberra Pact, commonly known as the Anzac Pact, which, he thought, differed from Western Union and the Atlantic Pact in having a greater community of ideals and interest. The Pact provided for the regional defence of the South Pacific within the framework of a general system of world security, a policy which corresponded to New Zealand's hope that the

United Nations would eventually take a leading part in establishing security. New Zealand had already accepted responsibility in regional arrangements for the defence of Western Samoa, the Cook Islands and Fiji, " the most important point in the defence plans." He pointed out that with the new emphasis on regional defence as a primary responsibility it was doubtful if, in a war with a major Pacific power, New Zealand could, as in the last war, send forces outside the Pacific or even outside the South Pacific. Another New Zealand delegate said later that it was only fair to add that there was no commitment that New Zealand's forces would be retained in the Pacific, and the general view was that they should be used in a war in accordance with general strategy. Military liaison between New Zealand and Australia was "particularly close," with each country having an army officer in close touch with the other's army headquarters, and attending meetings of the chiefs of staff or the Council of Defence when matters of special interest to his country were discussed. The United Kingdom also had a liaison officer in each capital and a Joint Planning Committee, on which all three countries were represented, had been announced in March, 1949. New Zealand's Minister of Defence had stated in 1948 that the Navy's "primary and immediate role" was "the protection, in conjunction with the Air Force, of trade and sea communications in the South Pacific." It was so organized that it could join with other naval units of the British Commonwealth to constitute an effective combat force. New Zealand had never attempted to maintain a standing army "ready to fight as an organized formation in war" but rather an efficient regular cadre responsible for organizing, training and equipping the Territorial Force and ready to serve as the "hard core" of land forces in the event of war. After consultation with Lord Tedder a target plan had been adopted for the Royal New Zealand Air Force which contemplated a Regular Air Force, a Territorial Air Force, an Air Training Corps and an Air Force Reserve. The Regular Air Force, when fully organized, would consist of Headquarters, a decentralized Command Organization, five squadrons and ancillary engineering, equipment and training units. New Zealand was also keenly aware of the importance of integrating science with defence. The government had created a Defence

Science Advisory Committee composed of distinguished scientists in government departments and the Universities; this body was linked with similar committees elsewhere in the Commonwealth. Steps were being taken to interest young scientists in this new field of research. The basis of New Zealand's policy had been decided by the Minister of Defence when he said:

In the past we have depended initially upon the Royal Navy and upon the active military strength of Great Britain. But in view of the lessons of the war and the march of events in the post-war world, we must ourselves make increasing provision for the defence of our own country and the strategic area vital to us stretching through islands to the north of New Zealand.

Details were also given on New Zealand's participation in civil aviation. She was represented on the South Pacific Air Council along with the United Kingdom, Canada, Australia and Fiji. This body was responsible for constructing or maintaining aerodromes in the Fiji and Cook Islands. These aerodromes, which could, of course, also be used for defence, were of interest to the United States, which had nominated Pan American Airways as a government-designated line using Fiji in its flights to New Zealand and Australia. In order to help to safeguard the interests of native peoples, New Zealand took part in the South Pacific Council, on which the United States and powers with colonial interests in the Pacific were represented. The Anzac agreement also called for considerable consultation on other matters than defence and external affairs. Consequently a permanent secretariat had been established in both Canberra and Wellington to facilitate the exchange of information on all matters. In this work Canberra, according to the speaker, appeared to be functioning more effectively at the present time. As the occasion required, conferences could be convened either at the ministerial or official level. One of the most important meetings under the Anzac Pact was the Canberra Conference of 1947 which had been attended by representatives of Australia, Burma, Canada, India, New Zealand, Pakistan, South Africa, and the United Kingdom. The Conference had exchanged views on the nature of a peace settlement with Japan. Like Australia, New Zealand was anxious "to recapture the interest of the United States in the South Pacific" and would welcome a South Pacific Pact, modelled on the North Atlantic Treaty, in which the United States would be a major partner.

The full statement of defence policy by the New Zealand delegation led to questions about Australian plans. It was stated that Australia had decided for the first time upon a general policy on a long term basis for a system of defence and an extensive research. An expenditure of £250 millions over five years had been agreed upon, with the expenses for the first year estimated at £60 to £65 millions. This figure was larger than had been originally anticipated and was caused by the high cost of defence research, as in the field of long range weapons. The Australian plan was integrated with United Kingdom and New Zealand policies and "the basic hope" was that the United States would eventually help. The speaker felt that Australia could still do more in this field and "quite well carry a greater amount of the United Kingdom burden." Full details of the plan were included in the delegation paper on strategy. A United Kingdom delegate observed that Commonwealth defence in the Pacific depended more than elsewhere upon retaining command of the seas and of the air above it. It was loss of this command of the sea, rather than the fall of Singapore, which had placed Australia and New Zealand in such serious danger in 1942. He did not regard a Pacific Pact as immediately necessary. If there did emerge a power capable of challenging the existing command of the seas he was sure the United States would be the very first to take up the challenge. Meanwhile it was important that Australia and New Zealand appreciated the importance of sea power and would make sure that command was retained. It was a source of satisfaction to the United Kingdom, which had had already to divest itself of responsibility for the defence of Greece and Turkey in favour of the United States, to hear that Australia was able to take a greater part of the burden in the Pacific. A Canadian pointed out that the difficulties which had arisen in the last war were partly the result of the democratic powers being entirely absorbed elsewhere. Once they could devote a considerable part of their strength to the Pacific, Japan was immediately in trouble. He thought it unlikely for a considerable time that Japan could again reach the advantageous position that she had occupied in 1941. Nor did he think it likely that Russia could play a comparable role in the Pacific as long as the present balance lasted. There were possibilities of infiltration by Russia southward on the mainland of Asia and crossing, with air power, to the islands. If that happened, the democracies would have difficulty in finding supply bases within reach of such an operation. But this was unlikely. "So long as we had a front in Europe, and so long as the United Kingdom and the United States were able to deploy a reasonable force in the Pacific the danger was remote." There did remain the problem of Russian political infiltration, with its economic advantages, which raised the question of the role of Japan, particularly on the mainland, in both politics and economics.

In commenting on the attitude of Australia towards Japan, Australian delegates said that the fear of Japan was deeply imbedded in the public mind and felt that this was "an over-emotional and rather irrational attitude." But they pointed out that it was the feeling of a country of seven and a half millions facing one with eighty millions of "extremely energetic people." Australia's views inevitably differed from those of the United States with a population of 150 millions. This distrust of Japan had caused Australia to refuse admission to Japanese consular officials until the Peace Treaty had been signed, and had even made her reluctant to sell wool to her. It had caused Australia to view with concern the change in American policy ". . . from holding Japan down to helping it to rise again." Australians remembered their economic tussles with Japan in 1936-37 and were afraid that Japanese goods might once again flood their market. But they knew that the Japanese were determined to survive, and, in spite of their doubts about American policy, realized that at the present time their best chance was "to string along with the United States." The United States faced a problem in Japan of the utmost gravity. It was difficult to see how she could control Japan's destiny without encountering the same difficulties which had befallen her in China. There might be real danger of a Communist Japan arising from continual repression. It was also possible that General MacArthur was over-optimistic in his estimate of Japanese democracy, but as one delegate put it ". . . there was no other way than the

MacArthur line of action." On the question of a peace Treaty with Japan Australia believed strongly that it should be discussed not only by the Big Four but by all the eleven powers who had participated in the Pacific War.

The New Zealand point of view was very similar. There too was "a widespread fear of Japanese resurgence," an apprehension which was linked with the fact that Japan—the only Far Eastern power which had had a powerful navy—was the country most likely to attack New Zealand and Australia. This explained, for example, why New Zealand was less fearful of a Communist China. New Zealand shared Australia's feeling that General MacArthur accepted too readily the sincerity of Japanese professions of democracy. Regret was expressed that Australia and New Zealand had had little influence, either in Washington or Tokyo, on occupation policy. Among influential and well informed people in New Zealand there was a fear that ultimately a Communist Japan might "join with a Communist China and the U.S.S.R. to form an unassailable force in the Far East, with a corresponding tendency to become aggressive." New Zealand appreciated that, with her need for markets and raw materials, Japan would inevitably be forced into close relationship with the mainland. It was obvious that the United States was trying to get away from subsidizing the Japanese economy. If Japan did work with the mainland countries the former situation of Nipponese domination might reappear or, what was more likely, Japan might work in conjunction with Communist China and the Soviet Union.

This suggestive analysis of the danger of a Communist Japan provoked Australian comments that the short run fear of a resurgent Japan was more important in public opinion, since it was based on war memories, trade considerations, and the pressure of population. But ultimately fear of Soviet domination might turn out to be stronger in Australia. The highly centralized nature of the government of Japan also added to the danger of Communism, but it was thought that the United States had foreseen this danger. A United Kingdom delegate raised the question of Japanese economic competition, a matter already causing concern to the British textile industry, which had suffered between the wars from Japanese dumping in Indian and dollar markets. Two United Kingdom delegations of employers and employees had recently returned from Japan with considerable evidence of such a danger. It was also suggested, but subsequently denied, that Australia had recently arranged to sell wool to Japan on advantageous terms. In the ensuing discussion the consensus of opinion was that Japan must achieve a large-scale export of textiles if she were ever to be able to balance her accounts, and that she was in a position that no other country could match to supply low priced goods for consumers in Asia and Africa who could not afford to buy anything else. This argument was supported by a delegate from Ceylon, who recalled the resentment in his country when, in the days before dominion status, a quota had been imposed upon imports of Japanese textiles. It had resulted in a considerable rise in the price of textiles that were essential for the people of Ceylon. Another United Kingdom delegate agreed that the Japanese economy must be restored but asked that in "this anarchic free world" precautions be taken "to guard against a greedy competitive scramble bringing down standards to a coolie level." The emphasis on "unfair competition" because of low living standards in Japan was thought to be a dangerous one, since it had implications for other countries than Japan, and might even be raised in the United States and Canada against United Kingdom standards. But illegal trade practices, stealing of patents, etc. could be prevented. Moreover, in view of the strain imposed upon her in financing Japanese recovery, the United States was bound to assist Japan in her search for markets. In response to a request from a United Kingdom speaker for a Canadian comment on the Pacific area, since the situation needed examination from the angle of the North Pacific as well as from the South Pacific, Canadians stated that their country wanted Japan to be effectively demilitarized and to achieve economic prosperity without returning to undesirable practices such as she had indulged in formerly in shipping and fishing. They shared the views of Australia and New Zealand that the treaty with Japan should be negotiated by all the powers concerned in the Pacific. Although Canada had not wished to share in the occupation of Japan, she was represented by a special liaison mission there. In 1947, at the invitation of General MacArthur, General Crerar, with a small group of experts, had visited the country to study conditions. But Canada was much more interested in Europe than the Pacific and was inclined to play a correspondingly subordinate role in that region. In any event as a North Pacific power her defence of that region was based on close co-operation with the United States. Canada was not prepared to undertake any substantial responsibilities in the Pacific. Her role in strategy and defence in the Pacific was "subordinate to that of the United States and much more reserved than that of other Commonwealth countries."

On the importance of Hong Kong and the attitude of their respective countries towards China, those delegates who took part in the discussion were in substantial agreement. An Australian pointed out that today Hong Kong was much more than a bastion of Empire. Its economic importance had greatly increased as its trade expanded with Siam, India and the Philippines. At present only 25 per cent of its trade was with China. The speaker thought that Hong Kong was performing a very useful service in the current confusion and economic disintegration in the Far East and asked for comment on the extent to which Commonwealth countries would be justified in supporting it. A United Kingdom speaker replied that Britain attached great importance to Hong Kong, as was evidenced by the number of troops she had sent there. She was determined to keep it open. Hong Kong was valuable not only for trade but as a source of information and a haven for refugees. He emphasized that the United Kingdom, despite limited resources, still regarded herself as a world power. She had no intention, he said, of "sliding back to the position of a small island". Britain had by no means lost interest in the Far East, and her continuing interest was not animated by greedy motives. The same speaker thought that although Soviet power should not be underestimated and the present ruler of China, Mao Tse-Tung, had been Moscow trained, the impact of Communism on the Chinese peasant might be rather different from its impact elsewhere. He did not think that the Foreign Office had lost all interest in China, and wondered whether the Commonwealth could suggest a constructive view of the situation in China. An Australian agreed that the position of Hong Kong was "entirely beneficial to all in the Pacific," since it provided a base of peace and order in a chaotic area. He emphasized the fact that there was no moral problem of colonialism, as was indicated by the absence of any movement for independence. Hong Kong was also an important defensive position which would be invaluable in the event of a transfer of Russian naval power to the Pacific. Australia, as Dr. Evatt had said, did not regard the door as completely closed to North China. A skeleton staff was maintained in the Nanking embassy, and the government was prepared to consider dealing with the Communists and not write them off as purely Soviet in form. It was quite possible that what might emerge in China would be a very different form of Communism. Australia was prepared to wait and see and not adopt the United States' attitude. This view was shared by a New Zealander who said that his country favoured having channels of communication with Communist China. There might be some difference of opinion over the use of New Zealand troops to reinforce Hong Kong, and the trade unions might offer opposition, but the government had made it clear that it recognized its own responsibility. A delegate from Ceylon said the decision to hold Hong Kong had not caused any hostile reaction in his country. He declared that the people of Ceylon appreciated that the position was entirely different from the situation in Indonesia where the Dutch had "practised a particularly undesirable form of colonialism." A Canadian said that his country had also kept its mission in Nanking. He deprecated the opinion of other speakers that the United States had entirely written off China; it was waiting, he thought, for the "dust to settle" before formulating a policy. In support of this argument he pointed to the studies which were being made in the State Department by a special committee under Mr. Jessup, and to the views of a powerful element in the Republican party which wanted a more aggressive policy. Another Canadian speaker also took issue with some of the doubts and fears that had been expressed about the ultimate objective of the United States in the Far East. If any people should fear American imperialism it should be the Canadians, but they did not do so because fear had been eliminated by daily contacts. To stem the Russian advance in the Far East, it was necessary to raise living standards and assist the Asian countries to establish freedom and democracy. In view of the crippling sacrifices made by the United Kingdom to preserve freedom, assistance for Asia could come only from the United States. He maintained that the least price for this assistance would be acceptance of the United States as it is. There had been great strides in United States opinion in recent years. The Marshall Plan was one of the most generous gestures in history and isolationism was dead or dying. But the United States needed time to adjust itself to its new position of carrying the load. We all had a responsibility to try to mould the United States opinion to a realization of its new role in the world. A generous United States people would continue to respond if approached the right way. The last American election showed that the American people were in control and they had a very big heart. With that reminder, of the vital part which the United States must play in every quarter of the globe, the Conference closed its discussions of policy and strategy.

6

Currency, Commerce, and Colonies

Although economic topics had been given their due place on the original agenda, the speed with which the financial situation had deteriorated for the United Kingdom in particular, but necessarily for all of the Commonwealth, led to these topics receiving more emphasis that had been originally intended. In contrast to preceding discussions there were more differences of opinion *within* delegations, and an inevitable variation in outlook between Canada and the other Commonwealth countries. Nevertheless, the measure of agreement reached upon the nature of the problem was impressive. It was agreed that the economic problems of the Commonwealth fell into two broad groups. These were the problems of adjustment to the conditions of the post-war world, and the problems of achieving sufficiently rapid economic progress in under-developed countries of the Commonwealth to give stability to democratic institutions and to combat the attractions of Communism.

The Conference first examined the problems of adjustment. As a United Kingdom delegate pointed out in a lucid analysis of the situation, the central problem was the balance of payments between the sterling area and North America. This balance had been disrupted by the war and the consequent loss of assets, rise of prices, and changes in the terms of trade. To restore it very big structural changes were required not only in the United Kingdom but in the whole sterling area. One major legacy of the war was an international division of labour quite inappropriate to the new conditions, the new terms of trade and the new levels of mutual indebtedness. Although particular solutions might simplify the problems of making these necessary adjustments, no ingenuity could avert the necessity of making very large changes. Such changes depended upon the extent to which several alternative lines of policy would be adopted. These included efforts to sell more to North America, to obtain more dollars elsewhere through multilateral trade, to induce North America to invest abroad, and to reduce imports from North America.

On one thing the delegates were in general agreement. The more the nature of these changes and their necessity could be realized and the more the different countries concerned could act in harmony and avoid "beggar-my-neighbour" policies, the greater was the possibility that a solution satisfactory to all the Commonwealth countries could be worked out. They had in common a dependence on overseas trade, involving a large measure of interdependence on one another. Because of her important trade with the United States, Canada was not quite so dependent on overseas trade. Britain, however, obtained two-thirds of her imports from overseas and one-third from Europe. Figures of a similar character would be applicable to other Commonwealth countries. Regional solutions for balance of trade problems might be acceptable for countries with numerous and lengthy land frontiers; they were not satisfactory for Commonwealth countries. An Australian pointed out that, Canada excepted, the Commonwealth countries also had in common a pool of sterling and dollars which was managed by the United Kingdom.

It was also agreed that an essential feature of any satisfactory solution for the United Kingdom was a balance of payments with North America at a high level. This was realised to be immensely desirable from the point of view of the United Kingdom and from that of the North American countries. In that respect, said a United Kingdom speaker, trade relations with Canada were fundamental. There was "no economic problem half so important to the United Kingdom as that of solving the problem of trade with Canada." If a balance was achieved at a low level, by cutting down United Kingdom imports and reducing the whole level of trade between North America and the rest of the world, the results would be disastrous for everyone. What was true of the United Kingdom was equally true of Europe. Western Europe is an area which depends on imported foodstuffs and raw materials. Without them it is virtually impossible to feed the large populations and to maintain them in employment. There is a real risk that failure to secure a balance which will permit large imports of food and materials will breed unemployment and Communism. From the North American point of view a high level balance is equally important. Without it, there would almost certainly have to be very painful adjustments of the agricultural output of Canada and the United States, and a danger that with growing misunderstandings, the world would fall not into two but into three great areas of possible conflict.

There was agreement too, and the delegations' papers had shown the same unanimity, that any satisfactory solution would need to be on a multilateral basis. Not only Canada but also, though in less degree, most of the other countries of the Commonwealth depended on a pattern of trade for which exports to one market bought imports from other markets. A Canadian remarked that Canada was in the unhappy dilemma that, while a large portion of its economy was dependent on the European markets, it was also largely dependent on imports from the United States. Before the war, United States dollars, which Canada, for example, used to pay for its imports, were earned by selling Canadian products for sterling and converting the sterling, with the help of surpluses of dollar earnings in the Far East or in the British Colonies, into dollars. The restoration of a multilateral pattern of trade was universally accepted as desirable. Although it was recognised that the range of commodities—rubber, tin, cocoa, coffee, etc.—which contributed to this multilateral earning of dollars was not large, and that sometimes, notably in the case of rubber, there were difficulties in restoring the pre-war volume, yet no one doubted that a multilateral solution should be the objective; all were of the opinion that the bilateral tendencies which had recently been in evidence should disappear as soon as practicable. Though she had been driven to bilateralism, said one speaker, the United Kingdom was "deeply wedded to multilateral trade." A Canadian added that although he recognized many bilateral agreements made by the United Kingdom and supported by sterling area payment restrictions had been unavoidable, they might even retard a solution. Without North American competition, prices in the sterling area would go higher, and incentive to export to North America would be reduced.

At the Strasbourg meeting of the Council of Europe there had been suggestions that Commonwealth countries should come inside a trade area which would discriminate against the dollar area. In commenting on this suggestion, a United Kingdom speaker argued that "the development of a multilateral low tariff world along the lines of the International Trade Organization" seemed to be a better solution than "the building of fences around Europe." The Conference discussed at some length the contributions which all the countries concerned might make to the working out of a satisfactory solution.

These discussions took place before devaluation had become a reality and many matters that were then thrashed out have since ceased to have the same significance. But certain points of more permanent importance emerged. First, it was recognized that the United Kingdom could not hope to hold large markets in North America unless its cost structure could be brought into alignment with that of the North American countries and maintained in alignment permanently. This was bound to involve continuous pressure to improve efficiency, productivity, delivery and design. Some Canadians expressed concern at the lack of enthusiasm of some British manufacturers for the idea of entering the North American market and competing there, and wondered if there had been sufficient attempts to reduce the attractiveness of non-dollar markets. The more freely the United Kingdom might be in competition with the North American countries, the more rapidly these technical advances might be expected to take place. These advances were all the more important because of the prospect in the near future of German and Japanese competition in exports. A United Kingdom delegate pointed out that in British industry output per head was 10 per cent greater than in pre-war years and had shown in 1948 an increase of 15 per cent over the previous year. When the United Kingdom was described as indolent and backward he felt her people were understandably aggrieved. But he realized that increased productivity did not necessarily steer goods towards the dollar area. Another speaker pointed out that nearly one-quarter of the national product in the United Kingdom was being used to improve capital equipment. The Anglo-American Committee on Productivity had not found the British workman so much inferior in personal effort but had seen the crux of the problem to lie in the field of management and in the increase of mechanization.

Secondly, it was recognized that devaluation would not in itself solve the problem. Devaluation, said a United Kingdom speaker, meant raising the prices of all imports and involved pulling out the stabilizing pegs and hoping to put them in again at levels which would make exports cheaper. If higher import prices were reflected fully and quickly in higher money wages and higher manufacturing costs in the United Kingdom, the only effects of devaluation would be a higher structure of all prices and the loss of the competitive advantage in the dollar area which devaluation afforded. Devaluation would need to be reinforced by measures to hold down prices. This implied that a sufficient degree of disinflation was a necessary adjunct to devaluation. It was also emphasized that, if the United Kingdom alone devalued, it would be difficult to prevent price rises. If all other non-dollar currencies followed in devaluing against the dollar, then a 25 per cent devaluation might mean only a 5 per cent increase in average sterling prices, and there would be a real prospect of containing the price rise and stimulating dollar exports. There would, of course, remain what one speaker called the "great uncertainty." Could we, he asked, "count on the United States and Canada keeping their tariffs unchanged if we cheapen British goods?"

Thirdly, it was stressed that, if devaluation were to take place, there would be a very special responsibility imposed on the United Kingdom to expand its capacity to provide exports of the required types to both the dollar area and the sterling area. The Asiatic countries would need machinery and equipment which recently those countries have been buying to an increasing extent from the United States. For them, as well as for the United Kingdom, dollar machinery will have become more expensive. As an Indian speaker pointed out, if devaluation were of the order of 25 per cent to 30 per cent, the effect on the sterling area would be "to increase dependence on the United Kingdom market." They would be gravely concerned lest this difficulty, combined with the limits of capacity of United Kingdom industries, should greatly slow down their rate of economic expansion. On the other hand, the main purpose of devaluation was to stimulate exports to the dollar markets. This might necessarily imply that, in cases where the total supplies were limited, more should go to the dollar markets which devaluation had made more profitable, and less to sterling and other "soft" currency markets. It was in the general interest of the sterling area for the United Kingdom to steer her exports in the right direction. The effect would vary in different types of industry with the volume of production and the price. A final and satisfactory solution could only come from a sufficient expansion of capacity and exports to meet all needs and give more punctual deliveries. In short, as a United Kingdom delegate summarized it, devaluation could only be undertaken as a long-term policy, with the knowledge that there were reserves which could last until its effects were fully felt, and with preparations for reinforcing it with other measures.

Many speakers discussed the extent to which the growth of the welfare state in the United Kingdom might be held to be an obstacle to her recovery and to the development of her export industries. On this question, inevitably, the Conference reached no sort of agreement. The critics urged with force that large resources were being devoted to ends which, however desirable in themselves, ought in present circumstances to be regarded as secondary. A United Kingdom speaker argued that his country had gone too far and too fast in government expenditure, and that the resultant taxation not only diminished savings but was a drag on incentive throughout all classes of the community. He felt that it was not possible to carry at the same time huge government expenditures, a programme of capital development, both government and non-government, current consumption, and unrequited exports. It was imperative to reduce commitments, particularly in government expenditures, and probably by some restriction of capital expenditure. He believed that disinflation was also necessary in other sterling countries but that Great Britain had a special obligation as banker for the sterling area to do all she could to maintain the reserves and credit of the area. "For the very sake of the welfare state" the balance of payments had to be restored, for no social security could exist if currency collapsed. On this last point another United Kingdom delegate said that there were inflationary pressures in the sterling area outside the United Kingdom. In 1948, for example, the total deficit of the sterling area in all currencies was £500 to £600 millions net but the United Kingdom deficit was only £120 millions. A third United Kingdom speaker agreed that the present rate of taxation could not be maintained indefinitely, because it deprived the worker, and especially the manager, of incentive. He thought a reduction of defence costs could be achieved through rationalization and pointed out that the Chancellor of the Exchequer had been placed in a very difficult position by the Minister of Health's allowing enormous and apparently uncontrolled expenditure on the Health Services. Some United Kingdom representatives vigorously argued in rebuttal that a healthy country was more productive, that many of the health services were themselves productive by improving the efficiency of workers, and that a sense of equality and fair treatment had been a strong bulwark in the United Kingdom against the progress of Communism, which was on a lower level there than in almost any other European country. One of them pointed out that only one-twentieth as many man-hours had been lost in strikes in the period after the second world war as had been lost in the same period after the first world war. Taxation for welfare expenditures, said the same speaker, compelled every individual "to spend money on things socially valuable."

The Conference next turned to what other countries in the sterling area might do to increase their dollar earnings. Recent trends of United States imports had shown fairly rapidly increasing imports of food and raw materials, but declining imports of manufactures. It was thought that Australian wool, Pakistan jute and Indian hides and skins, as well as a number of the products of Indian handicrafts might find substantially higher markets in the United States. A Pakistan delegate believed his country could considerably increase exports of jute if machinery for manufacturing it could be obtained. India hoped to increase jute exports from East Bengal and also expected to increase her exports of cotton as more waste land came under cultivation. But at present India had a deficit of dollars owing to her need for very large food imports. It was the view of a member of the Indian delegation that, until her food problem was solved, India could not be a net dollar earner as she had been in the past. He also added that India had been turning to the dollar countries for capital equipment, which had been difficult to get in the United Kingdom, and which was necessary if India were to become more industrialized. A Pakistan delegate was quick to point out that his country was almost self-sufficient in food-stuffs, and did not have a drain on dollar resources like India. It was in accordance with these trends to try to develop more exports to the United States of colonial products of every kind but especially of copper, tin and cocoa. Special concern was felt with regard to rubber. It was hoped that a revision of the United States policy on stockpiling strategic materials, and less use in industry of synthetic rubber, might appreciably increase the dollar sales of that commodity by the sterling area countries. This idea was of special interest to Ceylon, whose rubber industry, as one of her delegates stated, was in danger of collapsing. Like India, Ceylon had become increasingly interested in United States machinery, particularly for irrigation and hydro-electric power schemes.

Although it was generally recognized that a great responsibility lay on the United Kingdom and other sterling area countries to get their costs into alignment with North American costs, it was equally widely agreed that a great responsibility lay on the United States and Canada. It was their duty to see that the door was open—and kept open—if sterling area imports were available at the right prices, in the right quantities and at the right time.

In the case of the United States, anxiety was expressed by a number of speakers from sterling countries lest the long tradition of resistance to imports might show itself in further political and economic obstacles if large volumes of imports really began to flow in. An Australian remarked that the reaction of Congress to a lobby is "the biggest unknown factor in the world." He questioned the assumption that the United States could offer stability in trade dealings as did Canada. Although the United States tariff had been greatly reduced and was not now very high on the goods which actually entered the United States, there were many types of goods which the United Kingdom and other European countries could export competitively to other areas which still encountered almost prohibitive tariffs in the United States. A United Kingdom speaker gave as an illustration the experience of the lace industry of Nottingham. On fine lace, which was not manufactured in the United States, there was a duty of 60 per cent. On coarse lace, which was manufactured in the United States, the duty had been raised to 90 per cent. It was very much hoped that as a means of furthering a satisfactory high level solution of trade the United States would find it possible to make further tariff reductions. Canadians agreed that the United States had not yet recognized her full obligations as a creditor nation, but emphasized the substantial changes that had taken place in public opinion and deprecated a defeatist attitude. They questioned the "simplified notion" that if one developed a new trade Congress simply clapped on a new tariff; they said further that much of American trade was bound by international agreements and could not be changed unilaterally by Congress.

As far as Canada was concerned, speakers from the Canadian delegation were hopeful that if prices and supplies could be got right, considerably increased sales in the Canadian market would be forthcoming. One Canadian was of the opinion that Canada could take a "very major increase" in United Kingdom exports. Over a period of two or three years, if goods were available and prices in line, the increase might be as much as 50 per cent.

Indeed, the hope was held out that with increasing Canadian exports to the United States and increasing Canadian purchases from the United Kingdom, the point might be reached where the sterling area's balance with Canada would not depend on a transfer of United States dollars and the grave difficulties of earning them. But, in view of her lower tariff, Canada could not do as much to help the sterling countries by tariff reductions as the United States, which had less reason for the degree of protection which was afforded to its domestic industry.

The discussion of the prospects for increased sales to Canada from the sterling countries provided an opportunity for a Canadian delegate to explain why Canada could not join the sterling bloc or seek closer integration with it, but had to remain in the difficult position of being linked to both the dollar and the sterling blocs. He began by pointing out that 70 per cent of Canada's imports came from the United States; 50 per cent of her exports went to that country, as well as an even larger proportion of Canadian invisible exports. The United States had invested $5 billions of American funds in Canada as against the $1.5 billion of United Kingdom investments. With such a flow of American capital it was natural that Canada's industrial structure should follow an American pattern. Besides these close economic relations between Canada and the United States there were innumerable social and cultural ties, family relationships, thousands of daily border crossings, and the influence of American radio and press to leave their mark upon Canadian ways. Inevitably they predisposed the Canadian consumer to think in terms of American goods. But the fact that 70 per cent of Canadian imports came from the United States was more than a reflection of "superficial whims." Imports from the United States of basic fuels such as coal and oil, cotton and other raw materials, component parts of manufactures and capital goods were vitally essential to keep the Canadian industrial machine running.

To join the sterling area would mean that Canada should freely accept sterling for current transactions and severely curtail her imports from the United States in order to eliminate most of her American dollar deficit. There was no doubt, said the speaker, that such a policy would "create very great difficulties."

To restrict severely the types of key imports he had described would mean unemployment, would make the economy creaky and would make Canada a less efficient country. It would be difficult, at least in the short run, for the sterling area to fill the gaps in imports, and there would probably be a substantial increase in exports to the sterling area whereas imports from the sterling area might be substantially less. Perhaps even more important would be the reaction of the United States. Canada's joining the sterling area might appear to American eyes almost like "economic encirclement," since she was the only Commonmealth country which had not greatly restricted American entry into her domestic market. Since Canada is much the largest consumer of the United States, such a move would have significant economic effects on that country. Moreover, to Americans it would look like drawing a much sharper line than has hitherto existed between the Commonwealth and the United States. It would undoubtedly greatly weaken Canada and undermine whatever influence she possessed with the United States. Canadians strongly believed that such an action would be just as detrimental to the Commonwealth as to Canada. They considered that the basic problem is to bridge, and not to widen, the gap that exists between the dollar and sterling areas. As the speaker put it, "if there is any clear pattern in Canadian economic and political policy it is to try to prevent the divergence of sterling area and United States policies. The future of the Commonwealth depended on closer integration with the United States." This lucid exposition was well received by the Conference. One United Kingdom delegate remarked that it was "wholly impractical for Canada to join the sterling area."

Considerable thought was given to the question of international investment and the part which it might play in facilitating the balance of payments with the United States. There was very general agreement that the situation of international investment was of great importance. It was quite hopeless, said a Canadian, to try to balance the world economy today without the international movement of capital, nor could standards of living be maintained, or in certain regions raised. Anything which could lead to stability of currencies and mutual confidence between countries would greatly help the flow of investment, which in turn would be a means of bridging short-term gaps. There are very great needs for capital investment, both in the under-developed areas of the Commonwealth and in the colonies. On the other hand, it is unlikely that the United Kingdom, now a debtor nation, will be able to supply a volume of capital at all comparable to that which she was accustomed to invest in the early years of this century. A delegate declared that United Kingdom control of capital issues was certain to continue for a considerable time, not only of external issues (which did not exist at present) but internal issues also. One of the central problems was, therefore, how to stimulate the flow of United States capital into the Commonwealth. This flow might either be direct, or it might be indirect, with investment by United States concerns in the United Kingdom and the release of United Kingdom resources for investment in the Commonwealth.

A United Kingdom speaker said that in the twenties and thirties the American private investor had rushed "with the best intentions" into the export of capital abroad and had suffered heavy losses which he had not forgotten. He feared that the political insecurity of Europe, particularly owing to Soviet policy, the uncertainty about the stability of sterling and other currencies, and the present state of "this impossible world" were too great to tempt the American again to invest overseas. Canadians were not as pessimistic, and thought there were "real possibilities" of private investment from both the United States and Canada. One delegate even said that he could foresee the time when the bridge to the sterling area would be "largely built by capital exports from Canada." But the Canadians warned that investment depended on a favourable environment both in the sterling area and on this continent. As one of them argued, "if profits were to be regarded as exploitation, while at the same time investors were required to bear their losses, private investors were not going to invest". Another asked, since international investment had gone political was it so certain that we could have a private investment today comparable to that of the inter-war period?

It was appreciated, however, that there was a danger of overestimating the extent to which United States investment might solve the problems of dollar shortage. At present, the United

States has an export surplus of about $6 billions per annum. There are few American observers who expect that the United States annual commercial investment will be on a much larger scale than $1 to $2 billions. Consequently there is bound to remain a large gap that can be filled only by government loans through the Export-Import Bank and the International Bank, by loans and grants as under Marshall aid, by increased exports to the United States, or by reduction of purchases from the United States.

These problems of investment were very closely related to another great economic problem to which the Conference gave attention, that of the development of the under-developed countries of the Commonwealth.

As on previous occasions the representatives of India, Pakistan and Ceylon stressed the very great effects on the rate of economic progress which their people had anticipated from the coming of independence. There had been a great upsurge of popular opinion which expected a rapidly rising standard of life, and looked to the existing democratic governments to provide it. This demand for an improvement in living standards was intensified by the disastrous effects of the war upon the cost of living. An Indian delegate declared that the inflation in India, resulting from the effect of war finance upon the country's economy, was much higher than in other dominions. He said that the general price level stood at 380, as compared to the pre-war figure of 100, and that the cost-of-living index for the big cities was between 300 and 400. The delegate from Ceylon described inflation there as "of an unparalleled order," and quoted a paper issued by the Economic Commission for Asia and the Far East in support of his assertion. Food prices in Ceylon were so high that very heavy subsidies were necessary and had to be retained "to avoid the perils of Communism." From the Pakistan delegation came the same story of rising prices, and an equally firm conviction that inflation there caused by war conditions was the worst in the Commonwealth. The resistance of democratic institutions to the rise of Communism in the East, it was argued, depended very greatly indeed on the rate of economic progress which could be achieved. Unless there was help in development, there would be an "unwelcome change" in the political complexion of the government of Ceylon, the delegate from that country warned the Conference.

For their economic development the Asian countries face three closely inter-related requisites: trained and experienced men to handle the technical and managerial problems of building up their new industries; the assurance that adequate supplies of machinery and equipment will be available as needed; and the prospect of financial support at home and abroad. Considerable progress is being made with the provision of trained staff. To some extent, the countries concerned are looking to the United States, but they look also to the United Kingdom and the other Commonwealth countries with which for a variety of reasons their links are closer. As an Indian said, Indians knew the British and the British knew the Indians. They could work with the British, and it was easier to accept help from them than from countries outside the Commonwealth. Technical training has been and is being provided, not only in the United States and in the United Kingdom, but also in Canada and in some other parts of the Commonwealth. Speakers from Australia, New Zealand and Canada described what was being done by their universities in training Indian students, and expressed the hope that more scholarships would soon be available. But as the expansion of industries progresses so will the needs also increase. Hope was held out that these increasing needs can be met.

The second problem is the great need for the provision of actual machinery and equipment. Here again it was India's experience that the war had aggravated her difficulties through the necessary over-utilization of her capital equipment. Thus her textile mills had worked three shifts a day, and her railways had been so heavily burdened that there was a serious deterioration in her locomotives. When a mission from the International Bank had visited India, it had been much impressed by the damage done by the war to India's equipment. An Indian remarked that, unfortunately—in one sense—his country had not been occupied by the enemy so that India had not been eligible for assistance under UNRRA. Nor had there been a Marshall Plan for Asia. He declared that equipment was desperately needed by India "merely to get back to her pre-war position." A delegate maintained that because of the unbalanced nature of her economy

Pakistan's need for industrialization was greater than that of either India or Ceylon. Acceleration of industrialization would hasten the rise of living standards of 80 million people; industrialization was also, in his opinion, "a high strategic necessity for the Commonwealth and for Pakistan itself." Both India and Pakistan urged the importance of a planned program of capital development worked out with the other Commonwealth countries. An Indian delegate, who wanted an "intra-Commonwealth Point Four," suggested that the United Kingdom, Canada and Australia should work out the problem involved in the same manner as the OEEC countries did in Europe. Specific schemes should be drawn up in consultation with engineers, he said, and when the picture for five or ten years had been obtained, the Commonwealth governments should influence their economies as circumstances made it possible for them to make supplies available over a period of time.

With these suggestions a United Kingdom speaker concurred, but thought that in such a plan agricultural machinery should come in the first category, because only by expanding agriculture could the large populations described by earlier speakers be supported. Speakers from Australia and Canada expressed sympathy with the needs of the Asian dominions but pointed out certain difficulties. An Australian said that the whole of Australia's available resources was going to the building up of new sterling sources of supply for the United Kingdom. This investment amounted to approximately $500 millions a year. If Australia diverted part of her production to capital equipment, there would be less for the United Kingdom. It would therefore be a question for mutual consideration. What considerable part of Australian production could be devoted to India and the other Asian dominions? Canadians said that during the war Canada had given help to India under Mutual Aid, and had also continued to produce ships and locomotives to meet Indian requirements under long-term contracts. But Canada had already run into serious balance of payment difficulties as a result of trying to do too much in the way of what might be called the ERP type of aid. In future she could only participate on any sizable sca'e "as part of a joint effort with the United States."

India, Pakistan and Ceylon have all been making fairly considerable purchases of machinery in the United States. A further complication would, it was pointed out, arise from the devaluation of sterling. If sterling were devalued, and the rupee with it, the cost of dollar machinery would automatically rise, and the Asian countries would then be thrown back to a still greater reliance on the United Kingdom and other European suppliers. It is from their point of view most important, as was previously stressed, that capacity shall be expanded in the United Kingdom's industries sufficiently rapidly to provide for their needs, as well as for the necessary increase of trade in the dollar area. It is also important that the equipment itself shall be as suitable and as well-serviced as that which they have been buying in the United States. All Asian speakers reiterated the wish of their countries to remain in the sterling bloc. They felt that the United Kingdom provided a more stable market for their exports than the United States. A Pakistan speaker did express, however, some dissatisfaction that dollars earned by his country were turned over to reserves over which Pakistan had no control.

The problem of finance and savings presents substantial difficulties. Although it was possible, theoretically at least, that savings could be found from the internal resources of these under-developed countries by reducing consumption, any such solution would conflict with the urgent necessity to raise living standards. Consequently it is most unlikely that much can, in fact, be found from this source. It therefore becomes a question of utilising the alternative possible sources. Hitherto a large part of the capital needs of India, Pakistan and Ceylon have come from the running down of sterling balances. In India's case these balances originated partly from the exports of gold to the United Kingdom; partly from trading surpluses that accrued during the war and since its end because of the fact that the goods India normally imported were not available; partly from reimbursement for her war effort as defined by a wartime financial agreement; and partly from payments by allied governments to India for war goods. Ceylon's sterling balance had been built up through the convertibility of Indian rupees into Sinhalese rupees and their exchange for sterling. Pakistan acquired her share of the sterling balances after partition. All three countries were unanimous as to the necessity of the United Kingdom's continuing to release sterling balances to meet their pressing needs. As the delegate from Ceylon said, his people realized "the deeper effects of creating mammoth sterling balances," but the need to utilise them in countries like his own was so great that there was no other way.

Obviously these sources cannot last indefinitely. The sterling balances are not themselves inexhaustible, and the time will soon come when no substantial surplus will remain above the necessary working balances. What have not very appropriately been called the "unrequited exports" from the United Kingdom, paid for by these balances, have greatly increased the difficulties of the United Kingdom in reaching a balance with North America. It is important, therefore, to find a more permanent source from which capital investment can come. Delegates from both India and Pakistan were hopeful that Canada was in a position to advance considerable financial assistance, but Canadians, while sympathetic, could not hold out much encouragement. The limits to the capacities of the United Kingdom were also generally recognized. Although small amounts might come from other Commonwealth countries, it was agreed that it was unlikely that they could be a major source of supply. It was generally recognized, therefore, that some means of increasing the flow of funds from the United States to these Asian countries was urgently needed. Although suggestions were made as to the way in which such funds might be made available, this was clearly a matter beyond the competence of the Conference itself.

Comparatively little time at the Conference was devoted to the question of Imperial preferences. There was widespread feeling that for the time being their importance had receded because of other factors. As a Canadian put it, "under conditions of pre-emptive buying, of state purchase, and of licensing," they have lost their meaning. If, for example, no licences to import were granted by the United Kingdom, a tariff preference for a Commonwealth country meant nothing. He thought that the basic principle was "highly valued" in Canada but in response to a question added that, if the United Kingdom had to make economic arrangements with Western Europe which cut across preferences because of her involvements there, they would be accepted in Canada. The Pakistan delegation, as its delegation paper indicated, was more critical of the existing preference. A delegate described the existing agreement as a "hindrance" to Pakistan, and said that one-half of Pakistan imports were United Kingdom products entering under the preference, whereas only four or five types of exports from Pakistan entered the United Kingdom under the preference. He thought the situation would have to be reviewed. It was recognized that considerations of "hard" and "soft" currencies, of resulting currency restrictions, and the like, were, for the moment at least, of greater significance. It was not clear as yet whether, if trade returned into freer channels, the importance of preferences would be as great as it had been before the war. But there was a general consensus of opinion that they might still be an important instrument in fostering intra-Commonwealth trade.

A reference to bulk purchasing during the discussion of Imperial preferences produced an interesting discussion on the United Kingdom policy of state purchase, a policy which also involved bilateral trade agreements. Canadians were inclined to be critical of methods which, they argued, tended to destroy the price system. One of them said that Canadians were often ignorant of the details of United Kingdom bilateral deals, but when information was available they were "staggered at the price tags tied to the deals." He understood such agreements were mainly with Eastern European countries. There was, he added "some anxiety and soreness" when the United Kingdom offered to export to other countries "goods which Canada needed, or received imports from other countries which Canada could provide." One United Kingdom delegate replied that controls would have been necessary in Britain no matter what party had been in power. He thought it might be possible to utilize the price system with North America, while trading with the rest of the world on a planned basis by means of bulk purchases, long term contracts and payment agreements. He declared that such arrangements were "absolutely imperative," particularly with the Colonies who wanted co-operative marketing for bananas, cocoa, sugar and rubber, and bulk purchases in order to avoid economic collapse. He described the policy of the British government as designed "to blend planning with the price mechanism." There were, at present, controls due to shortages which could be relaxed as surpluses developed, and also controls due to policy considerations. The latter were an effort to get away from "the anarchic conditions of the free market" in order to ensure stability and maximum production. The delegate insisted that "conscious government direction" was "the only way to insulate the nation against the recurrence of a world depression originating in the United States." Although Britain was eager to increase her trade with the dollar area, she did not want to develop "a fundamental reliance upon such an unstable market" or to throw away her trade relations with the non-dollar countries. The speaker summed up his argument by saying that in any case, the flow of resources had to be guided and, as a result, "controls were an essential part of British economic theory". Another United Kingdom speaker did not think that either Britain or the entire non-dollar world could insulate itself against price collapses. He recognized that because of the shortage of dollars Britain was at present necessarily undertaking bilateral agreements and protective zoning, but would himself prefer to keep close to world prices wherever possible. He thought that most traders preferred to rely on market changes and hedging rather than on government-regulated changes of price. A third United Kingdom speaker added that no economist knew whether it was possible to maintain a high level of employment when recessions occurred elsewhere, but the United Kingdom was going to try to do so. He did not think that the United Kingdom assumed it could sell abroad other than on a competitive basis. A South African delegate suggested that marketing boards were also a valuable means of protecting the domestic primary producer and said they had worked well in her country. A Canadian remarked that, in his experience, West Indian producers had said they would like a competitive free market, but that if they were compelled to buy their equipment and fertilizers in a high price market, they would want to have long-term agreements. He suggested that there are "other ways of helping colonial producers than by falsifying the price system." He also pointed out that in a policy of bulk trading it was necessary to ensure a smooth flow of supplies, and this problem had caused difficulties for Canada in purchasing vegetable oils from the United Kingdom government.

From the South African delegation came an earnest appeal for support of the policy of securing a higher price for gold, which, it was claimed, would not only solve South Africa's problems, but would bring relief to the sterling area as a whole. The Union of South Africa was the world's greatest gold producer and gold constituted 50 per cent of her exports. Gold production was handicapped by the fact that the price of gold had been kept fixed while other prices had risen. Thus, the maize which was required to feed the native mine workers had gone up from eight shillings and sixpence per bag to between twenty-three and twenty-five shillings per bag. Imported machinery cost more, wages had gone up, and the cost of providing social services in the industry had greatly increased. A South African said that the mines were among the most efficiently run industries in the world, but unless a change for the better came soon, many of the low-grade mines in South Africa wou'd go under, "with disastrous consequences for the communities and industries which have grown up around them." He thought that even a slight increase in the price of gold would keep many of them going for a long time. To have the gold mines close down would be "almost literally a case of killing the goose that lays the golden eggs." Although South Africa had experienced an increase in the cost of her imports of 100 per cent since 1939 the value of her gold exports had increased by only 15 per cent. If the price of gold were increased, it would automatically increase the value of the gold reserves of the Western European countries, a result which would give these hard-pressed countries a breathing space. It would also induce the gold hoarders, of whom there were believed to be many in France, to disgorge. A rise in the value of gold would also increase the purchasing power of many countries which, like South Africa, had been compelled to cut down their imports from the United States. The general price rise that would develop would affect for the better the value of such ster'ing area exports as rubber and cocoa. The speaker realised the force of the American arguments against an increase in the price of gold but contended that, without some such aid as he proposed, American exporters would suffer severe losses. He argued that although the evils of inflation were great, those arising from deflation were greater, and it was the latter with which the United States was now confronted. Not further price rises, but falling prices and rising unemployment was what Americans now had most to fear. Other speakers welcomed the idea of an increase in the price of gold. As a Canadian assured the South African delegate, he was speaking to the converted. An Indian delegate thought that a higher price for gold would bring out large private hoards in his country. A United Kingdom speaker said that European countries were very conscious of the pre-war importance of gold in helping to bridge the gap in their balance of payments. But, in the light of the known views of the American administration, the United Kingdom would, he thought, be hesitant to suggest that gold should be revalued. An Australian summed up the general feeling when he said that the decision hardly rested with the Commonwealth but that the United States would "turn to this inevitable remedy."

From these discussions certain points clearly emerged. Foremost among them was the great and necessary concern of all the Commonwealth countries in the wellbeing of each other. For all of them Commonwealth markets were of major importance. The Commonwealth countries in the sterling bloc had a vital interest in the internal affairs of the United Kingdom since the United Kingdom was responsible for the banking system which held their currency reserves. In turn the United Kingdom was vitally interested in them because their surpluses or deficits greatly affected the possibility of a balance with North America. Thus, there was a clear recognition of the importance of mutual discussion of these inter-related problems. But when the Conference went on to discuss the extent to which delegates thought that a Commonwealth economic policy was desirable, there was an equally unanimous feeling that such a policy was out of the question. A Canadian pointed out that the experience of the Ottawa Conference had shown that the ideal of a common policy did not go very far when the details were examined. He summed up opinion when he said that the setting, the traditions and the aspirations of the Commonwealth countries varied too greatly. The realizable objective was thought to be frank discussion and consultation, combined with complete freedom to interpret policies and to work them out as each Commonwealth country might think best. As a United Kingdom delegate put it, free discussion of problems of adaptation, and some awareness of where we were going and what our contribution might be was needed.

Although one delegate suggested that there was some difficulty in persuading United Kingdom public opinion that informal measures would work "as well as the organized formal agencies developing in Europe," organized forms of co-ordination were not thought to be desirable. One delegate said that South Africa was traditionally suspicious of any fixed form of relationship, economic or otherwise, but would agree, however, to consultation and to meeting problems as they arose. The impression was general that there already existed a great deal of machinery for mutual discussion of problems. The marked increase in the number of High Commissioners and Trade Commissioners in the various Commonwealth countries had greatly improved Commonwealth contacts. The United Kingdom-Canada Continuing Committee was cited as an illustration of a new type of agency which had made a "fairly good beginning" at bridging the gap between state purchase and a free market for such commodities as sisal, sugar, and vegetable oils. It was not thought necessary to add substantially to this machinery, or to create any formal economic secretariat to handle the existing problems. But there was general support for the view that more frequent meetings of senior ministers and officials from the various Commonwealth countries would facilitate the working out of independent policies in general harmony. An Indian delegate suggested that a Commonwealth economic conference was desirable. He argued that there were very great problems in both of the broad fields that have been indicated above which called for urgent solution. His arguments received considerable support from delegates in a number of other countries. Delegates from Australia, Canada and the United Kingdom were dissatisfied with the amount of information which was available to the public on Commonwealth policies in the economic and other fields. A United Kingdom speaker remarked on "the reluctance to publicise the present Commonwealth organization and the liking of officials to work in obscurity." As an example he pointed out that at the Prime Ministers' Conference in October, 1948, there had been an announcement that measures for closer consultation would be recommended to the respective governments, but that nothing further was heard of this until the Commonwealth Finance Ministers met in July, when it was said that their meeting had been agreed upon by the Prime Ministers. He disapproved of the way in which information dribbled out in this fashion. Another United Kingdom speaker suggested that there would be no harm in the United States' knowing more about Commonwealth co-operation. An Australian thought that a much better exchange of information, coupled with publicity, would prevent "half-baked comment." He believed that "a Cominform rather than a Comintern" was needed. A Canadian said that the Canadian public was unaware of the extent of consultation which already existed. It was suggested that a great deal could be done, on the unofficial level, by the Institutes of International Affairs in the Commonwealth countries.

The economic discussions clarified even more than their predecessors the very close inter-relations between economic, political and strategic considerations. Economic progress may be a stronger weapon in combating Communism than the weapons of war or of diplomacy. Politics and strategy may be ineffectual if the economic base is not firm. Such considerations particularly affect the relations of the United Kingdom to the Commonwealth on the one hand, and to Europe on the other. The decisions which the United Kingdom will have to face in the near future will be of the very greatest importance not only politically but also economically to the Commonwealth. The very foundation of economic progress is a sense of confidence in political stability and the prospects of peace. The economic issues, the political issues and the strategic issues in the ultimate are all inextricable from each other and are no more than different aspects of the same problem.

When the Conference turned to discuss colonial policies and racial discrimination, the feeling engendered by the latter soon tended to overshadow the importance of the former. If they were regarded only on the basis of material interest, the colonies were important to the United Kingdom as providing American dollars through the sale of their raw materials and as the source of almost 10 per cent of her imports. This importance had been recognized in the Colonial Development Act of 1945, which had authorized the expenditure of £120 millions over a period of ten years. Of this sum approximately £65 millions had already been allocated. In addition to this grant from the Treasury the colonies were also appropriating, in their own budgets, substantial sums. But the United Kingdom was equally concerned with political progress in the Colonies. "We recognize," said a United Kingdom speaker, " that duty and moral right take precedence over national and material interest." All political parties were agreed that the colonial peoples should be assisted and encouraged to advance, as soon and as fully as possible, to the position now occupied by Ceylon. This new policy reflected the lessons gained from mistakes in the past, and was fully accepted by United Kingdom commercial and financial corporations interested in the Colonies. A United Kingdom delegate maintained bluntly that it was necessary to treat the new citizens on terms of equality and grant them the same fundamental rights that we demanded for ourselves. There must be no mental reservations. In Africa, where the situation was described as "the keystone of Colonial policy," there were already unofficial majorities in the Legislative Councils of the West African colonies. A new world was opening up in Africa, thought the same speaker, in its possibilities comparable only to the development of North America in the past century. The rapid advances in transportation and education and the impact of the war, which had brought American troops to Africa and sent African troops to far off lands, and which had concentrated all the forces of science and industry in the erection of various strategic bases on African soil, were largely responsible for the increased tempo of change. With their mineral resources largely untapped, their agricultural resources capable of much greater development through the application of science, and the manpower available to develop resources, the peoples of Africa were on the threshold of a remarkable development. This development afforded unlimited scope for investment, but in order to have efficient workmen the first investment must be in health and education. The political stability needed to attract investment by creating the right environment could only be achieved by conceding the legitimate aspirations of the native peoples.

Since the peoples of Africa were only emerging from a tribal system, every man was an African and regarded every other African as his brother. There was, for example, no such thing as a Nigerian under these conditions. The reactionary policy now being pursued by the South African government in handling its native problem was of much more than local significance. It impinged upon the attitude of fifty or sixty millions of natives north of South Africa. Presenting as it did the racial problem in its most intense form, it involved the welfare of the majority of the population in South Africa itself. Neither side had a monopoly of justice in the controversy, but from the material point of view, as one delegate warned, "a minority without hope is a dangerous cancer on the body politic, a majority without hope causes one to shudder." He expressed sympathy with the problems confronting the South African government but said that sympathy should not prevent disagreement being expressed with the manner in which that government was endeavouring to cope with the situation. This pointed reference to the tenor of current South African policies, which another United Kingdom delegate described as "rolling out the red carpet for Communism," at the time when Dr. Malan was stating his country's willingness to combat by force in alliance with other countries the threat of Communism, inevitably provoked a debate charged with emotion, but conducted on a high plane.

As a consequence the discussion of colonial policy did not receive the attention that it deserved. One United Kingdom delegate was, however, somewhat sceptical of the possibilities of proceeding rapidly to full self-government in the African colonies, and was also uncertain of the extent to which the natives were capable of running, entirely by themselves, a modern technical and industrial civilization. That could be done by the peoples of Ceylon, India and Pakistan, but he thought some white direction would be needed in Africa, where there would certainly be slow development in many parts. In reply, the speaker who had opened the debate said that the colonial policy of the United Kingdom was no "wildcat scheme," and that both colonial administrators and commercial people were agreed that the training of the colonial peoples in self-government was successful. Capital had not been frightened away by the advance of self-government. On the contrary, as he knew from personal experience, United Kingdom companies were seeking more avenues of investment in the colonies. These corporations realized that the days of British domination were drawing to a close and were training their own men in the new spirit. This delegate also said that African businessmen, who were succeeding in competition with European corporations, were taking an interest in politics and thereby offering a guarantee that the agitators would not get full control and dissipate capital. In West Africa, which was the pattern in both politics and economics for all of the colonies, native peoples had been interested in trading for centuries. Their businessmen were just as anxious as the English to build soundly and would employ European technical advisers for many years to come. He thought that there was unlimited scope for development in the colonies if funds were wisely invested. Capital from the Commonwealth and the United States, as well as the United Kingdom, would be needed. In that connection he suggested that Canada should examine opportunities in the West Indies where she had a special interest. The heavy investment of American funds in copper mining in Northern Rhodesia showed that United States businessmen realised the opportunities that existed. A South African suggested that there was a great need for an investment in skills, as in education and medicine, if the African colonies were to develop. The whole problem of opening up Africa, he said, depended on scientific advance and on trained personnel in the first instance. South African soldiers, who had traversed the continent during the war, had seen the needs for technicians and agriculturists. In West Africa, Khartoum and Kampala he himself had seen higher educational institutions being handicapped in their development because there were not enough students coming up from the lower grades. South Africa, which was already supplying anthropologists and technicians for the whole continent, had been asked to provide more facilities for medical education and was establishing a medical school primarily for that purpose at the University of Natal. There was shortly to be held in Johannesburg a large scientific congress of representatives from all territories south of the Sahara. In summary a United Kingdom speaker stressed that British colonial policy was a matter of constructive statesmanship based upon faith in the future, and those in touch with the natives knew that they had the same faith.

In commenting on racial discrimination a delegate from Ceylon said that he had tried very hard to see the problem through South African eyes, but did not believe that there had been "a proper relation of policy to the object in view." South Africans might hush the voices of Indians and Africans by restricting the franchise but he did not see how they could hush their minds. He warned that it was "impossible for them to oppose the forces arrayed against them throughout the world and to defy the march of time." Eventually the colour problem must disappear and it would be solved either by democratic or Soviet methods. Colonial peoples realized that one day they would reach their goal of self-government, but the immediate problem was "whether present policies would prevent these peoples from becoming good members of the Commonwealth." Although Ceylon was not affected by the day-to-day irritations of South African policy to the same extent as India with her considerable minority in South Africa, there were occasional happenings of "grave emotional disturbance" to the people of Ceylon. A United Kingdom speaker agreed that the racial policy of Dr. Malan might cause "very great disharmony" in Commonwealth policy. She enumerated several points on which liberal opinion in the United Kingdom had been gravely concerned, and in explanation of this concern quoted extracts from press reports of possible administrative and legislative measures under consideration by the Malan government, and of resolutions presented at the provincial congress of the Nationalist party in the Transvaal. She added that the new South African citizenship regulations had also completely undermined the position of a large section of the European community. All this was "discrimination with a vengeance," which, in her opinion, was an invitation to Communism. Quite apart from Communism and the respect for Human Rights to which all were pledged by the Charter of the United Nations, Dr. Malan was "surely sowing the seeds of doom" in a country where there were two million whites and nine million members of other races. The natives might be backward, undeveloped and primitive, but so were children and as children of the world, the natives were entitled to "protection, education and the fullest chance of self-development." The delegate concluded by saying:

Politically and economically the Africans are advancing. If instead of building road blocks and fighting a hopeless rearguard action, South Africa would lead and guide their onward march, what a glorious page she might write in her own history and in the history of the Commonwealth.

A Canadian, who had studied the living conditions of the natives in South Africa at first hand, had been impressed by what he had seen on a native reserve and doubted whether the natives of Swaziland or the Gold Coast, which he had also seen, were any happier than those in the reserved areas of Zululand. On the other hand he could not defend the condition of the natives in Johannesburg. Another United Kingdom speaker pointed out that the racial problem was not just a bilateral relationship between two races but often, as in Malaya, involved three or more races. Some research had been done in this field, but there was still a very wide gap in knowledge and study of the facts and possible solutions. He hoped that the various Commonwealth Institutes of International Affairs would give a high priority to the study of these problems and keep one another in touch on the subjects under review. It might be possible to associate them with a Commonwealth Institute of Race Relations.

The South African speakers, who regretted the absence of a member of the Nationalist party to state the government's case, urged that their country's problem, the economics of a multi-racial society, was one of enormous complexity. The classic liberal pattern of development which applied to the United Kingdom, said one of them, could not suitably be applied to a community in various stages of civilization. There were, according to the South Africans, four separate problems to be faced: those of the tribal native, the urban native, the "coloured" people and the Indians. In the tribal group, which covered about eighty per cent of the total, the natives were under their own chieftains. In the native territories there were systems of government at different levels with native councils, such as the Bunga in the Transvaal, where, a delegate said, debates were conducted "with decorum and efficiency worthy of any Commonwealth parliament." The urban group included natives who had come to the cities for employment and were in a transitional stage because of their contacts with Europeans. The "coloured" peoples, who numbered about 900,000 and were the descendants of West African slaves, Malays and some whites, had long been established in the Union and were European in culture. Although socially segregated, they could hold property, were not barred from the skilled trades, and had the franchise. They elected three European members of Parliament and four senators, who had a specialized knowledge of native affairs. There were also four senators nominated by the Governor General. The threat to abolish the coloured franchise hangs like the sword of Damocles over their heads. The Indians who had come to Natal eighty years ago as labourers had prospered and considerably increased in numbers. They resented the restrictions on their right to purchase land which were embodied by the Smuts government in a "Pegging Act." As a result they had refused to exercise their franchise for direct representation in the Provincial Councils and indirect representation in Parliament. The Indians had then appealed to the United Nations, where the South African request that the question as to whether or not this was a domestic issue should be referred to a judicial body had been disregarded. It was claimed that more than anything else the emotional discussions in the United Nations had provided propaganda for the Nationalist party which had helped them to win the elections of 1948. Real progress was being made in the realm of education, where large sums were set aside for native education; at the present rate of increase it would not be long until all natives of school age would be in school. At the present time the rate of increase in attendance at native schools was twice as great as the rate of increase in the native population. Here was a qualitative as well as a quantitative improvement that few countries could equal. The percentage of Indians attending university was four times as great as in India. This educational advance was regarded by one South African as a prerequisite to the attainment of democratic rights.

As an indication of the views of the rank and file of the white population in South Africa, one speaker referred to the South African delegation paper No. 6, which summarized the views of 150,000 soldiers, of whom the majority were Afrikaans-speaking. Their answers to a carefully drawn questionnaire indicated that most of them favoured more liberal treatment of the natives. He himself believed that a white population could not hope to survive merely by insulating itself from the native majority. As he put it, the only way to preserve the white civilization was to spread it as widely as possible. Another South African delegate pointed out that Dr. Malan's party represented only forty per cent of the European population. She denied that any political party deliberately subscribed to a policy of oppression. What the Nationalists favoured was a policy of *Apartheid,* by which they meant a separate system of parallel development for the Africans in their own areas. She regretted that so far the Malan government had concentrated on the negative side of its *Apartheid* policy. But they had not yet eliminated native representation from parliament, or abolished the coloured franchise. They had wiped out the communal representation given to the Indians, mainly because the latter had been unwilling to accept the legislation previously enacted by the

Smuts administration. The speaker stressed the fact that both white parties in South Africa were determined to maintain white civilization, and to maintain their racial integrity at the foot of a vast continent where races in an admittedly lower stage of development were numerically preponderant. It was clear that the Africans needed European guidance for their development. Although the condition of the natives left much to be desired, and much remained to be done, it was nevertheless true that, in General Smuts' phrase, South Africa, because of its higher wage rates, was the "Mecca" of Africans from the north.

7

The Future of the Commonwealth

By common consent Part III of the Agenda, which dealt with the "Post-War Evolution of the Commonwealth and Its Implications", provided the most significant topic for discussion. At the last conference on Commonwealth Relations in February, 1945, it had been too early to assess the significance of the changes in Commonwealth policies and attitudes that had occurred since the outbreak of the second world war. But the delegates at Bigwin Inn had the experience of a decade before them for examination. One thing was clear. The adaptability of the Commonwealth to a rapidly changing world had been repeatedly and impressively demonstrated. Once again it had stood the test of a world war and had emerged battered but victorious and with a deepened sense of comradeship.

The Canadian delegate who opened the discussion began by emphasizing the change that had taken place in the atmosphere of Commonwealth discussions through the emergence of three Asian states who were completely free to be comrades in war or neutrals, to stay in the Commonwealth or to leave it. These new partners had ancient and indigenous cultures and religions which differentiated them from the older Dominions. They did inherit, however, British concepts of parliamentary government and democracy without which their membership would have had little meaning. The older Dominions, in spite of cultural diversities in Canada and South Africa and, to some extent, within the British Isles, had a common heritage of Western European culture. Between the two world wars the partner governments in the Commonwealth had operated with a maximum of informality, as befitted a family of nations. It remained to be seen whether the entry of the Asian Dominions into the family circle would lessen the informality and introduce a greater tendency to spell out details. It would be natural that they should ask more urgently the meaning of the Commonwealth. It was also natural that they should insist upon the Commonwealth presenting a united front against racial discrimination. The older Dominions also had their questions to ask. The configuration of power in the Commonwealth had been changed to an extent which it was still impossible to assess. Were the strategic bulwarks of the Commonwealth in the Indian Ocean, for example, weakened or strengthened? Could the Commonwealth operate in its traditional fashion, when there still existed between two of the Dominions "an intense and ugly friction embittered with memories of bloodshed"? It was the speaker's view that the spirit of the Commonwealth, which was to settle such quarrels within itself and not seek help elsewhere, was being violated.

A second point of importance in Commonwealth relations was described as "the significant development of multilateral relations between the older members." Before 1939 consultation was primarily between Britain and the individual Dominions, but since then the interchange of High Commissioners had considerably facilitated multilateral communications and consultation. Although London remained the focal point, Commonwealth members on the periphery were becoming much more aware of each other's problems. There were vast opportunities for development of this new tendency, and the future of the Commonwealth might depend upon how they were utilised. The Canberra Pact was an illustration of what could be done in developing useful regional arrangements between two Dominions, and a valuable precedent.

For his third point the Canadian selected the development of closer relations between the Commonwealth and the United

States. He ascribed it to the war-time co-operation in the hard struggle against Germany and Japan, and to the postwar threat of aggressive Russian Communism. Since the latter was likely to continue, the Commonwealth might look forward to and seek closer co-operation with the United States. Together they could give the world its only possible real guarantee of peace.

In commenting on the meaning of the Commonwealth, the speaker asserted that its political dynamic was its liberal democratic ideals and institutions. As he put it:

Against the revolutionary ethics and tactics of Russian Communism it represents ideals of constitutionalism, gradualism, peaceful change, reform by discussion, and confidence in peaceful solutions, either within the state or in the Commonwealth sphere.

The Commonwealth stood for the association of free nationalities, "each permitted to shape its institutional life according to its spirit and traditions." Here was a finer doctrine of nationality than that subscribed to by Stalin, since it provided for genuine freedom and repudiated the ideal of a super-state.

In response to this challenging statement, the spokesmen for the Asian Dominions spoke equally frankly. The Pakistan leader said that his country entered the Commonwealth believing that such a course meant entering a group of nations with the same outlook on moral and political questions, animated by a "warm feeling of kinship and irrational sentiment," and recognizing the leadership of Great Britain. He thought that this leadership was due to Britain's traditional position as head of the Commonwealth, her strong faith in democratic ideals, and the fact that she was the only world power in the Commonwealth. He paid tribute to Britain as the greatest exponent of democracy the world had ever seen, particularly in the domestic field, and described her as "the freest country on God's earth today." Britain's moral leadership was of great importance, as it was from their contacts with her that the people of Pakistan judged the other parts of the Commonwealth with which they had had no contacts. The war had been a great shock to British leadership in the whole of Asia, but past mistakes and failures had been redeemed by the great gesture of giving freedom to India and Pakistan. Morally Britain had "redeemed herself and become a great and noble nation."

After these generous compliments, the speaker turned to describe three shocks which he said had been given to the initial faith of the people of Pakistan in British leadership. The first had arisen from the circumstances of partition which he described as "ill-conceived, incomplete, and ignoring the situation of the Muslims." The second shock had been the manner in which the boundary was fixed by the Commission with India, when a very important district peopled mostly by Muslims and contiguous to West Pakistan had been awarded to India. This allotment, he said, seemed "more than accidental." The third great shock had come when Britain suddenly reversed her policy on Palestine. Up till then Pakistan had thought herself in step with Britain. The speaker said that he realized the exigencies of the moment had perhaps dictated the British attitude towards the birth of the new state of Israel, but it was felt that if the Commonwealth placed the exigencies of the hour in first place it would cease to have a meaning to its members. Despite these shocks he hoped that future developments would purge the bitterness that had been generated in the past. He claimed that the Muslims and the British possessed a much greater temperamental understanding of each other than Hindus and British, an understanding which he attributed to a common unitarianism in religion, and the same robustness of outlook on domestic and world affairs. Pakistan's faith in the Commonwealth as a whole had also suffered a shock at the outset of the dispute with India over Kashmir. To Mr. Jinnah's inquiries of each member of the Commonwealth as to what were the rules, what was the traditional procedure in such cases, not a single reply had been received. There was no bitterness over this episode, but it had created perplexities which still existed.

The speaker stressed the fact that overriding all these considerations was the impending danger of Communist Russia which had become clear to his countrymen. Ways and means must be found for stopping this menace. In that connection he suggested that a possible danger for the future might arise from the treatment of Muslims by the government of India. If that minority was unfairly treated, it would probably look towards Russia. He argued that neither Pakistan nor India could assume leadership in the Middle East or South-Eastern Asia. Such badly needed leadership must come from the Commonwealth as a whole, and could only be given if the perplexities which had been described were removed.

An Indian delegate concurred in the tribute paid to British progressive ideals and said that if Britain remained in the future what she had been in the past, she is "certainly entitled to the moral leadership of the Commonwealth." He said that India's decision to remain within the Commonwealth should not be underestimated in view of recent history and the background of India's political leaders, most of whom had "often tasted His Majesty's hospitality." India had remained in the Commonwealth, once independence had been achieved, because she realized the similarity in ideology and politics and institutions between the two countries. Britain, and to a lesser extent, Australia, were the only Commonwealth countries that she knew. The speaker wondered what would keep the Commonwealth together, with the King no longer the unifying factor, and a lessening of racial and cultural similarities. The speaker also ventured to offer some purely personal conjectures which were admittedly unlikely to receive endorsement in New Delhi. He speculated whether the tendency which had led towards independence might not be reversed, and whether a Commonwealth citizenship involving political, economic and military obligations might not develop. This, he said, was an essential condition for the growth of the Commonwealth. In time there might even appear a Commonwealth federation of nations which would be superior to a regional federation, in that it would solve the dangers of colour and of continental wars. India brought to the Commonwealth her strong tradition of anti-colonialism and her equally strong desire to prevent discrimination between races. She realized that there was a vacuum of power in the Indian Ocean and that there should be "military links and a common strategy by India, Pakistan and South Africa in order to defend common democratic ideals." But the Commonwealth should likewise realize that it had a responsibility for the economic development of the backward areas and for raising the living standards of people who were essential for military purposes. He recognized that the differences between India and Pakistan, and India and South Africa, would have to be settled, and thought this settlement might best be achieved by refraining from making a frontal attack on the problems. It is "the art of constructive statesmanship to emphasize identities and consciously to deprecate differences." Thus India and South Africa could get together on their common strategic problem, while at the same time India and Canada could co-operate on economic matters.

Another Indian speaker, who was himself a Muslim, replied to the statement of the Pakistani delegate on the position of the Muslim minority in India. He thought that the professions of sympathy for this minority which came from Pakistan, were "a stick to beat the Indian government...[to] be thrown away when it was no longer needed." It was his view that:

Indian Muslims are nothing more nor less than Indian citizens. They are not being patted or petted and they must face their new situation like men for it is only as men and citizens willing to co-operate with their fellow-citizens and to serve their state to the utmost that they can make a significant contribution to Indian life . . . The Indian government has little experience, and the tasks before it are stupendous. There is discontent, but it is not confined to Muslims. Indian Muslims are in duty bound to join in building up the life of the nation, and they should not be turned away from a duty which they are competent to perform. They should not be distracted nor deceived.

The delegate from Ceylon joined in the tribute to the qualities of Britain, whose liberal ideals he described as "the cementing quality which welds the Commonwealth together." He did not agree with the term "New Commonwealth," which had been used by some speakers, as it implied a loss of traditions and imponderables which were the essence of the Commonwealth. The dynamic and flexible attitude which had kept the French Canadians of Canada and the Afrikaners of South Africa within the Commonwealth would, he hoped, enable Ceylon to find her place in the association. If she did not feel at home after a few years, she could secede, while continuing to live in friendly amity with her former partners. He believed that it was vital to keep co-operation on a functional level and to deal with problems as they appeared without any loss of sovereignty. The march of the Commonwealth towards federation, he declared, should be "a gradual process of growth and not an intellectual agreement."

Ceylon did not regard the Commonwealth as either a commercial or philanthropic institution. She expected that if one of its members were attacked the rest would show their resentment in varying degrees. She had contributed her naval bases for the strategy of the Commonwealth and hoped that Britain and the Commonwealth would need these bases for a long time.

The tributes to the United Kingdom by the Asian delegates were warmly acknowledged by United Kingdom speakers. One of them quoted Mr. Churchill as saying that the Indian decision to remain within the Commonwealth was one of the most generous gestures he had witnessed in his whole political career. The speaker in commenting on the Pakistan invitation to Britain to retain the moral leadership of the Commonwealth, emphasized the vitality of British political life. "My country," he said, "is not an ageing parent of a robust family. It is eternal and intends to remain so." The United Kingdom had no intention of abandoning its position of world leadership, and, as recent events in Malaya and Hong Kong had demonstrated, its power in Southeast Asia, was far from being at an end. She realized that leadership could be shared in the Commonwealth, a realization which made the task easier. There were some problems that had to be solved domestically by the partner governments such as the "most teasing problems of race and caste" which confronted India. He believed that, although not every one could go as far as Mr. Lionel Curtis in his advocacy of federalism as the solution for world problems, and although sovereignty could not perhaps be ceded at this stage, it would be possible to create "a strong and permanent structure for the Commonwealth" which would preserve its ideals and institutions, and to have an ultimate objective which he defined as seeking to bring together the Western democracies, the Asian powers and the United States.

Another United Kingdom speaker offered an important interpretation of the significance of the Declaration of the Commonwealth Prime Ministers on the status of India. He believed that the admission of a Republic was an essential step in the growth of the Commonwealth. The problem had long been before it and had now been resolved on the basis of full membership and full representation for the Republic of India. In the past it had been easy "to snatch at the shadow and lose the substance" as had been demonstrated in the relations of the United Kingdom and Ireland. There it had been proved that "forms excellent in themselves, if uncongenial," are "a barrier to free co-operation." The speaker recalled the views twice formally expressed at Commonwealth conferences in 1921 and 1926 that there was a danger in trying to establish the nature of the Commonwealth, and doubted if the task could be profitably undertaken at Bigwin. He also thought that the term "New Commonwealth" suggested something "fundamentally untrue." Although it was immensely changed and strengthened, its character was fundamentally the same, and, for that reason, the new Asian dominions felt they would have a place in it. The essence of the Commonwealth lay in its spirit, which was dangerous and difficult to define, and not in the letter of its relationships. It was an "international democracy" dependent upon free discussion, out of which came a sense of common purpose. It was also "absolutely dependent" upon free and equal partnership which, he again emphasized, must not be hampered by forms that might destroy the spirit.

To the question, "What were the springs of the future evolution of the Commonwealth?" the speaker thought the answer lay not within the Commonwealth but without. As long as its members preserved the integrity of the liberal-democratic spirit it would be a mistake to concern themselves with the remote future. "All generations are equidistant from eternity."

A third United Kingdom delegate also addressed himself to the problem of the meaning of the Commonwealth. He doubted if it could be found in the form of a common aspiration or objective, since many of those suggested in that connection were vague and by no means peculiar to the Commonwealth. On the other hand, common purposes were, if not the cause, at least a condition of the Commonwealth holding together. Thus the defence of the Commonwealth, which was now in danger, had confirmed a common interest, even if it had not created it. He regarded the Commonwealth as the product of history "flowing from several sources into one stream," and agreed with the delegate from Pakistan who had stressed the importance of sentimental forces. He defined the Commonwealth as a group of sovereign states, unlike such groups as the United Nations and OEEC, which had been described as in a state of "chartered impotence." The Commonwealth was unchartered and therefore, in some respects, less impotent. Its members had permanent relations of friendship and confidence which were the basis for their habit of consultation. To consult and to understand each other was a "vital duty," as was also the assurance of permanent friendly relations. For that reason the speaker agreed with the Indian delegate as to the need for solution of the Kashmir dispute. A second feature of the Commonwealth was the tendency of its members to treat their mutual relations as peculiar to themselves and not shared with other countries. They did not fear that such a policy would result in their being accused of "ganging up" as a bloc in opposition to others. They accorded each other tariff preferences which were at the moment commercially less significant than formerly; but the right to make such treaties afforded the members a privilege which could not be claimed by foreign countries. They were developing machinery of cooperation distinct from diplomatic relations with foreign countries, as well as a variety of unofficial contacts through conferences such as the present one which were "vitally important in building the fabric of common interests and mutual understanding." The speaker believed that the Commonwealth had an organic unity which meant that it was a living unit, not "a mere collection of units but a thing in itself." Although the Crown as "an institutional binding force" had no weight, and the idea of allegiance had been carved up by the division of sovereignty arising from the Statute of Westminster and other instruments and conventions, British opinion regarded the Crown as a symbol of unity. By accepting, in the Declaration of 1949, the King as a symbol of association, as the Head of the Commonwealth, India had, in his opinion, indicated that the Commonwealth was not regarded by her as "a mere collection of units." The speaker pointed out that the Commonwealth was in effect the only world organization except the United Nations. It spanned all continents and was instrumental in preventing separation into regional groups based upon purely economic or strategic considerations. The Commonwealth brought into the democratic world new countries with whom it might be otherwise difficult to build up contacts. Its common language and other affinities gave it a unique ability to maintain and strengthen close association with the United States. It offered the best opportunity and milieu for resolving differences in race, religion and outlook among countries, differences which were just as dangerous as ideological differences and more certain to endure. The Commonwealth possessed a great asset in its flexibility, which could well be illustrated by the manner in which Australia and New Zealand were adapting themselves to new conditions in the Pacific. In conclusion the speaker asked what could be done with the Commonwealth, and gave as his own reply:

We can admire but neglect it; we can talk about it but do nothing; or we can follow the parable of the talents and use the Commonwealth constructively in the service of mankind.

During the lively discussion two other speakers presented points of view which rounded off the opinions of the United Kingdom delegation. One of them gave a personal comment from the standpoint of the younger generation whom a Canadian had described as having no conception of the Commonwealth. He agreed that the Commonwealth was organic in its nature and resembled a family or a church more than a state. The climate of opinion at the conference and the absence of inconvenient rules was in contrast to the atmosphere at the Strasbourg meeting of the Council of Europe which he had just attended. With the realization of complete independence, a sense of community had grown which illustrated the well known psychological phenomenon that it was easier to agree once the obligation to agree was removed. He had been struck by the fact that the spiritual community was reinforced by the material interests which were apparent in the political, economic and strategic fields. But if permanent machinery to limit sovereignty were discussed, there would be a tendency for each partner government to think of instances where it might prove inconvenient, and to focus attention on potential conflicts rather than upon existing community of interest. For that reason any suggestion for "formalizing the relationship by machinery" would be likely to wreck the Commonwealth and weaken its influence. The speaker also pointed out that since all the Commonwealth states had stronger formal ties with their neighbours than with the Commonwealth, that fact demonstrated it was not a closed association or an exclusive society, and would not ultimately develop into a super-state. The last United Kingdom speaker on this topic suggested that the younger generation could be reminded that we had seen one world body, the League of Nations disintegrate, while the Commonwealth had withstood severe testing, and remained with the United States the greatest force for peace that the world had yet seen. He admitted that the concept of the Commonwealth might be more difficult for the next generation of the new member states to understand, and thought that this need should be stressed. He would add one characteristic to the list of Commonwealth qualities—the spirit of tolerance which had been demonstrated in the treatment of South Africa after the Boer War. That example might be encouraging in view of the bitter memories referred to by delegates from India and Pakistan.

For a veteran member of the Australian delegation, who thought that the conference represented "as fair a cross section of the Commonwealth as was likely to be assembled together," the most striking features of the discussions were the increasing emphasis on survival and the decline of interest in formal organization. These changes reflected the devolution of the Commonwealth and the disintegration of the world where law and order limped but no longer ran. It was his judgment that a fully informed and candid debate on the questions raised by the speakers from the Asian countries would lead at best to the conclusion that "association in the Commonwealth, whether formal or not," would probably give each other "a better chance of survival for a limited time and a somewhat better material standard of living" than if they were outside it. The speaker appealed for an interest as well in "wider and more neglected values" outside politics, economics and strategy, values in which were to be found the mainsprings of life. In an age in which the achievement of Western science had caused the world to stand mesmerized like a frightened bird before a snake, it was urgent that the Commonwealth and the Institutes should pursue a wider synthesis. As he pointed out, there were many eminent thinkers, especially in the United States, who were particularly concerned "with the possibility of creating that new awareness and wider faith in terms of a union of East and West." One of his colleagues in the Australian delegation said it was impossible to define the Commonwealth and even "a bad thing" to try to find its meaning. It was better to keep the present concept of Commonwealth relations and let a decade go by in which the new forces would clarify themselves. The essential nature of the Commonwealth might be described as a "holy mystery" justified by its works. Any attempt at rational analysis might create difficulties, misinterpretations and, perhaps, even introduce perplexities that were not already there. As he put it, "We know blindly, or rather we feel, that there is something peculiar and we feel that it is worthwhile."

With this feeling a Canadian agreed "whole-heartedly" and compared it to membership in a club which one valued without knowing precisely why. He took "mild issue" with the United Kingdom speaker's belief that a symbol was necessary for the Commonwealth. In Canada the Crown caused no difficulty, but there were other countries that would find it a symbol difficult to accept. He suggested that citizenship might be an alternative point of attraction, and referred as an illustration to the statements by the Prime Ministers of the United Kingdom and Canada at the time of the passing of the Republic of Ireland Act, namely that Ireland and their respective countries would not regard each other as foreign countries and their citizens as aliens. That, he believed, was "just about as far as we can go." An Irishman agreed that Ireland was anxious to keep its special association with the Commonwealth, as both Prime Minister Costello and Mr. De Valera had made clear. Her decision to become a republic had had the full approval of the Commonwealth governments. Ireland could make her contribution to world peace, especially to European recovery and above all to the defeat of Communist ideas. He endorsed the views of some British delegates that OEEC was not enough and thought that economic stability could not be expected unless there was closer co-operation between the OEEC and other great producing countries. It was his conviction that if other Commonwealth countries, especially Britain, would "take a little more interest in the Irish question and not regard it as a purely local problem,"

Ireland might make "more progress than in the last twenty-seven
years or even in the last seven hundred." A second Irish speaker
said that what India was doing today was what Irish plenipo-
tentiaries had suggested in the negotiations with Britain in 1921.
Because of the difficulties arising from the terms of the Treaty
of 1921, the Irish people became anxious "not only to be independent in fact but to make the forms and theory conform to
the facts." Like other delegations the Irish recognized the value
of the Commonwealth as an association of independent states,
an association created through history, even though it had been
sometimes a history of quarrels. He expressed the belief that
if Ireland were to be united, it should "certainly not baffle
the wit of man to find a link with the Commonwealth for an all-
important island lying alongside Great Britain." A third speaker
from Ireland went even further and said that he had always
believed in the Commonwealth idea, and that Ireland could
play a greater part in world politics if she were a member of it.
Nevertheless he was an Irishman first and had accepted the
decision to leave the Commonwealth. He thought that Ireland
might have remained a member, if the practice of living by
friendly consultation had been applied at the outset to the Irish
question; but instead every attempt had been cold-shouldered,
as he knew from personal experience. He hoped that in the
future Ireland would remain closely associated with the Commonwealth and be able to take part in such conferences as the
present one. The speaker appealed to the members to find some
way of helping India and Pakistan to settle their differences
without direct interference, and hoped that the loss of faith in
the United Kingdom which had been described by a delegate
from Pakistan would not blind the Asian members, as had happened in Ireland. Further disintegration in the Commonwealth
would be disastrous, as it was the only world organization now
operating and continuing to work for peace.

From the South African delegation there came a significant
comment on the acceptance of the Republic of India's continuing to be a member of the Commonwealth, an observation which
was at variance with the general approval. The speaker pointed
out that this decision was more important for South Africa than
for any other part of the Commonwealth because of the strong

sentiment in South Africa for a republic. She felt that approval of India's policy would reinforce those anxious to turn South Africa into a republic, and, if one were to judge from the blue prints issued during the war by its adherents, a South African republic would not be of the democratic type as in Ireland or perhaps India, but rather of the old Boer model. The Prime Minister had promised that there would be no republic without a referendum but had not made clear whether the kind of republic proposed would appear in the referendum. Although Dr. Malan had categorically stated that he would like South Africa, if it became a republic, to remain in the Commonwealth, there was a strong section of his own party which favoured a republic outside the Commonwealth. The speaker also referred to Dr. Malan's statement after he returned from the Prime Ministers' Conference in 1949, namely, that he had placed on the record in London a declaration that the expression "the King as head of the Commonwealth" did not alter any of the existing rights of the various members of the Commonwealth and did not endow the King with any new constitutional function. As Dr. Malan had said in the Assembly:

I feel that the resolution that was adopted there has once and for all put this matter beyond any doubt and that the position will never be misinterpreted again in the future.

She thought that this statement was another indication of the centrifugal path South Africa was following in Commonwealth affairs, and gave further proof of South Africa's suspicions of any suggestion of legislation which could be termed legislation for a super-state. As she put it, South Africa could accept no legislation which would perpetuate the Commonwealth in written form.

The doubts previously expressed by an Australian about the wisdom of examining the nature of the Commonwealth were re-echoed by a speaker from Ceylon. He agreed that the ties which linked the Commonwealth together should be strengthened, but believed that it was fruitless and even dangerous to analyse moral ties and urges too far. This was not the view of the speaker from Canada who had opened the debate and was asked to comment on the views which had been expressed.

He could see no more harm in clarifiying the nature of the Commonwealth than in clarifying anything else. He regarded the Commonwealth as an association which had no single government and defied all Austinian categories of sovereignty. Like all real associations, membership involved moral obligations, to preserve the Commonwealth, for instance, and to endeavour to further its purpose. There was no legal compulsion to take such a step but its members were under a moral law which had more significance. This might seem to be mysticism but he regarded it as "merely practical morality."

It was noticeable that no speaker during the debate advocated immediate steps towards federation, while many were strongly opposed to it. One United Kingdom speaker thought that what he described as the "numerous offers of marriage" which the United Kingdom had received from different parts of the world and which involved various kinds of federal union were based on "a very great fear of Russian antagonism and the strength of Communism." He thought that the United Kingdom should be very receptive to proposals but was bound to be somewhat cautious lest entry into a federal group prove a false step and result in the federation being exposed to such strain that it could not survive. His formula for United Kingdom policy was:

We should pursue the present course, maintaining the closest possible co-operation, binding ourselves by the spirit of freedom and recognizing that association with the United States is vital to us all. We should also pursue close co-operation among the United Kingdom, the United States, the Commonwealth and Western Europe.

A Canadian thought that policy would be substantially the same in his country. He said that their experience in working out difficulties of federation at home predisposed Canadians against taking federation schemes seriously. There was a general belief in Canada, shared by all political groups, that the federal idea would embarrass the development of pacts between one or more of the Commonwealth members and other free countries such as the United States. Informal and flexible institutions, he said, were more effective in linking up states anxious to preserve their sovereignty and independence. An Australian believed that Commonwealth ties were more effective if undefined and that none was more binding than voluntary association. So long as the members of the Commonwealth maintained that mutual respect which its partnership demanded, its force would never weaken. With these views a United Kingdom speaker concurred, stating that he had once thought that spiritual ties might be bettered by legislation for federation, but had come to the conclusion that spiritual ties were much better left alone by governments.

In support of this argument the delegate referred to the situation created by the various Commonwealth countries adopting Citizenship Acts. Previously there had been common citizenship, which enabled people to pass freely to and fro in the Commonwealth, although there was nothing to prevent one, if he were a Canadian, from saying robustly "I am a Canadian." The United Kingdom had been forced through the action of the other governments to pass the British Nationality Act which he described as a "confused piece of legislation." In his judgement the less nations interfered with sentimental ties by legislation the better it would be for everybody. The same point of view was expressed by another United Kingdom delegate who thought that such measures diminished the effect and power of underlying common status which he felt was the basis on which something could be built. The people of the United Kingdom had been told when the Act was passed that there was no intention of injuring the common status, whereas Dr. Malan had denied that a common status existed. They had not been prepared for such legislation, which had been decided upon "in a hole and corner fashion" at a meeting of the Commonwealth Prime Ministers because of a widespread desire in the Dominions. A delegate from Ceylon, who had attended the Conference of Experts on Nationality in 1947, said that at the time he had pointed out the dangers of stirring up this question and thought that his predictions had to some extent come true. The fact that South Africans were not necessarily British subjects showed that the purpose originally envisaged by the Prime Ministers had not been achieved. Before the South African Citizenship Act had been passed an Englishman was automatically a South African citizen after two years in that country. Now he must reside for five years and his citizenship was subject to veto by the Minister. This description of the South African legislation was confirmed by delegates from that country who added that the Act omitted for the first time any reference to Commonwealth citizenship and made a South African nothing but a South African citizen. One of them added that it would not be unfair to say that the Act was used to reinforce the strong urge towards complete South African nationality, unhampered by ties of empire, which was inherent in the present government.

The case for separate nationality acts was put by speakers from Canada, New Zealand and Australia. One Canadian admitted that some people looked a little askance at the effects of the Canadian Citizenship Act, but justified it in terms of its value for young people inasmuch as it gave them a sense of individuality, and offered them a symbol of democracy. He believed that it was important to give a sense of community to the young people of the Commonwealth. Another agreed that the Act helped to create a healthy positive Canadianism for young Canadians and also for new citizens. He described what he termed a "deep-seated psychological difficulty" in that some young Canadians, some new ones, and perhaps, a few older ones, found it "difficult to reconcile Canadian citizenship with any sense of reality about the Commonwealth." The Canadian Act had clarified this situation by the categorical statement that a Canadian citizen was a British subject. A New Zealand delegate believed that national legislation for citizenship which had been considered at the Conference in 1947 was as inevitable as the passing of the Statute of Westminster. In his opinion it was not brought about solely by the passing of Canadian or Irish legislation but was "a sign of the development of the Commonwealth." He pointed out that it had been necessary for New Zealand when negotiating agreements for abolition of visas with foreign governments to be able to define very carefully the person to whom such agreements would apply. It was also true that legislation such as was adopted in the United Kingdom did not involve a sharp break with a common code, but reaffirmed the principle that citizenship of each part meant citizenship of the whole and that admission to Commonwealth citizenship was secured through citizenship in a dominion. A delegate from Australia said the Australian Nationality and Citizenship Act which came into force on January 26, 1949, paralleled the New Zealand and Canadian ones in stating that an Australian citizen was also a British subject. It was regarded as of great importance for immigrants and those who were becoming naturalized. It was thought in Australia that a formal procedure of naturalization would encourage new citizens to feel that they were accepting obligations as well as privileges.

In the discussion of the question, "How far can we or should we have a common foreign policy?" there was general agreement that foreign policy must also be handled by individual governments who could share common purposes, but could not have a single policy. Domestic factors, which varied widely in the different countries, and regional interests precluded any centralization of policy. A Canadian pointed out that it was better, for instance, to have his country negotiate directly and individually with the United States on such topics as civil aviation, than to have the subject treated as one phase of a common policy in which the strong bargaining position of Canada might be seriously weakened by the current economic difficulties of the United Kingdom. Similarly it was wiser to have Canada and the United Kingdom participate individually in the North Atlantic Organization than to have the Commonwealth as a whole give it lukewarm or divided support, because the problems of the North Atlantic area were remote from the immediate interests of India or South Africa. On the other hand, Canada had not been much interested in Middle East problems, which concerned all other partner governments, until the question of Palestine had been brought before the United Nations. The speaker added that there were cases when a secondary power such as Canada might be asked to assume major responsibilities, as in the occupation of Germany, without being permitted any prior share in the formation of policy. This had been true of the Armistice negotiations with Germany and the preparations for the Minor Peace Treaties. It explained in part the withdrawal of Canadian troops from occupation after a brief period, and accounted, to a considerable extent, for the unwillingness of the Canadian government to share in the provision of air crew for the Berlin air lift. But there had been a tremendous development in Canadian foreign policy away from the pre-war attitude of "Yes, we have no commitments" to an assumption of responsibility as in the North Atlantic Pact. Canada had been active from the beginning in negotiating that treaty and had been the first country to complete its ratification. He concluded by saying that in forming her foreign policy Canada had always to consider the role of the United States, and to work as closely as possible with her.

Other delegates said that Canadian opinion was not unanimous on the question of maintaining occupation forces in Germany and taking part in the air lift. One of these delegates thought there would have been differences on the first, but an overwhelming majority would have favoured taking part in the air lift. Another said that although there were difficulties in the way, he believed that when there was a job to be done and the capacity to do it, it was "up to the government to find a way of doing it and not find excuses for not doing it."

Although United Kingdom speakers felt that Canadian participation in the occupation of Germany would have been "of great psychological value," they were in agreement that a common foreign policy was impossible. What they preferred for the Commonwealth was "the greatest possible degree of consultation and the utmost degree of co-operation in implementing the decisions adopted as a result of that consultation." There had been instances "of complete and inadequate consultation for political purposes." One of them in commenting on the relation of military commitments to foreign policy said there was no question of automatic military commitments in the Commonwealth since co-operation was voluntary, but it was possible to negotiate specific bilateral agreements involving contributions for joint defence. Examples of these were the Canberra Pact and the agreement between the United Kingdom and Ceylon. He regarded these as of "immense value" since they indicated the willingness of governments to make common commitments. When independent action was taken, as in Malaya or Hong Kong, it was of limited value for political purposes. The speaker said that he found it strange that:

There is no limit to the commitments we are prepared to make with countries outside the Commonwealth whereas this is not the case when it comes to Commonwealth commitments.

Another speaker from the United Kingdom stated that the Commonwealth faced one outstanding military problem—how to avoid domination by Russian Communism. He believed that war could be avoided "if we act sensibly," and suggested that a popular Nazi slogan might be reversed so as to read "Joy through Strength." In facing Communism the Commonwealth had to strengthen its internal position and to study the vital battleground. In his judgment it was essential to think more fully about the possibility of a Russian advance southward in Asia and Africa, and to strengthen the Commonwealth nations in those areas. The Commonwealth was not a single unit for military purposes and no one part of it could stand alone. If there were those in India who thought they could stand alone they would be "suffering from a delusion." Peacetime arrangements for military consultation were fairly good, were developing in the right fashion, and would be strengthened by the machinery to be set up under the Atlantic Pact. The speaker added:

There is a feeling in the United Kingdom, however, that when it came to peacetime military commitments of the kind that inevitably face a great power in the world the burden is still left to us exclusively. No one can fail to recognize the assistance which the United Kingdom has received in the economic field but the moral effect of Commonwealth participation in common military tasks will be very great even if the participation is small.

He gave as instances of action demanded from the United Kingdom, the occupation of Germany and the Berlin airlift, the defence of Hong Kong, and the occupation of Japan. He realized that there had been some co-operation from the Commonwealth countries, but more was required. The phase of "no commitments" had passed in Canada, but closer consultation must be furthered. The United Kingdom appreciated the immense economic assistance which it had received from Canada in the years since the war, but the additional benefit of Canadian help in the military field would be enormous. As he put it, this did not mean that the Commonwealth must have a common foreign policy, but that members should so direct their actions that the whole Commonwealth would be strengthened in face of the danger confronting it. Such a forthright statement was bound to evoke comment but perhaps not as much as was hoped. Previously a Canadian, who had been intimately associated with the British Commonwealth Air Training Plan, had discussed the lessons to be gained from its operation and his remarks were pertinent to the question that had been raised. After paying tribute to the exceptionally high quality of the personnel from other Commonwealth countries who had helped to administer the Plan, he discussed some of the problems created by the majority of R.C.A.F. personnel's being incorporated in R.A.F. units. He was almost certain that the lesson learned was that never again could Canada "consider letting individuals serve in units of any other Commonwealth or foreign country." Canada would operate her own forces, even though they were closely incorporated with the forces of other countries. Another Canadian said that fullest consultation in the military field was required, and that the situation had considerably improved over the days before 1939. In Ottawa there was a careful linking together of defence and foreign policy, illustrated by the creation of a Defence Liaison Division in the Department of External Affairs and by the presence of officers from that Department at the National Defence College in Kingston both as students and teachers. He pointed to the greater commitments for military action which Canada had assumed under the North Atlantic Pact. A United Kingdom delegate, who said that he rejoiced to hear of the developments in Canadian foreign policy, agreed that common foreign policies did not necessarily mean identical policies, and that it was sufficient to have a common purpose for individual policies. He believed that such a purpose must be the "preservation of our democratic way of life" but that it would be unwise "to base our common purpose on the purely negative terms of military strength." Since we could not beat Communism merely by military action, it was necessary to advance on the social and economic front. If that were done, advance on the military front might not be necessary. It was his conviction that:

The improvement of social welfare and the development of a stable economic system which will bring our people out of the morass of poverty by making the best use of our technical equipment, our knowledge and our resources is the answer to Communism.

An Indian thought that there was some misunderstanding about the position of his country and set out to make it quite clear. He pointed out that the Indian government was very strongly opposed to the Communist movement, and that the Indian people had no love for a Communism which was identified with atheism. Prime Minister Nehru had been attacked both by the Russian press and radio, and the Indian Trade Union movement had been criticised by Russia and her satellite states in the Economic and Social Council because it had withdrawn from the World Federation of Trade Unions to join the new and more democratic international trade union movement. India had a traditional fear of Russia and the Indian people were not unaware of the Russian menace. But the facts of geography must not be forgotten, and India was in a difficult position. The speaker wondered, for instance, whether Canadians would make strong statements about the United States should the United States turn hostile to the United Kingdom, when they realized that Canada might "get it in the neck" by so doing? The emergence of a Communist China, for which he thought the Western powers were largely responsible, had also made the situation more dangerous than ever before. India did not begin with the assumption that war was inevitable and that the world was divided into two. She would like to know whether it was not possible for all the countries to get together to see if the rift could not be healed and the U.S.S.R. and her satellites made to feel not completely isolated. If such a split was irrevocable it was obvious that India would not side with Russia, and it was even possible that she might not remain neutral. The Indian view was not inconsistent with a policy of military co-operation; the speaker declared in fact that this sort of co-operation already existed " to a very great degree."

An earlier comment on instances of inadequate consultation prompted an inquiry on the extent to which the Commonwealth countries consulted together at the United Nations before

making policy decisions. Doubts were expressed whether consultation was as close as it might be. An Australian thought
that not only was there very little consultation but that at times
it was even deliberately avoided. One of his colleagues said
that in Australia there were two inconsistent tendencies, "a
desire to promote co-operation, and at the same time an equally
strong desire to assert the Australian right to take independent
action if necessary." He ascribed the latter sentiment as arising
from the recent achievement of nationhood, the "robust and
independent character of Dr. Evatt," and the traditional attitude
of the Australian Labour movement. Furthermore, it sprang to
some extent from the Australian faith in the democratic system
of free discussion. Although this principle might have been
carried too far by the Australian delegation at the United Nations, it should not be assumed that his country was unfavourable to the principle of Commonwealth consultation. A New
Zealander said he understood that Commonwealth delegations
did meet sometimes at U.N. meetings for a preliminary exchange
of views and did seek to reach agreement, but always with the
understanding that if agreement were not possible, they were
at liberty to express their different views in the U.N. discussions.
This was also the view of a Canadian who thought Commonwealth discussions of an informal character were constantly
taking place, not only at Lake Success but through the various
High Commissioners. He said that for example, Canada when
on the Security Council had tried to keep in touch with the
views of the Commonwealth countries most concerned during
the negotiations by the "neutral six" Council members on the
Berlin Currency question. But Canada always wished to avoid
the appearance of a bloc policy from which the United States
was omitted, and had previously made this desire manifest in
the Prime Minister's comments on Lord Halifax's "ill-advised"
speech of 1944. A South African thought there was less exchange
of views in the UN than there had been in the League of Nations,
where it had been customary to discuss together the agenda for
the next day's meeting, and where contacts had been more
frequent through dinner parties. She thought that the change
might be due to the fact that the United States had not been
a member of the League but was a member of the UN. An

Australian did not think there was much difference in the degree of consultation then and now, and suggested that it was not only a case of avoiding a bloc against the United States but against any other country as well. This avoidance of forming a bloc might have been pressed too far but was "not entirely unreasonable."

At this point a United Kingdom delegate intervened to protest that discussion was being too much directed upon minor details and was getting away from the general purpose of the Commonwealth in the world. The fact, he observed, that economic crises and war were infinitely more destructive than ever before made the necessity for averting them greater than ever, and required a high degree of planning and conscious effort for a world system. He thought the Commonwealth was well suited to help to achieve this new system, which must be based upon the free consent of all the peoples concerned, because each of its members was a leader in its own area, and each had special links with the United States, which was imbued with the same spirit as bound the Commonwealth together. He maintained that Soviet Russia should not be viewed solely as a menace. There had been slumps and wars before 1917. As Arnold Toynbee had suggested, the U.S.S.R. provided a useful pressure which forced us to do the things we ought to do but would otherwise have done more slowly. There were other problems emerging, such as the integration of Germany and Japan into the democratic world. Asia and Africa must be linked to the Western world in a viable economy. Although Russia, "the physical embodiment of Nemesis," would take every possible advantage of our failures, the danger would be less if we maintained a tremendous preponderance of power. He thought there was a danger that during conferences among Commonwealth countries these long-term problems might become buried by the more immediate ones.

In the discussion of how methods of consultation among the partner governments could be improved, general satisfaction was voiced at the steady growth in contacts through the exchange of High Commissioners and the expansion of the Trade Commissioner services. An Australian raised the problem of the possibility of a Commonwealth secretariat, with more limited powers than those which had been suggested for it in the past by Prime Minister Curtin or Lord Bruce. He pointed out that Commonwealth governments had accepted a secretariat in the United Nations and that permanent machinery would develop under the North Atlantic Pact. The latter might affect the Canadian attitude, which had previously been hostile to any proposal of a secretariat on the ground that it would lead to a common policy. Alternatives to a secretariat, such as government to government consultation and the High Commissioner system were subject to grave difficulties. The first method was "spasmodic" and sometimes did not occur at all, a failure for which all members of the Commonwealth were equally to blame. The High Commissioner system, as had been shown in the Australian delegation paper, had not developed the full degree of diplomatic consultation and discussion which existed between foreign countries. The speaker admitted that Australian opinion was by no means unanimous on the subject but asked for a reasoned reaction—"not a mere frightened shying away"—to his proposal. One Canadian said that he thought Canadian opinion was not so much basically opposed to the idea as uncertain what it actually involved. Such questions as the composition and function of the secretariat, the locale, the nature of its relation to the Commonwealth Relations Office, and the provision made for contacts between its personnel and their home countries needed examination before an opinion could be expressed. There were immense practical difficulties before we got to the question of what the secretariat would do. In the case of the Atlantic Pact, Canadian participation was the easier because the dominant partner was the United States and contacts would be convenient with a secretariat located in Washington. Other Canadians stressed the degree of consultation which already existed through the present agencies, and spoke from personal knowledge of the satisfactory results that had already been secured through Commonwealth committees of a functional type, or through proper use in political liaison of the High Commissioners and their staffs in the various capitals. They felt that much could be gained by making continual and more effective use of all these. One Canadian pointed out that if the secretariat was completely removed from control of policy, it became simply "another machine for communication less direct than the present method." A United Kingdom speaker thought the original concept of the secretariat should be that of a continuing agency to follow up meetings of Commonwealth Prime Ministers or other senior ministers and to study questions that had arisen from these discussions. As he put it, the object should be "machinery serving the interests of Commonwealth meetings from the highest level down." In the opinion of another United Kingdom delegate there was much to be gained by increasing the personal contacts between responsible ministers, contacts which had been used very infrequently but which achieved much that could not be gained by exchange of cables and despatches. An Indian delegate agreed with previous speakers that the establishment of a Commonwealth secretariat was not essential and suggested proposals for the strengthening of the High Commissioners' Offices, particularly in the economic field. He favoured more regular meetings of the Ministers of External Affairs in the various capitals with the resident High Commissioners for exchange of information. He also thought that the meetings of Prime Ministers should not always be in London, and that Dominion Prime Ministers of long experience should endeavour to make a farewell tour of other Dominions before retiring from office.

An Australian advanced practical reasons why Ministerial consultations could not be too frequent. Constant travel placed a terrific strain upon the Ministers concerned, as the experience of the Australian Cabinet had shown. Ministers were sometimes reluctant to attend meetings to discuss policy at a high level because of the difficulties in making decisions which might not find popular support in their home countries. For that reason he believed that meetings on the official level were the most useful. The same speaker offered no answer to the questions about the Commonwealth secretariat which had emerged during the discussion. He thought that its functions might be those described earlier by a United Kingdom speaker; that its personnel should be separate from the governments of the countries represented, in a relationship analogous to that between the United Nations Secretariat and the General Assembly. It might possibly include representatives of the Prime Ministers or Ministers of External Affairs, although he realized that such an arrangement might be open to criticism on the grounds that it was coming too close to bringing about a common foreign policy. He held no strong views on the location of the Secretariat, but, personally he favoured Bermuda.

When an Indian delegate opened the discussion on the extent to which the Commonwealth could or should unite for economic purposes, he began by saying that it was "unrealistic" to talk of one Commonwealth economic policy, but added that it would "not be unfair to ask, however, that the Commonwealth countries . . . consider, when framing their own economic policies, the incidence of these policies on both the highly developed and less developed members of the Commonwealth." He believed that there was great need of a proper study of the resources and needs of the Commonwealth as well as a better understanding of the effects of the war on the economies of the member nations. For that reason he referred to the suggestion he had previously made of the desirability for a Commonwealth economic conference. The speaker did not think that it was necessary, or even desirable, that it should be a government conference but felt that government support would be "both useful and necessary." Such a conference should examine the effects of the war on all parts of the Commonwealth, the aspirations of the native peoples, the economic interdependence of the Commonwealth countries, and a long term solution to the dollar gap. He believed that it would make the Commonwealth realize that the economic development of the underdeveloped areas was "essential in the fight against Communism." He repeated his previous description of India's needs for capital investment and its relation to the sterling balances, for expert advice on methods of economic development, and for technical training along the lines of what had been done for the young Indian "Bevin boys" who had gone to England during the war. What was needed was an evolution of a Commonwealth Point Four, based upon the recognition by the Commonwealth countries of "a mutual interest in each other and a determination to meet the requirements of others in order to raise the standard of living of all the peoples in the Commonwealth."

With this suggestion the other Asian delegations were in complete agreement. A Pakistan delegate said that if the Commonwealth had any meaning for the Asian countries it could "only be expressed in concrete measures for their economic improvement." Aid to these countries, which would help to give them a sense of community of interest with the rest of the Commonwealth, would involve, in addition to the methods proposed by the Indian delegate, "a close examination of such questions as foreign investments and the revision of tariff laws and conventions." He was prepared to propose the creation of a permanent advisory body representing such Commonwealth countries as were willing to join a committee which could offer advice and undertake various measures for the economic development of member countries. He pointed to the pressing needs of Pakistan for industrialization and her corresponding need of "friendly guidance and technical and financial help of the Commonwealth"; he even went so far as to say that Pakistan would "without hesitation place her raw materials and other resources at the disposal of the Commonwealth and thus help to evolve a common dynamic of economic development of the Commonwealth as a whole." The delegate from Ceylon supported the Indian suggestion, and said that in his country, in the field of investment events were getting ahead of advocacy. He described a large economic project in Ceylon which was being financed by equal amounts of Sinhalese and British capital, and administered by an equal number of directors from each country. This was one illustration of what was already under way; he thought that more British and American capital would soon be invested in Ceylon.

A delegate who said that New Zealand felt strongly the need for consultative economic machinery gave an interesting illustration of the complexity of economic interrelationships within the Commonwealth. New Zealand's prosperity was vitally dependent upon her dairy industry, for which the United Kingdom was the main market. At present a government subsidy on butter in the United Kingdom stimulated New Zealand sales, but because of this critical dependence New Zealand was anxious to explore the possibilities of other markets. It might be possible to supply dried milk to India, but a large capital outlay would be required in the dairy industry before such a switch in production could take place. So far it had not been possible to secure a long-term agreement to justify such an expenditure. Consequently New Zealand could not go further until the policy of the United Kingdom and the response of India to the project were clarified. Such a situation reinforced New Zealand opinion upon the importance of having a definite machinery of consultation on economic problems which would be on a continuing and not an *ad hoc* basis. A South African agreed with the previous Indian speaker upon the need of surveys of natural resources but thought that the knowledge gained from them should be pooled with the United States in view of the American Point Four programme, and that American technical aid should be called upon where necessary.

Delegates from the other Commonwealth countries were inclined to examine the problem in a still wider setting. A United Kingdom speaker emphasized the immense economic problems which confronted all Commonwealth countries and the "mortal dangers" which would arise unless they were solved. He described the "anguish of thought" with which the experts had faced the problems of European economic co-operation at Paris in the autumn of 1948. So far as Europe was concerned these problems could be solved only by achieving a high level of balance in international trade. Unless this level was reached Canada could not avoid "the tremendous, far-reaching, and most painful series of agricultural adjustments in her economic history." It was to be hoped that the United States would open the door for a joint solution, but the Commonwealth countries and others had to be willing to realign their entire foreign trade and "be ready to go through the door." He favoured a Commonwealth economic conference to thrash out the details of economic co-operation, but would prefer a more official conference, since its practical effects upon their governments would be greater. On the other hand he agreed that the conference should be "formalized to the least possible extent." A Canadian heartily supported this argument and pointed out that on the one hand Canada could not join in a common economic policy for the Commonwealth because of her close ties with the United States, while, on the other hand, the new Asian Dominions needed investments which were quite beyond the capacity of any single Commonwealth country to provide. It was his view that:

Commonwealth economic policy does not make very much sense without close co-operation with the United States. This is an absolute necessity. Given this close co-operation, a tremendous amount can be done which can best be carried out in an informal manner.

He agreed with the Indian delegate about the need for knowing each other's economic problems, and felt that the Conference had made all of the delegates, and particularly the Canadians, aware of one another's "profound ignorance of problems, difficulties and opportunities." He thought that Canada could offer technical co-operation and possibly some capital investment and was interested in the markets in the Asian countries. The speaker went on to express concern at the tendency he had noticed in the Conference of drawing "a sharp and real line of division between the British Commonwealth and the United States." He felt there was a tendency on both sides of the Atlantic to over-emphasize the differences, with North Americans believing that socialism was at the root of the British crisis, and some Europeans visualizing the United States as "run by Wall Street financiers and pot-bellied capitalists." The United States had changed radically in the last decade, perhaps as much as the United Kingdom, if not quite in the same direction. It was his view that the talks which had been going on in Washington had shown that "our divergencies do not prevent us from working together." Other Canadian speakers followed the same line of argument and pointed to the growth of welfare legislation in North America, the use of controls, and of floor prices for agricultural products, and the fixing of prices for international commodities, such as tin and rubber, to show that as compared to the United Kingdom there were "differences in ways but not so much in the trend of government intervention." One of them gave illustrations from his own industry of what would happen to Canada if a high level of trade were not established. He was worried over the tendency to establish a high cost structure in the non-dollar world in order to conserve dollars, and said that "to use the analogy of the log-jam we can hardly blow it up with dynamite. We must pull out the individual logs and get the stream flowing." Another Canadian followed up this simile by adding that the one country strong enough today to abandon protection was the United States, and this made it the key log in the present jam. He urged that Canada examine her own position courageously and see if she could lower tariff barriers so as to give a lead. It was his view that Americans would be more prepared to help if they felt that Canada was doing more. As he said, we would get nowhere as long as we kept saying what the United States ought to do. We could not dictate to the United States.

The trend of argument developed by the Canadian delegates evoked some interesting comments. One United Kingdom speaker insisted that, if federation were achieved and the fear of war thereby removed, all the economic problems would then be easy to solve. Another one strongly supported the Canadian view on the danger of contrasting capitalist United States with socialist countries. He said that such a notion had contributed to the arguments for a "Third Force" which would be politically Socialist and would mediate between capitalist countries and Communist Russia. In practice and theory that had proved "complete nonsense," since Socialism was the main enemy of Communism. In the United Kingdom the Labour government had seen that it would not solve its problems without co-operation with the United States, and had found that there were fewer differences between the United Kingdom and the United States than, for example, between the United Kingdom and the Italy of Signor De Gasperi or the South Africa of Dr. Malan. A third United Kingdom delegate ascribed the difficulties which the Conference had discussed to political insecurity and "terrible instabilities" in currency which arose from the huge chasm between the great creditor and the debtor countries. He realized that both debtor and creditor had to make a concerted effort, the one to be a free trade area and to welcome imports from the debtor countries, the other to provide exports to North America of the right price and quality and at the right time. If such an effort were made, a high level of trade equilibrium could be achieved and the necessary investment of capital on the part of the creditor would be stimulated. A Canadian agreed with this diagnosis, but said that one of the obstacles to expanding private investment was the inadequacy of machinery in North America and, as the period between wars had shown, "a lack of fundamental principles." An Australian concurred and wondered if there could not be some method of combining British "financial know-how" with American capital in the rehabilitation of the world. He thought it would be especially important for the Asian Dominions. A United Kingdom delegate said this point had often been considered by New York bankers, but they had never seen their way to adopt British methods. He pointed out that the great American banks had had large branches in London for very many years. The same delegate said, in commenting on a suggestion that American capital might be "canalized" to the Commonwealth through direct investment by United States concerns in the United Kingdom, that there had been some instances, but that such firms were "showing audacity in the face of the present position of sterling and with the present very high taxation of profits and dividends."

This discussion of investment ended with a Canadian's comment on the suggestion that Canada should give a lead to the United States in overseas investment. He agreed that it was desirable, but pointed out some of the difficulties. The Canadian capacity to produce an exportable surplus for investment was severely limited by the amount of American dollars needed for essential imports. To get them elsewhere than in the United States would involve greater discrimination against American imports than was now the case, and would not be likely to increase the desire of the United States to co-operate. The only other method for securing a surplus for investment was to reduce domestic consumption and cut internal investment. Such a policy involved political considerations and would require more controls, to which he thought Canadians would "strenuously object." It was his belief that in the long run concentration on the development of Canada would permit improvement in the standard of living both at home and abroad. In the short run Canadians would feel that they should keep in step with the United States. In 1947, Canada had, relatively speaking, got ahead of the United States, and as a result, her dollar reserves had very nearly disappeared. It had then been necessary to reduce the drawing rights of the United Kingdom on the credit extended to her, and to ban many United States imports, a policy which had been unpopular in both the United States and Canada. If the United States made dollars available for investment, he believed that Canada would "more than match them in her relative contribution." In the immediate future it should be Canada's role "to try to increase United States assistance by close consultation with that country, and by pointing out that Canada was prepared to do as much as the United States." If Canada tried to do something on her own she would be involved "in far more serious restrictions of United States imports."

It was to be expected that the Irish delegation would not discuss Commonwealth economic policy. One of them did point out, however, that Ireland was a member of the sterling area and stood or fell economically with the United Kingdom. He thought that Ireland could make an indirect contribution to United Kingdom recovery through her agriculture. Under Marshall Aid Irish agriculture, which had suffered during the war from the inability to import essential feeds and fertilizers, was being assisted in expanding production. He reminded the conference that ninety per cent of Ireland's exports went to the United Kingdom and were chiefly composed of food products. By 1952-53, given favourable conditions, exports of agricultural produce from Ireland would increase from $110 millions to $262 millions. Another Irishman followed this up by saying that his country bought eighty-eight per cent of her imports from Commonwealth countries, and asked for greater reciprocity in solving economic problems than existed at present. Ireland was anxious to increase her industrial employment and had adopted certain tariffs "to prevent dumping, keep her workers employed and protect the funds of her investors." He asked that if nations entered into agreements, they should "keep Ireland's position in mind and not sign agreements harmful to small countries." Believing that the best way to combat Communism was to give a decent standard of living to all, the Irish government was making strenuous efforts to achieve this aim.

For its final item on the agenda the Conference discussed the question of "Commonwealth public relations," a topic which had not appeared on the agenda of previous meetings. Its inclusion arose from the realization that the members of the Commonwealth did not know enough about each other, or about the Commonwealth as a whole, and that the rest of the world did not know enough about the nature of the Commonwealth. On this latter aspect of the question there was little discussion, although some reference was made to the special importance of the United States' understanding the Commonwealth better. A New Zealand delegate, the only delegate present who had lived for several years in the United States, said it was true that the people of the United States were generally ignorant of the Commonwealth. She thought that the Dominions had done a better job than the United Kingdom in combating this ignorance, and believed that there was more sympathy for India in the United States because of the increased publicity that had attended her attainment of independence.

Because of their tendency to play down Commonwealth meetings, part of the blame for inadequate appreciation of the Commonwealth was placed upon the governments. One delegate said that before leaving the United Kingdom he had been struck by the view of pressmen that public relations on Commonwealth matters had not been well handled. Another United Kingdom delegate said he was against publicity campaigns which were not based upon policies and achievements that made news. The Prime Ministers' conferences had been failures in that respect because of the inadequate arrangements for publicity, the brevity of the communiqués that had been issued during the meetings, and the scanty debates in Parliament. A Canadian criticised the "coy and cautious atmosphere" which attended official announcements in Canada of Commonwealth talks or meetings. He said that every time those announcements were made the government hastened to add a sentence explaining that such talks would be "informal, unofficial and exploratory." He agreed that there was "no use loading a cart with publicity stunts if there was no horse to draw it." Another United Kingdom speaker thought that the inadequate publicity given to the Prime Ministers' conferences had been due to "an exaggerated concern for the sensibilities of the members of the Commonwealth." Now that the constitutional questions and problems of status had been cleared out of the road, it was time for the Prime Ministers to scrap the old tradition of silence and be ready to produce "the horse for the cart." On the other hand, it was pointed out that the great value of the Prime Ministers' meetings was "their quiet informality" and much of this would be destroyed by publicity.

With the publicists present agreeing, with unexpected modesty, that deeds and not words were more important in bringing the Commonwealth together, the Conference proceeded to examine various proposals to achieve that purpose. "How we treat one another," said a Canadian, "will be reflected in how we write about one another." In commenting on this argument one delegate put it neatly when he remarked that Commonwealth public relations depended upon successful private relations. Periodic meetings of such bodies as Trade Unions, Bar Associations, the Empire Press Unions, Women's Institutes, and the Commonwealth Parliamentary Association could do much to improve Commonwealth relations. In this work the various Commonwealth Institutes of International Affairs could and should take the lead, as they had already done in promoting the four unofficial conferences.

It was also agreed that the basis for better understanding must be achieved through education. Suggestions ranged from a strengthening of the curricula on Commonwealth affairs in the schools to the expansion of adult education, which might possibly be aided by the Information Officers attached to the staffs of the various High Commissioners. Much would be gained, it was felt, by a wider exchange of radio programmes "designed to demonstrate Commonwealth co-operation and to show the Commonwealth as a family," by a development of short wave broadcasting, the production and distribution of documentary films (of which the delegates saw some examples during the conference) and by the development of travelling exhibits of arts and crafts in the various Commonwealth countries. An Indian delegate suggested that it might be possible to have a "Commonwealth Council" with similar objectives to those of the British Council. Several delegates favoured an increase in the number of travelling fellowships for study in Commonwealth universities by graduate students, and more encouragement for research workers to visit laboratories in other Commonwealth countries than their own. As a South African said, such measures would help to establish "a sort of intellectual lease-lend in the Commonwealth." It was pointed out that the Association of British Commonwealth Universities at its meeting in Oxford in 1948 had endorsed proposals for exchanges of staff and students. The need for more chairs of Commonwealth Relations in the Universities was stressed, but a warning was sounded by one delegate against the danger of having teaching in this field sharply separated from the study of international relations. The same delegate stressed the serious lack of documentary material on Commonwealth affairs. There was considerable agreement with the suggestion of a United Kingdom delegate that it was time for a fact-finding survey, conducted by the national Institutes in each country, to ascertain what was known about other countries of the Commonwealth, what agencies were at work in this field, and the extent to which Commonwealth subjects were being covered by the press and other publications. A South African delegate summed up the discussion by saying:

A common task and common experiences constitute the basis of an *esprit de corps* between members of the Commonwealth. This is the fundamental lesson which the last war has taught us, and which should be capitalised by all those engaged in propagating Commonwealth solidarity.

PART III

THE CONFERENCE IN RETROSPECT

To judge by the remarks made both publicly and privately after the discussions were over, and by the comments that subsequently appeared in the periodicals[1], the Bigwin Conference was generally regarded as the most successful to date of the unofficial Commonwealth conferences. The two veterans of all four conferences, others who had participated in more than one, and novices who in some instances had arrived as "doubting Thomases" and later admitted freely their conversion—all of them agreed in expressing gratification with the meetings and a keen desire to see them continued. Such harmony of opinion did not arise from the complacency of a little Jack Horner feasting in a Conference corner and regarding the rest of the world with smug superiority. Those at Bigwin were too well aware of the seriousness of the problems which all the Commonwealth countries faced, and had had too wide experience in meetings of all sorts to succumb to such a fond delusion. Since the Conference was barred by its very nature from reaching decisions or endorsing policies, satisfaction with its results could not be based upon gratification at having scored a victory in "getting some thing done." It developed rather from the delegates' gaining a clearer appreciation of what the Commonwealth was and might be, and what were the problems which confronted it.

Although extremists of the Right or the Left were not to be found in any of the nine delegations, those present either made an earnest attempt to describe their point of view when that was necessary, or had arranged for its depiction in the delegation

[1] Cf. Nicholas Mansergh, "New Voices From Asia," *The Observer,* September 25, 1949; H. V. Hodson, "The Commonwealth Is Alive," *The Sunday Times,* September 25, 1949; "The Commonwealth Confers," *The Economist,* October 1, 1949; The Rt. Hon. R. A. Butler, M.P., "The Bigwin Conference," *International Affairs,* January, 1950, pp. 11-21; "The Commonwealth Relations Conference—A Canadian View," *The Round Table,* December, 1949, pp. 21-28; R. G. Trotter, "Bigwin and the Changing Commonwealth," *International Journal,* Winter, 1949-50, pp. 22-30; George Caiger, "The Bigwin Inn Conference," *The Australian Outlook,* December 1949, pp. 229-236; V. K. R. V. Rao, "The New Commonwealth—Will It Endure?" *India Quarterly,* Vol. VI, No. 1, January-March, 1950.

papers. With minor exceptions the Conference was remarkably
representative of informed public opinion in the various countries.
But the Conference was more than a mirror. Its members felt
themselves in duty bound to expound the views of their countries
and did so without fear or favour. Possessing a common language,
even though it was spoken with a wide variety of accents, trained
in the same techniques of discussion, and sharing the same concepts of government, the delegates quickly got to the heart of the
matter in the successive round tables. They were frank without
giving offence, critical of each other's policies without imputing
political motives for being so. The arguments over the partition
of Ireland, the Kashmir dispute, and racial discrimination in
South Africa lacked nothing in passionate sincerity or sharp
divergence of opinion. Delegates made these problems come
alive without creating the atmosphere of a Donnybrook fair. In
some instances they helped to create a sense of proportion, in
others a regret that such discussion was not feasible elsewhere.
Here was the kind of ventilation of a grievance which an official
conference seldom achieved, and which a protest meeting only
exacerbated. To vary the metaphor a meeting like Bigwin was
valuable in revealing "soft shoulders" that needed attention on
Commonwealth highways. Thus Professor Mansergh wrote in
The Observer:

One of the most lasting impressions of this conference is that
Britain should not allow herself to drift or be forced into reactionary policies by the threat of Communism in Europe, for by so
doing she would risk losing far more on balance in Asia where
her prestige and potential influence are now higher than ever
before.

This cautionary function of such a conference as Bigwin is all
the more important because of the increasing tendency of official
Commonwealth conferences whether of Prime Ministers, Finance
Ministers or Foreign Ministers to achieve informality and intimacy at the expense of public enlightenment. The kind of *com-
muniqué* issued, for instance, after the Colombo conference,
which one of the delegates at the meeting satirized, may be
necessary to preserve the frankness of discussion and to encourage
attendance at Commonwealth meetings, but is almost useless

in making the peoples of the Commonwealth aware of the nature of the urgent issues under discussion. For that reason an unofficial but well-informed Commonwealth conference, whose members are in a position to influence public opinion in their respective countries, and whose proceedings can be published in considerable detail, serves a very useful purpose.

As the first unofficial conference at which all three Asian dominions were represented, Bigwin gave their delegations an opportunity and a challenge. They were able to enlighten the other delegates on the seriousness of the economic problems which confronted their countries, and, sometimes unintentionally, gave a hint of why their needs for help under a Point Four or by some other device were complicated by national attitudes. The Asian delegates warned the others that unless the present ruling classes could "deliver the goods" by raising the living standards of their peoples, the Commonwealth would find their successors much less prepared to follow the accustomed paths of reform. They made it plain that the intensity of their dislike of colonialism had not blinded them to the motives of the Communists who exploited that dislike. At the same time they were less prepared than their Western colleagues to concede the inevitability of the division of the world into pro- and anti-Communist forces. But the men of the East did more than warn and inform the others. They challenged them to explain what the Commonwealth really was, to explain why its procedures had been abandoned in the Kashmir case, or why its ideals had been violated in Africa. It was clear that they were interested in retaining the intimacy of the past, even though the British Empire had dissolved into a Commonwealth of Nations and the Republic of India was replacing the British Raj. They freely conceded Britain a moral leadership in Asia, which could be retained only by exercising it, but challenged Canada and Australia to translate into material assistance oratorical generalities about Commonwealth values. In short the Asian delegates expected the Commonwealth to demonstrate its adaptability to changing conditions without becoming a "New Commonwealth" which would lack the essential features of the old. It was noticeable that although they were as much opposed as any group to centralization of policy or to a single Commonwealth policy, the

Asian delegates were prepared to go a considerable distance in furthering discussions about Commonwealth economic problems and increasing Commonwealth co-operation.

It was to be expected that the Canadians should speak with an American accent on many of the problems that came under discussion. They demonstrated the element of truth in the repeated platitude that Canada is the interpreter of the United States to the Commonwealth. Such a statement does not mean that the other Commonwealth states are not in touch, diplomatically and otherwise, with American policies. It does not overlook the fact that the United Kingdom and the United States talk the same language as Great Powers. But it was apparent at Bigwin that environment, attitude of mind, and increasing economic intermingling with the United States gave the Canadians an appreciation of the American scene which no other group possessed and from which all could benefit. It was also noticeable that the enormous changes in the climate of opinion in the United States had in turn reacted upon Canadian thinking and made possible clearer decisions and bolder policies than were attempted in the thirties. No delegation questioned the need for American assistance in the areas of economic action, foreign policy and defence. None denied the similarity of ideals which the United States and the Commonwealth shared. This greater sense of partnership, as well as of need, was one which at times the conference almost took for granted, but to which Canadians repeatedly returned. It did not, however, preclude comments, especially from Asian speakers, that the Commonwealth could and should do more for its members, particularly in economic matters, and not wait too much upon American assistance. On the other hand it evoked suggestions from the United Kingdom and Canada to the delegates from Australia and New Zealand that their countries should not march too far ahead of the United States in their advocacy of pacts or policies in the Pacific.

By common consent the delegation from the United Kingdom was recognized as the most representative in character and the most impressive in the technical competence of its experts. In the debates on economic policy the differences within its ranks were neither concealed nor over-stressed, and materially contributed to the searching character of those discussions. On other topics, strategy, foreign policy, and to a lesser extent on colonial problems, the area of agreement within the delegation was almost complete. There was no lack of frankness in admitting the restrictions that harsh necessity had placed upon the exercise of British power in regions where once the United Kingdom had held predominant influence. But there was an equally firm and reiterated insistence that the United Kingdom had no intention of settling down as a retired empire builder to cultivate her green and pleasant land. She was a Great Power and intended to remain so, even though super-powers armed with atomic bombs might tower above her and further complicate her problems which clamored for solution. By their past record and what they placed on the Conference record the members of the United Kingdom delegation offered convincing proof that the decline in the relative strength of their country was not paralleled by a corresponding decline in will or capacity. To judge from their observations there was more readiness than in the past to concede the possibility of their country becoming a junior partner in the firm of Uncle Sam and John Bull, and a growing scepticism about the likelihood of ever securing any real measure of co-operation from the U.S.S.R. in building one world. Lastly, through its spokesmen the United Kingdom, at a time when European wooing of her was never more ardent, displayed a greater awareness of the part that other Commonwealth countries could and might play in world affairs, and a greater willingness to discuss co-operation with them on a regional basis. Such co-operation would not preclude, as the North Atlantic Pact had already demonstrated, association with other countries in the same region inspired by the same motives.

Dollar shortages and other factors had made the delegations from Australia and New Zealand less broadly representative in their character than in the past. They did not prevent the Conference from forming a clear conception of what was being said and thought about the Commonwealth in the Antipodes. The effect of the impact of the second world war upon these countries was marked. They were no longer concerned about the disturbing views on status held by Irishmen, South Africans or Canadians. They were much more alive to the urgency of the problems which faced them in the Pacific and no longer inclined to look towards the Mother Country as their sole protector. They were in sympathy with Asian views on the passing of colonialism, and with Canadian views upon the inescapable necessity of securing co-operation from the United States. Although there lingered vestigial survivals of past yearnings for Commonwealth machinery such as were expressed in the suggestion for a Commonwealth secretariat, and although there were veiled doubts (less veiled in the delegation papers) about the feasibility of intimate consultation in a less homogeneous Commonwealth there was an obvious eagerness to try to make a go of it under present conditions and to develop regional associations much wider in their scope and intent than the Anzac Pact.

Whether by accident or design, the South African delegation gave to the Conference a picture of a country which was the most "inward-looking" of all those represented. Grimly aware of the seriousness of its native problem, and of the disapproval with which the policies of its government were viewed in the United Nations and by its partners in the Commonwealth, the delegation did all that could be done to bring out the mitigating factors in the situation. It pleaded for time and for toleration. Repeatedly the South Africans reiterated their country's hatred of Communism and willingness to co-operate, by force of arms if necessary, in stemming its advance. But differences with their neighbours and Commonwealth partners made South Africa less in a position to negotiate viable regional agreements than countries like Australia or Canada. Bitter domestic disputes made their delegation more able to offer warnings than to give encouragement when Commonwealth policies were debated.

After all that has been said and summarised it only remains to add that the Bigwin Conference furnished solid grounds for reasoned optimism about the future of the Commonwealth. It would be folly to deny the existence of explosive issues that still divide Commonwealth countries or threaten their internal unity. It would be dangerous to ignore the seriousness of the military and political threats to the security of the partner governments, threats which the Commonwealth cannot meet alone. It would be stupid to minimise the critical nature of the economic difficulties which harass so many of the Commonwealth countries and which are still far from solution. But the existence of a sense of comradeship, the legacy of cherished traditions, and the appreciation of common purposes are intangibles whose strength should not be ignored. It was surely a sign of grace that men and women from nine countries could assemble from all parts of the earth to debate their problems so frankly and vigorously in such an atmosphere of shared and communicable experience as no other international meeting could duplicate. They might call themselves citizens of a republic, a union, a dominion or a kingdom. Their homeland might be a crowded island or an entire and alarmingly empty continent. But all were proudly aware that they held in common ideals which during the second world war they had successfully defended against seemingly hopeless odds in "their finest hour," and which made their Commonwealth one possible nucleus of the free world of tomorrow.

APPENDICES

Appendix A

SPEECHES AT THE OPENING SESSION OF THE CONFERENCE

Address of Welcome by Honourable Brooke Claxton, Minister of National Defence, and Acting Secretary of State for External Affairs

On behalf of the Government of Canada I extend a cordial welcome to all the delegates to the Conference meeting here in Canada for the second time. To "survey the position of the Member Nations of the Commonwealth in the postwar world and to consider the changes that may be required in their policies and the contribution they can make to world order and progress"—this constitutes, as I am given to understand, your terms of reference.

I know your deliberations will be useful—the free and frank exchange of views between friends is always useful—and I hope your stay in Canada will be enjoyable. While I realize that public and private business will be exercising urgent pressure for your return home as soon as the conference is over, may I express the hope that you may see something more of Canada. In the best traditions of the local greeter may I say that if any of you are interested in the work of the Department of Defence, with which I am directly concerned, I would be glad to arrange visits to any of the service establishments or to make arrangements for you to see any of our great industries. I should also be glad to see that similar arrangements with regard to other government agencies are facilitated in every way. Above all I hope that it may be possible for you to visit Ottawa. Parliament will be in session and I hope that the comparative unanimity you will see there will be matched in your own deliberations.

It gives me particular pleasure personally to extend this welcome because I was present at the first conference which was held in Toronto in 1933. The second took place at Lapstone, near Sydney, Australia in September of 1938; the third at London in 1945. Mr.

E. J. Tarr, K.C., who is with us today, is the only person who was present at all the other conferences as a delegate and played a major part in the arrangements for all of them. He will, I am sure, be glad to join me in a particular welcome to our friend, Mr. Ivison Macadam, who is, I believe, the only other to have attended all four conferences and whose work contributed so much to their success.

It is particularly happy that this fourth conference is being held in the year marking the 30th birthday of the Royal Institute of International Affairs. Among your number is Mr. Lionel Curtis, for whom this occasion must be a great source of satisfaction, and whom we honour as a founder of Chatham House, the home of the pioneer Institute.

It is hard to exaggerate the part played by the Royal Institute of International Affairs and its sister institutions in the countries of the Commonwealth in developing an understanding of international affairs. When the Canadian Institute of International Affairs was formed in 1928 the shelves of our libraries showed precisely one book on Canada's foreign policy. In Parliament the subject was hardly mentioned.

The Institute interested men of different occupations, many of whom took an active part in public life and (very important) it included leading publishers and journalists. The position already gained by the Institute was shown in the Canadians who took part in the 1933 conference—they included Sir Robert Borden, Sir Robert Falconer, Newton Rowell, John W. Dafoe, Sir Joseph Flavelle, Senator Louis Cote, J. S. Woodsworth and Sanford Evans, to mention with respect and regret only those who have ceased to be among us.

Certainly the conduct of public business as far as I have been concerned has been helped by friendships made in 1933 with such men as Walter Nash, Philip Noel-Baker, Sir Ramaswami Mudaliar, Sir Mohammed Zafrulla Khan and Alfred Stirling.

We will all have read the observation made by the Prime Minister of the United Kingdom at the Guildhall banquet last July that: "If there were a Chatham House in Warsaw, in Prague, Bucharest and Sofia, how much more hopeful the world outlook would be." With this assertion all will agree. The value of these unofficial conferences is immeasurable. The frank and dispassionate examination and discussion of affairs by delegates representative of various sections of opinion play a vital role in any free society. During this last year Ireland, by the decision of her government and Parliament, has decided not to remain a member of the Commonwealth but to maintain a specially close relationship with members of the Commonwealth; and we welcome here the Irish representatives who have come here on the basis of that special relationship and I may add of friendship.

Since the last conference too the march of events has brought independence to our sister nations of the Commonwealth, India, Pakistan and Ceylon. I am sure I speak for everyone here when I say that we watched the birth of these new nations out of their ancient civilization with anxious concern and that we have observed the progress already made with sympathetic understanding and admiration.

The association we call the Commonwealth is as we know an elaborate texture of relationships, constitutional arrangements and economic activity. The Commonwealth has its severely practical and realistic aspects, but its unique character derives from the fact that it is also an association heavily charged with emotions and sentiments. It is for this reason, more than any other perhaps, that from time to time each of us should examine it with clear and realistic mind.

There are those who have found that the binding tie of empire is the common crown, which for many is more than a symbol—it is the very personification of an essential kinship and unity.

There are those whose red blood was stirred at the sight of the red on the map as at the sound of the trumpet or the glory of a flag.

There are others who have found the secret of the Commonwealth in its long common history and in the great inheritance of common culture, traditions and ideals.

In Canada because of our racial complexion the Commonwealth aspect of our national life is both an inherited and an acquired characteristic.

But the Commonwealth today can still be best explained in the often overlooked part of the Balfour Declaration of 1926, where it was said:

Free institutions are its lifeblood. Free co-operation is its instrument.

Is this not true?

The members of the Commonwealth have a feeling of community because, irrespective of their origins, they seek their security and their happiness in the framework of the reign of law and with the assistance of parliamentary institutions. Those institutions are justly called "British Parliamentary institutions" and they have been a great working instrument of government that is honest, efficient, just and free.

The evolving Commonwealth has been more vital and much more useful than the attempts to describe it in static terms.

One could give a number of examples of efforts to confine the Commonwealth in a straight-jacket of words.

At the 1933 conference it was asserted and apparently generally accepted that no nation of the Commonwealth could be neutral without severing its connection with the Commonwealth. Now it may be recalled that almost ten years ago today Canada entered the war as the act of her own government with the approval of her Parliament and she did it seven days later than Britain. During those seven days the neutrality of Canada was recognized by the United States, and very useful it was too, as anyone would agree who saw our four or five thousand miles of undefended frontier crossed daily by munitions which could still be sent to us but not to Britain.

The Irish went even further in proving the point by staying in the Commonwealth as a neutral as long as the war lasted.

Another example of the dangers of prophesy was shown in 1927 when the late Lord Bennett, then Conservative leader of the opposition, opposed the appointment of a Canadian minister to Washington. His words were:

This country apparently is entering on a great adventure, the last great adventure in our relation to the British Empire. I am wholly opposed to the establishment of this embassy at Washington. It is but the doctrine of separation; it is but the evidence in many minds of the end of our connection with the empire. For that is what it means. It means nothing else ultimately because if we are a sovereign state we cannot belong to the British Empire.[1]

Shortly after Mr. Bennett came into office in 1930 it was his own brother-in-law, Mr. Herridge, whom he appointed minister to Washington. Mr. Herridge occupied his important office with praiseworthy distinction and there was no adverse change in Canada's relations with the Commonwealth.

When we are dealing with an association which is warmed by friendship and stirred by vitality, we do well to be cautious in accepting prophesies of doom or legalistic definitions. The Commonwealth is not a constitutional monstrosity; it is simply unique in

[1] (*House of Commons Debates*, April 13, 1927, p. 2472).

that its ties are founded on freedom and thus enable it to make its great contribution to the security and happiness of mankind.

As you begin your discussions today, you do so against the framework of a world which has become extremely complicated from many points of view, but in which certain simplifications have become increasingly clear.

In the first place, at the 1933 Conference we were concerned with finding a way of harmonizing a Commonwealth system of diversity with a collective system of security. Today, no one can be concerned about the diversity and questions of status are no longer relevant.

In the second place, there is of course complete acceptance of the importance of the United States in the world today. Any consideration of the defence of the Commonwealth or any part of it without taking into account the position and power of the United States would be quite unrealistic. The meetings now proceeding at Washington emphasize the paramount importance of measures to bring the areas of the pound and the dollar into the same trading community. On collective action with the United States depend both security and prosperity.

A third point worth remarking is that within each country of the Commonwealth there appears to be greater unity with regard to external relations than ever before. All are agreed, for example, that support of the United Nations is a cardinal point in foreign policy. We are already committed to co-operation in a wider field. Almost all are agreed on the necessity for taking measures of individual and collective defence against Communist aggression.

Communist Russia's revelation of the unlimited nature of her ambitions has arrayed the forces of freedom as the League of Nations never succeeded in doing. Peace will be secure as long as the Russians know that they cannot win a war of aggression against the forces of freedom. Peace will continue to depend on strength (though of course not on strength alone) until there are other developments not presently visible on the distant horizon.

This attitude is necessary because we regard liberty as fundamental to our happiness and to our progress. Indeed the maintenance of peace by strength must be regarded as a means to that end. We must never regard the Iron Curtain as inevitable or necessarily permanent. If we are true to our belief in our democratic institutions, then it follows that, given time, democratic principles will prevail. Democratic principles will prevail because they are better and more efficient than is any dictatorship; and we must make and keep them better and more efficient.

The corollary to personal liberty is personal responsibility. The basis of good relations is the steady and persistent cultivation of friendships based on understanding. In the last resort, peace and freedom, progress and prosperity are the affairs of individuals and they must be worked for and the battle won all over again ... every day. In that the members of the Commonwealth will play their part, and it is no small one. The free exchange of views at this conference will strengthen the foundations of understanding. Only the free can be friends.

In welcoming you to this conference I do so in the confidence that your contribution to the cause we all have at heart of ensuring the peace and enlarging the prosperity of all our different peoples will be assisted by your deliberations.

Opening Address by R. M. Fowler, Conference Chairman

It is now my privilege and pleasure, on behalf of the Canadian Institute of International Affairs, to welcome all the delegates to this Conference.

In one of the Canadian data papers—I think that written by Dr. Brady—the suggestion is made that Canadians are not as ready as their friends in other Commonwealth countries to talk about their enthusiasm and faith in this unique association. Perhaps it is true that we are not prone to put into words our interest in Commonwealth affairs; but I believe Canadians have by their actions on many occasions shown their concern in, and have played a part in solving, Commonwealth problems. Possibly the enthusiasm with which the Canadian Institute welcomed the opportunity to act as hosts for this Conference may be regarded as a minor evidence of Canada's active interest in Commonwealth relations.

We are indeed very happy that we can again act as hosts of a Commonwealth Conference. The Canadian Institute, only a few years after it was founded, had the honour of inviting the first of these conferences to Toronto in 1933. We participated with interest and benefit at the meetings at Lapstone, Australia, in 1938 and at London in 1945. Each succeeding conference has noted major changes and the development of new problems since the preceding meeting, but I doubt if there has previously been such an accumulation of perplexities and difficulties as the last four years have brought. It is peculiarly appropriate that representatives from this group of like-minded peace-loving nations should meet again for informal discussions of their relations with each other and with the world at large.

Our welcome extends with sincerity and impartiality to all delegates and their associates—and also, where we are so fortunate as to have them with us, to the wives of members of delegations. I know that the delegates from the United Kingdom, Australia, New Zealand and South Africa will understand if I place special emphasis on our welcome to our friends from India, Pakistan and Ceylon, whose countries have, since the conference in 1945, attained full independence and full membership in the Commonwealth. Those developments have given new proof of the virility and adaptability of the Commonwealth concept and hold out the hope of joining the East and West in mutual understanding and recognition of common democratic objectives. It is with all this in mind that I take special pleasure in welcoming the delegation from the Republic of Ireland as a full member of this Conference. You will recall that last November on the passing of the Republic of Ireland Bill in the Dail, Mr. Costello made it clear that "Ireland does not intend to regard the citizens of Commonwealth countries as foreigners or their countries as foreign countries." There was, he said, a specially close relationship between Ireland and the nations of the Commonwealth. We all recognize that closeness based as it is on history, geography and a common outlook on international questions. It would be impossible for us to regard the citizens of Ireland as foreign or alien to the purposes that have brought us together and we heartily welcome the Irish delegates to this Conference as friends.

It would be impossible for us to meet here in these unofficial discussions without having constantly in our minds those official meetings that are taking place at this moment in Washington. We must all be conscious of the momentous nature of these economic discussions between the United Kingdom, the United States and Canada. Since the end of hostilities in 1945 we have unhappily been forced to recognize that the hopes of creating a workable One-World system could not be realized—at least for the moment. We have seen the emergence of two competing, unfriendly blocs of nations in the world. At best, there is only an uneasy equilibrium in this Two-World system. But in recent years, and with mounting acceleration in the last few months, a further subdivision of the world has appeared as a possibility. In economic matters, there is today increasing difficulty in trade betwen the so-called sterling area and the dollar area. I do not myself believe that economics are everything—that trading difficulties must inevitably lead to political and human misunderstandings. But it is beyond doubt that economic and trading relations, if they are sound and healthy, contribute to friendly political relations between nations; and the reverse of that proposition is equally true. Therefore, it may not be too extreme a statement to say that the discussions now taking place in Washington will largely determine whether we are to have a Two-World or a Three-World system among nations.

In the face of such momentous events taking place elsewhere, it might be easy for us to feel that our discussions at this Conference were somewhat unrealistic, and even trivial. I think this would be a great mistake. No one can reasonably expect that the Washington meetings will produce a quick answer to the difficulties of world trade. President Truman has already warned against the hope of any "trick solutions." The best we can hope for, and probably the most desirable thing in the long run, is that a start should be made at Washington on fundamental long-range solutions of trade problems. There will be needed great effort, much understanding, and considerable imagination by the peoples of all nations —and much determination and patience, too—if the suggested solutions are to be effective and permanent. I hope that the work of this Conference may contribute to that result, both in increasing the understanding of all delegates of the problems of our several nations and possibly also in promoting co-operative action between our governments in seeking and speeding the solutions of international problems.

It is no matter of national pride—and certainly should be no cause of envy to other nations—that Canada has as great a stake as any country in the world in the establishment of an effective and efficient international order. Both politically and economically we are dependent on the maintenance of peace and multilateral trade as perhaps no other nation is dependent. At least, for us no alternative seems possible or feasible if we are to continue our growth as a nation and an effective member of the world community. Geography has given us a strategic importance that is unique for a country of twelve or thirteen million people. Our geographic position involves us in the relations between the United States and Russia, in the relations between the United States and Western Europe, and in the relations between the nations bordering on the Pacific. Our history ties us to the United Kingdom and France and the culture of Western Europe; yet we are a North American nation inextricably bound by deep friendship and economic inter-

dependence with the United States. Our economy and our
standards of living are dependent on multilateral trade; fortunately,
we have many resources and many strategic materials that the
world needs, but our whole well-being is bound up with the ability
of other nations to continue to satisfy these needs from Canadian
sources. For these reasons, the Canadian delegation comes to this
Conference with a desire to contribute all it can and with high
hopes for its success.

I do not intend in these opening remarks to discuss the agenda
of the Conference, or Canada's views on the various headings in
the agenda. These views can be better given at the round table
meetings over the next ten days and by others in our group who are
more competent to speak on particular subjects than I am. I will
only remind you of the basic terms of reference of this Conference
which are defined as follows: "To survey the position of the
Member Nations (here represented) in the post-war world, including the relations between them, and to examine what changes may
be required in their policies in the interests of world order and
progress." With these comprehensive terms of reference and with
the detailed subjects listed in the agenda, I fancy we will be hard
put to complete our discussions in the time we have available. I
imagine also we will come upon many items on which we will agree,
and also on many subjects on which we will find ourselves in considerable disagreement and heated opposition—and these differences
of opinion are likely to cut across the membership of different
delegations. I venture to think that is all to the good, as I am
a great believer in the power of what I may call expository and
illuminative controversy.

I have sought for some basic principle that might serve to guide
us at the outset of our discussions, and I found it—as one might
have expected—in the words of a great Scottish divine. When
questioned on the difficulties of handling great masses of men
divided by doubts or by honest differences of opinion, he made
this reply:

There are, concerning any great body or organization which is in
general agreement on substantials, two things required of anyone
who would serve it. One is to keep the mass together, avoiding,
so far as may be, its disintegration or falling asunder; but yet to
do this in such a way as always to help the mass forward, making
its centre of gravity advance.

I venture to think that that might well be the guiding principle of the group of like-minded nations here represented, and of all of us in our forthcoming discussions.

Replies by Delegation Heads to Address of Welcome

MR. E. C. DYASON replied on behalf of the Australian delegation. He felt he must not take advantage of the alphabetical priority of Australia to make an undue draft on the encomiums which those who followed would wish to bestow on the host Institute. The Australian delegates greatly appreciated the warmth of the welcome. He thanked the Canadian Institute for the hospitality they had already enjoyed and expressed a lively sense of gratitude for the favours to come.

Australians, Mr. Dyason said, felt happy and comfortable in Canada. In spite of the difference in "mutilation of the Oxford vowels," Canadians and Australians basically felt about each other and about the United Kingdom in the same way. They shared those wider loyalties to which the world aspired but could not as yet realize. There were differences as to forms and procedures in their relations but those were relatively unimportant. Australians shared with Canadians the sense of the imperative need of good relations with the United States. They believed it equally important, if not more imperative, to continue the struggle for the realization of some suitable form of world organization to express the common aspirations of man.

But geography affected their respective visions. The seven and a half million Australians who lived on the last Island of the Asian Archipelago were deeply involved in the destiny of the more than one thousand millions who lived—in great part in want, fear and ferment—between Suez and Yokohama.

Although Australians believed in one world, they did not accept the current over-simplification of it into two competing halves locked in fatal struggle. Australians believed it should be widely recognized that, if we were compelled to accept groupings, there were at present four worlds—the Western Hemisphere, Western Europe, the totalitarian world and Asia. Australians did not believe that until the ancient cultures were united in one world significantly different from any of its present segmental cultures, Europe would lose its soul or Asia its authority in things that mattered more than we Westerners—in our absorption with material trappings—realized.

If it was true that the Schizophrenia in our national policies nowadays had its roots in the unnatural schism between the way modern science interpreted the world and the way in which we had learned, largely through Asia, to feel it right to be interpreted, we could see why there is no longer a compelling legitimacy in us. We could also understand why blatant and spurious absolutes continued to compete for the domination of mankind. The healing of that schism was something to which both East and West must contribute, not by the easy assumption of a veneer of each other's cultures, but by a new creative synthesis that would be of a different form from either.

This was something, however, that would require the patience of generations, and meanwhile the Commonwealth, not being one of those spurious absolutes but a relative and flexible congeries with the roots of its several parts deep in three of the four worlds already specified, had, because of that fact, an historic role to play in realizing the one world to which we all aspired. But Australians were naturally also deeply concerned with the more im- mediate strains, stresses and calamities which afflicted and threatened the world now. This was so, though themselves beset by fewer immediate risks and strains. The threat to world order by intense ideological differences, the grave uncertainties in Asia and the imminent threat of a breakdown in the economic (or preferably "financial") field in the sterling area, prevented Australians from feeling at all comfortable about the future.

But these were at the root of the questions that would be discussed in the Round Table. The Australian delegation would make its contributions to them against the background he had tried to draw, in a spirit of mutual enquiry and with respect for the views and rights of the other national groups represented at the Conference.

MR. L. M. D. DE SILVA, Chairman of the delegation from Ceylon, thanked Mr. Fowler for the particular warmth of the welcome he had extended to the new Asian Dominions. He stated that as representatives of a young Dominion and the tiniest member of the Commonwealth, the Cingalese delegation were thrilled· to be present at this Commonwealth "party."

SIR T. VIJAYARAGHAVACHARIYA, Chairman of the Indian delegation, stated that he was not a stranger to Canada. In fact his acquaint- ance with this country had begun 23 years ago when he was asked to inaugurate the Canadian National Exhibition in Toronto.

He felt that this conference was a proof of the unity of the three new Dominions with the rest of the Commonwealth. He welcomed the formula worked out in London last April, which secured the unanimous approval of the participating countries. As a result, although India would cease to be a monarchy in form, she would remain within the Commonwealth. This proved the flexibility of the Commonwealth. We should therefore not seek to give a precise definition or bind the Commonwealth to rigid formulas. He emphasized the historical importance of Britain willingly giving up sovereignty over India and stated that while Britain had thus abdicated an Empire, she had built one in the hearts of the Indian peoples.

SENATOR MICHAEL HAYES, Chairman of the Irish Delegation, stated he had proposed to explain the presence of an Irish Delegation at this Conference; this seemed, however, unnecessary after the kind reference of the Minister of National Defence and the warm welcome of the Chairman. Citizens of the Republic of Ireland were not aliens in Britain or in the Commonwealth, neither were British or Commonwealth citizens regarded as aliens in Ireland.

In fact, Ireland had been invited by virtue of its "unique relationship with the Commonwealth." That relationship extended to population, politics, economics and also to the realm of ideas. Like England, Ireland was a Mother Country, which gave it special ties with several Commonwealth countries. In Canada for instance, an Irishman, D'Arcy McGee, had played an important part in Canadian history. The political institutions of Ireland, particularly its parliamentary and cabinet system and its civil service, were on the British model. Britain was Ireland's best customer, absorbing 90 per cent of her exports. On the other hand, Ireland was, in proportion to population, Britain's own best customer. Quite apart from natural sympathy towards Britain's economic problems, Ireland was vitally interested in the future of the pound, having four hundred million pounds of sterling assets in England. Finally, like the Commonwealth, Ireland believed in personal liberty and responsibility, and like the Commonwealth it was opposed to atheistic Communism.

The Irish delegate then thanked Canada, not only for its generosity, but for the way in which this generosity had been shown. He wished to congratulate Mr. Tarr, Mr. Fowler, Mr. MacLennan and his assistants for the efficient organization of the conference and to thank Chatham House and Mr. Macadam for facilitating the Irish delegation's participation in the Conference.

He believed that the free and frank discussion which would

follow need not be unfriendly and would, he hoped, influence Ministers concerned with the making of grave decisions.

DR. GWENDOLEN CARTER presented with special appreciation the thanks of New Zealand for the welcome and hospitality extended by the Canadian Institute. New Zealand was a small country with fewer people than any other part of the Commonwealth. It was geographically more isolated. But the very smallness of its population had meant that New Zealanders could never be narrowly self-centred in their thinking. They had always looked out, particularly to the United Kingdom and Ireland, from which the vast majority of New Zealanders had come, but also to the United States and to the other overseas members of the Commonwealth. A meeting such as the present one was welcomed because it overcame the bars of geographical isolation, the more so because the circle of Commonwealth members had grown to include India, Pakistan and Ceylon.

New Zealand, because of its people, was rooted deep in the British tradition. Some contributions of their own had been added to the common stock, however, in the adjustment to a new environment. New Zealand had been a pioneer in social legislation, experimenting empirically and not unfruitfully, it felt, in providing a basic security for all its people. New Zealand too had had a great challenge and opportunity to find ways of working with the native peoples of the Pacific through its own Maori people who shared so fully in the life of the New Zealand community.

Partly because of this, partly because of the war, New Zealand was more conscious of its place in the Pacific than at any earlier period in its history. Yet regionalism would never command New Zealand's full allegiance. New Zealand looked on the region as only a part of the much wider international scene and on regionalism as only a partial answer to its needs. And because the Commonwealth held together countries from all over the world and of diverse backgrounds in the bond of common purpose, New Zealand believed that the Commonwealth contributed richly to the international purposes which it cherished and welcomed the more warmly the opportunities afforded by the Conference.

PROFESSOR A. S. BOKHARI, Chairman of the Pakistan Delegation, thanked Canada for its welcome. Pakistan was a new State and a new name in world geography, but although his country's birth was a very recent event and they had yet no great achievements to report, he was glad to say that the newly-born child was doing very well and Pakistan's contributions to the deliberations at the UNO and other international bodies would show that it was far from being apathetic to world problems. Embarrassed though it was at finding itself in the company of members who had been wearing long trousers for a long time, his delegation had nevertheless come here with the same enthusiasm and earnestness with which his country was trying to solve the problems of a new state. He hoped that they would learn much from this Conference and that their participation in it would be mutually beneficial. With the rapid shifts in the geo-political centres of the world, and after the inclusion in the Commonwealth of three New Dominions who were racially, culturally and traditionally different from the other members, the Commonwealth had acquired a new complexion. This required a new approach to Commonwealth problems and a new understanding of each other's viewpoint. A character in one of Shakespeare's plays had said: "Some are born great, some achieve greatness and some have greatness thrust upon them." Applying this to the Commonwealth, but in this family of nations it could not be said of any countries that Commonwealth shall be thrust upon them. If we recognized the great changes that had come upon the world and upon the Commonwealth itself since the Conference had last met and if by mutual understanding we adjusted our relations accordingly and succeeded in finding a new and even closer cohesion, the Commonwealth could make a great contribution to stability and order in the world. From that point of view it might well be that the Commonwealth today was at the threshold of a bold and indeed a brave adventure. He wished the Conference every success.

Dr. E. G. Malherbe replied on behalf of the South African delegation. He observed that this was his third visit to Canada. He warmly thanked the Canadian Institute for its welcome and hospitality. He spoke, he said, as a South African of French Huguenot descent on the Afrikaans-speaking side. His home in the Orange Free State had been burned down by British soldiers in the Boer War but that phase had been largely got over. It might be, however, that South Africa still suffered from too much history. Every time he had been in Canada he felt inspired by the way Canada seemed to be achieving solidarity and a true Canadian spirit amongst the diverse cultural elements in her midst. For example, he had been struck by the fact that on the same monument in Quebec one saw side by side the names of Wolfe and Montcalm, erstwhile enemies.

He hoped that this might one day be something one could see in South Africa too.

As a result of recent political events South Africa was very much in the limelight just now. With its very complex racial, political and economic set-up the problems of his country constituted in a sense a microcosm of what the world itself was suffering from and if a solution could be arrived at there it might serve as a pattern to be applied on the larger scale. He had a telegram from the South African Institute that extended an invitation to hold the next Conference in South Africa. It might be, Dr. Malherbe thought, that a greater sense of reality and understanding could be achieved by studying these complex problems close at hand.

In dealing with Commonwealth relationships he recounted a story of the King's visit to South Africa. In the rural Transvaal the King was met by a large commando on horseback most of whom were nationalist representatives. After chatting informally with them the King said: "How friendly you are! But you are, I hear, the people who want a republic." And the reply was: "Yes. But after meeting you, we wonder if you would like to be president."

While South Africa might be at present in an ideological ferment, its roots were sound. They reached deep down into Dutch and British democratic institutions.

Improvement in group relationships (whether it be of nations or races) could come about only if there was due recognition of two fundamental principles: (a) the practice of co-operation and (b) recognition of individuality. These two principles were correlative. Co-operation between persons or groups became difficult if there was not proper recognition of the individuality of each. South African history provided many illustrations of this point.

People learned to co-operate by actually co-operating. Let us therefore begin by concentrating on those goals in the achievement of which our differences (e.g. in race attitudes) were not relevant. A frontal attack on, say, differences in race attitudes often failed. One must outflank them. One could do that by tackling together objective problems as, e.g., greater production, better health and housing in which difference in racial attitudes are not germane. This might be a line to take also in this Conference.

The South African Institute had tried hard to get a representative of the Nationalist press to come here as a member of the South African delegation but unfortunately circumstances had prevented him from coming at the last moment. Nevertheless the delegation would do its best to live up to the high standard of objectivity set by the late Professor Hoernle and his colleagues representing all parties at previous conferences.

THE RT. HON. R. A. BUTLER replied to the address of welcome on behalf of the United Kingdom delegation. Mr. Butler, in voicing the thanks of the delegation for the hospitality and cordial reception afforded by the Canadian Institute, took the opportunity to praise the generosity of Canada towards the United Kingdom. He asked Mr. Claxton to convey his words to the government of Canada and to the Canadian people.

Mr. Butler made special mention of Sir Robert Borden, Mr. Newton Rowell and Mr. John Dafoe, Canadian delegates to earlier Conferences all now deceased. Mr. Fowler, the Chairman, was at the first Conference of 1933. He wished to join in Mr. Claxton's tribute to Mr. Lionel Curtis, the Nestor of the U.K. group. The presence of the daughter of Asquith and the son of Lloyd George should induce the head of the United Kingdom delegation to proceed with circumspection.

The timing of this fourth Conference was important. Mr. Butler drew attention to the general urge for the organization of international bodies that was abroad. Widely dispersed over the globe, the Commonwealth had interests in each one of these organizations. At the same time the Commonwealth itself was specially interested in its own growth.

He was especially glad to see present delegates from India, Pakistan and Ceylon. He could claim, he thought—though the point had apparently not been noticed and investigated by the Conference authorities—that he was himself a Pakistani by birth. He had travelled widely in India, as the sub-continent then was, and had many personal and family ties there.

Mr. Butler resumed his remarks on the Commonwealth by saying that to each of its member nations the playing of its own hand was an absorbing interest. Even more absorbing was the study of the influence which working closely together would exercise on world order and progress. Each Commonwealth country had its aims and purposes but that was not enough: it must work to a common and wider aim. Actions likely to make the wider aim unrealisable were just as undesirable as those designed to form a too restrictive or specific relationship. Mr. St. Laurent had said, "We should oppose developments in our Commonwealth relations which might be inconsistent with our desire to participate fully in the task of building an effective international organization on a larger scale."

Mr. St. Laurent had previously warned of the danger of "specific commitments." This was a great subject for debate and not one to be entered into on the present occasion. Certainly however we must beware of "restrictive practices," of monopoly and of isolationism, these were dangerously out of fashion. To refer back to the words of Mr. St. Laurent, we should avoid "developments in our Commonwealth relations which might be inconsistent with a wider objective." Such developments might, if they resulted in diffusion of effort and confusion of aim, be fatal to world peace. Clearly therefore we must follow a path of co-operation which retained the advantages of close association and which led towards a wide and generous objective.

In some ways the countries represented at the Conference were as close as they had ever been before. Mr. Butler cited the example of Eire, to whose representatives he wished to extend a special welcome. He hoped later to be able to counter the assertion of Senator Hayes that Eire was a mother country, by reference among other things to the Scottish people. The Soviet Union had obligingly brought the Western democracies and more particularly those of the United States and the Commonwealth, into a relationship, similar to that achieved in the Second World War. Nevertheless, while we were close together, other regional or individual groupings were proceeding. We must see to it that the policies or the growth of one sector did not so prejudice those of another area that the great and wide objective was made more distant. "There must be news from Bigwin and big winning news, as well as accounts of proposed economic and political ties from Strasbourg."

We should welcome, Mr. Butler said, the efforts of European countries to link their destinies after 300 years of effort. Indeed the removal of divisions in Europe might lead towards that peace which the Commonwealth so much desires. But we did not desire commitments in Europe to prejudice closer relations within the Commonwealth. Perhaps Europe might learn from the Commonwealth the art of close association which springs, not from cessions of sovereignty or of independence, but from a common spirit and shared sacrifice.

Co-operation in Europe and the Commonwealth must proceed together. But to be effective the time at this Conference must be used to know, understand and to state Commonwealth interests, whether political, economic or strategic. The Conference should therefore not stray over every problem that the pasture of the world provides but be concerned to enquire thoroughly into these Commonwealth interests.

Delegates were chosen representatives of their Institutes. In their representative capacity they had special responsibility. Let their work therefore be both effective and endure. Moreover, unofficial contacts had great value, especially those between the Institutes. Perhaps some continuing association between the Institutes could be arranged during the Conference.

Mr. Butler concluded by expressing his belief in the robust future of the Commonwealth. Its members had new tasks and new destinies. Indeed it might well be the role of the modern Commonwealth to lead towards a wider fusion of which the United States would form one element. In this way, perhaps, the splitting of an already divided world into three parts might, as was vital, be avoided.

Jeremy Bentham, although a Utilitarian, observed in what some say was an idealist mood, "Law and morals have the same centre but not the same circumference." The wisdom of these words should not be lost on the Conference. Let them not seek to enforce the application of set rules and regulations on the more distant circumference of the circle of free peoples. "But let us know no bounds to the extension of these moral and spiritual principles which have made our past history and which assure our future glory."

Appendix B

CONFERENCE AGENDA

THURSDAY, SEPTEMBER 8

10:00 a.m. - 12:15 p.m.　Formal Opening: Speech by Hon. Brooke Claxton; Opening Address by R. M. Fowler; Replies by Delegation heads to address of welcome.

Part I: The Position of the Member Nations in the Post-War World

4:15 p.m. - 6:30 p.m.　First Round Table Session: One member of each Delegation reviewed in general terms the position of his country. The Conference Recorder presented an extensive analysis of the preparatory papers which had been submitted by each Institute.

FRIDAY, SEPTEMBER 9

10:00 a.m. - 12:15 p.m.　Second Round Table Session: A continuation of the general reviews by Delegation members.

Part II: Current and Prospective International Problems and the Policies of the Member Nations Towards Them

4:15 p.m. - 6:30 p.m.　Third Round Table Session: The working of the United Nations with reference to: the organization of a world security system, including the control of atomic energy; and economic and social functions (Part II, a).

Chairman: Professor A. S. Bokhari
Recorder: Professor A. Brady

SATURDAY, SEPTEMBER 10

10:00 a.m. - 12:15 p.m.   Fourth Round Table Session: The working of the United Nations, cont'd. (Part II, a).
Political and strategic aspects of current international problems: the consequences of the division into two worlds; relations of the Member Nations with the U.S.A. and the U.S.S.R.; peace settlements with Germany and Japan (Part II, b).
Chairman: Mr. H. V. Hodson
Recorder: Mr. John F. Northey

4:15 p.m. - 6:30 p.m.   Fifth Round Table Session: Economic problems: post-war reconstruction and international trade and monetary problems; I.T.O.; International Fund and Bank (Part II, c).
Chairman: Mr. R. M. Fowler
Recorder: Professor E. A. G. Robinson

MONDAY, SEPTEMBER 12

10:00 a.m. - 12:15 p.m.   Sixth Round Table Session: Economic problems, cont'd. (part II, c).
Chairman: Captain R. G. Cavell
Recorder: Professor E. A. G. Robinson

4:15 p.m. - 6:30 p.m.   Seventh Round Table Session: Economic problems, cont'd. (Part II, c).
Chairman: Captain R. G. Cavell
Recorder: Professor E. A. G. Robinson

TUESDAY, SEPTEMBER 13

10:00 a.m. - 12:15 p.m.   Eighth Round Table Session: Regional security arrangements and other proposals for regional co-operation or integration: their political,

economic, and cultural implications. (i) Western Europe and the Atlantic Pact (Part II, d, i).
Chairman: Mr. L. M. D. de Silva
Recorder: Professor N. S. Mansergh

4:15 p.m. - 6:30 p.m.   Ninth Round Table Session: Regional security arrangements. (i) Western Europe and the Atlantic Pact, cont'd. (Part II, d, i).
Chairman: Mr. L. M. D. de Silva
Recorder: Professor N. S. Mansergh

WEDNESDAY, SEPTEMBER 14
10:00 a.m. - 12:15 p.m.   Tenth Round Table Session: Regional Security arrangements (ii) The Middle East, the Indian Ocean, the Pacific Ocean, the Far East. (Part II, d, ii).
Chairman: Senator Michael Hayes
Recorder: Professor N. S. Mansergh

4:15 p.m. - 6:30 p.m.   Eleventh Round Table Session: Regional security arrangements. Continuation of the above until 5:00 p.m.

Colonial policies and racial discrimination. (Part II, e).
Chairman: Professor R. G. Trotter
Recorder: Miss Lucy Sutherland

Part III: The Post-War Evolution of the Commonwealth and Its Implications

THURSDAY, SEPTEMBER 15
10:00 a.m. - 12:15 p.m.   Twelfth Round Table Session: The new Commonwealth — post-war changes and new members (Part III, a).
Chairman: Dr. E. G. Malherbe
Recorder: Mr. S. W. Jamieson

4:15 p.m. - 6:30 p.m.　　Thirteenth Round Table Session: What is the meaning of the Commonwealth? What are the springs of its future evolution? (Part III, b).
Chairman: Dr. E. G. Malherbe
Recorder: Mr. S. W. Jamieson

FRIDAY, SEPTEMBER 16
10:00 a.m. - 12:15 p.m.　　Fourteenth Round Table Session: How far can we or should we act together for economic purposes? (Part III, d).
Chairman: Rt. Hon. R. A. Butler
Recorder: Mr. S. W. Jamieson

4:15 p.m. - 6:30 p.m.　　Fifteenth Round Table Session: Can methods of consultation be improved? Commonwealth public relations —internal and external. (Part III, e, f).
Chairman: Rt. Hon. R. A. Butler
Recorder: Mr. Denis W. Healey

SATURDAY, SEPTEMBER 17
10:00 a.m. - 12:15 p.m.　　Final Business Session

8:30 p.m.　　Final Plenary Session: Presentation by Conference Recorder of his final report.

Appendix C

LIST OF DELEGATION PAPERS AND REFERENCE PAPERS

The following papers are available at Chatham House and at the headquarters of the Canadian Institute of International Affairs and of other Commonwealth Institutes:

Delegation Papers

AUSTRALIA
Special Problems of the Member Nations.
  I. Economic Problems. By R. I. Downing, P. H. Karmel, G. R. Mountain, John Marshall.
  II. Political Developments since 1939. By P. H. Partridge.
  III. Strategic Problems. By the Victoria and New South Wales Branches of the Australian Institute.
  IV. The Future of the British Commonwealth. By Sir Frederic Eggleston.

CANADA
  1. Canada's Economy in a Changing World. Edited by J. D. Gibson. 1948. (Toronto: C.I.I.A., 380pp., $4.50.)
  2. Canada and the Commonwealth. By Alexander Brady.
  3. Strategy and Policy in the Defence of Canada. By Eric Harrison.
  4. Canada and the North Atlantic Treaty. By a Winnipeg Study Group.
     Nos. 2, 3, 4, are reprints from *International Journal*, Summer, 1949.)
  5. Changing Pattern of External Trade. By J. D. Gibson (*Monthly Review*, August, 1949, The Bank of Nova Scotia, Toronto.)

INDIA
  1. Aspects of India's Foreign Relations.
     (i) Reciprocity in Citizenship Rights. By Sir B. N. Rau.

     (ii) Indo-American Political Relations. By Prof. M. Venkatarangaiya.

    (iii) India and the U.S.S.R. By Prof. M. Mujeeb.

    (iv) India and the Commonwealth. By Sirdar Gurmukh Nihal Singh.

2. India's Economy.

     (i) A Plan for Agriculture. By H. C. Sharma.

    (ii) Trade Relations. By M. V. Bhatawdekar. (Subsequently published in *India Quarterly,* Vol. VI, No. 2.)

    (iii) Industrialization of India and Commonwealth Co-operation. By Dr. Gyan Chand. (Subsequently published in *India Quarterly,* Vol. V, No. 4.)

    (iv) India and the Sterling Bloc. By C. G. Ramasubbu. (Subsequently published in *India Quarterly,* Vol. V, No. 3.)

3. Racial Discrimination. By K. P. Karunakaran. (To be published as part of *India In World Affairs* by The Indian Council of World Affairs, Karachi.)

PAKISTAN

1. Pakistan and the Commonwealth. By K. Sarwar Hasan.
2. The Economy of Pakistan. By Mushtaq Ahmad and S. M. Huda.
3. Genesis of Pakistan. By K. Sarwar Hasan.

   (The three papers to be published 1950 by P.I.I.A., Karachi.)

SOUTH AFRICA

1. The Present Economic Position of the Union of South Africa. By the Johannesburg Chamber of Commerce.
   The Economic Situation in South Africa. By L. H. Samuels.
2. South African Diplomats Abroad. By E. Rosenthal. 1949 (S.A.I.I.A.), Johannesburg.
3. South Africa and the United Nations. By J. W. Patten.
4. New Shape of the Commonwealth. By E. M. O'Dowd.
   The Union's Political Position. By D. E. McCausland.
5. Position of South Africa in the Strategy of the Commonwealth and the World. By three South African Students of International Affairs.
6. South African Attitudes on Racial Discrimination: Opinions of White Soldiers in the South African Army, Regarding the "Native Question." By Ernst G. Malherbe.

UNITED KINGDOM
1. The Commonwealth and the Nations: Studies in British Commonwealth Relations. By Nicholas Mansergh. 1948. (London: R.I.I.A. Toronto: Oxford University Press. 228 pp. $2.50.)
2. British Foreign Policy Since the Second World War. By Sir Charles Webster.
3. The United Kingdom's Strategic Interests. By Major-General Sir Ian Jacob.
4. The United Kingdom's Economic Problems. By E. A. G. Robinson.
   (Nos. 2, 3, 4 were subsequently published together in a single pamphlet entitled United Kingdom Policy: Foreign, Strategic, Economic. Appreciations by Professor Sir Charles Webster, Major-General Sir Ian Jacob, and E. A. G. Robinson. 1950. (London: R.I.I.A. 101 pp. 4s.)

Reference Papers (Miscellaneous)

UNITED KINGDOM
Consultation and Co-operation in the British Commonwealth. By H. J. Harvey, assisted by E. M. Meade. Parts I and II. (To be published in 1950 by R.I.I.A.)

IRELAND
1. Irish Aid to Europe.
2. Anglo-Irish Relations. By Sean MacBride. (Reprint from *International Affairs,* July, 1949.)

NEW ZEALAND
1. Publications of The New Zealand Department of External Affairs:
   No. 26—South Pacific Commission: Report of the New Zealand Delegation on the Conference held at Canberra, 28 January-6 February, 1947, for the Purpose of Establishing an Advisory Commission for the South Pacific.
   No. 30—The Conference of Paris: Report of the New Zealand Delegation on the Conference held to consider the Treaties of Peace with Italy, Roumania, Bulgaria, Hungary, and Finland. Paris, 29 July-15 October, 1946.

No. 33—United Nations: Report of the New Zealand Delegation on the Second Part of the First Regular Session of the General Assembly held at New York, 23 October-15 December, 1946.

No. 38—Japanese Peace Settlement: Report on British Commonwealth Conference, Canberra, 26 August-2 September, 1947, and comments and proposals regarding New Zealand Policy towards certain Issues of the Japanese Peace Settlement.

No. 39—Western Samoa, 1947: Reports to the Trusteeship Council by the United Nations Mission to Western Samoa.

No. 58—United Nations Conference on Trade and Employment: Report of the New Zealand Delegation on the Conference held at Havana, Cuba, 21 November, 1947-24 March, 1948.

No. 60—United Nations: Report of the New Zealand Delegation on the Second Regular Session of the General Assembly held at New York, 16 September-29 November, 1947.

No. 61—The United Nations: Report of the New Zealand Delegation to the Special Session of the General Assembly on Palestine, New York, April-May, 1948.

No. 65—Department of External Affairs: Annual Report, 1 April, 1947-31 March, 1948.

2. The Bretton Woods Agreement: open letter to the members of the General Assembly by C. G. F. Simkin and H. R. Rodwell.

3. Davidson, J. W., "Political Development In Western Samoa", *Pacific Affairs*, Vol. XXI, No. 2, June, 1948.

4. Beaglehole, Ernest. "Social And Political Changes In The Cook Islands", *Pacific Affairs*, Vol. XXI, No. 4, December, 1948.

5. Wood, F. L. W. "Report From New Zealand", *Pacific Affairs*, Vol. XXII, No. 1, March, 1949.

6. Report of speech by Mr. Walter Nash, New Zealand Minister of Finance at the Jubilee Dinner of the Auckland Master Grocers' Association, 9th May, 1949, *New Zealand Herald*, May 10, 1949.

7. "New Zealand's Chinese 'Minority' ". A Preliminary Report by Philip Matthews.

Appendix D

OFFICERS OF THE CONFERENCE

Chairman	R. M. Fowler
Vice-Chairman	Sir T. Vijayaraghavachariya
Acting Secretary General	Ivison S. Macadam
Honorary Treasurer	Harold Fry
Conference Recorder	F. H. Soward
Conference Press Officer	Victor Sifton
Organizing Secretary	Douglas A. MacLennan

CONFERENCE ORGANIZING COMMITTEE

Conference Chairman	R. M. Fowler
Chairman of the Committee on Arrangements and Agenda	H. V. Hodson
Acting Secretary General	Ivison S. Macadam
Recorder	F. H. Soward
Honorary Treasurer	Harold Fry
Press Officer	Victor Sifton
Organizing Secretary	Douglas A. MacLennan
Assistant Organizing Secretary	Edna Neale

Representatives of Delegations:

Australia	George Caiger
Canada	E. J. Tarr
	R. G. Cavell
Ceylon	L. M. D. de Silva
India	Sir T. Vijayaraghavachariya
Ireland	Harold J. Douglas
New Zealand	Dr. Gwendolen M. Carter
Pakistan	K. Sarwar Hasan
South Africa	Dr. E. G. Malherbe
United Kingdom	H. V. Hodson
Secretary of the Committee	Duncan C. Campbell

CONFERENCE STEERING COMMITTEE

Chairman - - - - - - - - R. M. Fowler
Recorder - - - - - - - - F. H. Soward
Secretary General of the Conference - - Ivison S. Macadam
Representatives of Delegations:

Australia	E. C. Dyason
Canada	E. J. Tarr
Ceylon	L. M. D. de Silva
India	Dr. V. K. R. V. Rao
Ireland	Michael Hayes
New Zealand	Dr. Gwendolen M. Carter
Pakistan	A. S. Bokhari
South Africa	Dr. E. G. Malherbe
United Kingdom	Rt. Hon. R. A. Butler

Secretary of the Committee - - - - Duncan C. Campbell

Appendix E

WHO'S WHO OF THE CONFERENCE

OFFICERS

Chairman
FOWLER, ROBERT MACLAREN. President, Canadian Institute of International Affairs. President, Canadian Pulp and Paper Association and of Newsprint Association of Canada. Born December 7, 1906, at Peterborough, Canada. Graduate of University of Toronto and of Osgoode Hall. Practised law in Toronto, 1931-45. Member of the staff of the Rowell-Sirois Commission on Dominion-Provincial Relations, 1937-39. Secretary and General Counsel, Canadian Wartime Prices and Trade Board, 1942-45. Member of the Board of Governors, Canadian Welfare Council, and of the Executive Committee, Canadian Chamber of Commerce.
Publications: Among others, *The B.N.A. Act and Nationhood* (C.I.I.A., 1944).
Address: 2279 Sun Life Building, Montreal, P.Q.

Vice-Chairman
VIJAYARAGHAVACHARIYA, SIR T. *Chairman,* Indian Delegation. Member, Federal Public Service Commission, 1926-29. Vice-Chairman, Imperial Council of Agricultural Research from 1929-35. Prime Minister, Udaipur State 1939-47. Chairman, Madras Government Committee on Co-operation 1939. Commissioner for India, British Empire Exhibition, 1922-25. Opened Canadian National Exhibition, August, 1926. Delegate from India to the F.A.O. Conference in 1946. Leader of the Indian Delegation and Chairman of the International Forestry Conference organized by the F.A.O. in Mysore, 1949. Address: New Delhi and Simla.

Acting Secretary General
MACADAM, IVISON STEVENSON, C.B.E., M.V.O. Director-General, Royal Institute of International Affairs since 1946. Born 1894. Educated Milville College, Edinburgh; King's College, London; Christ's College, Cambridge. Fellow of

King's College, London. Assistant Director-General and Principal Assistant Secretary, Ministry of Information, 1939-41. Secretary, Royal Institute of International Affairs, 1929-46. A Founder and Trustee of the National Union of Students. Member of Council of King George's Jubilee Trust. Editor of *The Annual Register*. Secretary of the British Commonwealth Relations Conferences, 1933, 1938, and 1945.

Address: Chatham House, 10 St. James's Square, London, S.W.1, England.

Honorary Treasurer

FRY, HAROLD. Partner, Fry and Company, Investment Dealers. Member of National Council and National Executive Committee, and Honorary Treasurer, C.I.I.A.

Address: 25 King Street West, Toronto 1, Ontario.

Conference Recorder

SOWARD, FREDERIC HUBERT, B.Litt., F.R.S.C., Professor of History and Director of International Studies, University of British Columbia. Past President, Canadian Historical Association. Chairman, Vancouver Branch, and Member, National Research Committee, C.I.I.A. Special Assistant, Department of External Affairs, 1943-46, Summer 1949. Member of the Canadian delegation to the Second British Commonwealth Relations Conference, Sydney, 1938, and of Canadian delegations to Institute of Pacific Relations Conferences, 1933, 1936, 1942.

Publications: *Twenty-five Troubled Years, Moulders of National Destinies, Canada in World Affairs, 1944-46* (C.I.I.A., 1950). Principal author, *Canada in World Affairs, 1935-39*, (C.I.I.A., 1941), *Canada and the Pan American System* (C.I.I.A., 1948).

Address: 1820 Allison Road, Vancouver, B.C.

Conference Press Officer

SIFTON, VICTOR, C.B.E., D.S.O., President *Winnipeg Free Press, Regina Leader-Post, Saskatoon Star Phoenix,* and of the Canadian Press, 1948-49.

Address: *Winnipeg Free Press*, Winnipeg, Man.

Organizing Secretary

MACLENNAN, DOUGLAS ALEXANDER. National Secretary, Canadian Institute of International Affairs since 1942. Secretary of the Canadian delegation to the Ninth Conference of the Institute of Pacific Relations, Hot Springs, Virginia, 1945. Organizing Secretary of the Canadian Conference at Montebello on "Canada and the Building of the Peace", Quebec, 1943.

Address: 230 Bloor Street West, Toronto 5, Ont.

DELEGATIONS

AUSTRALIA

DYASON, E. C., B.M.E., B.Sc. *Chairman,* Australian delegation. Economist, formerly Company Director. Son of late I. E. Dyason, Bendigo, Victoria; born April 8, 1886 at Bendig. Educated St. Andrew's College, Bendigo, and Melbourne University. Practised as mining engineer, 1908-20. President, Chamber of Mines, Victoria, 1918-22. President, Gold Producers' Association of Australia, 1919-25. President, Victorian Branch, Economic Society of Australia and New Zealand, 1926-28. President for Central Council for Australia and New Zealand of Economic Society, 1930-32. President, Section G., Australian and New Zealand Association for the Advancement of Science, 1932. Vice-President, Section A., A. & N.Z. A. Adv. Sc., 1934. Member, sundry unofficial committees set up by Commonwealth government, 1920-31, dealing with economic problems. Chairman, Bureau of Social and International Affairs, Melbourne, 1930-32 and 1934-39. Member, Melbourne Stock Exchange for several years. Formerly a partner of Edward Dyason & Co., Melbourne.

Publications: Joint author of *The Australian Tariff* and of papers on economic subjects mostly published in the *Economic Record.*

(The editors regret to report the death of Mr. Dyason on the ship which was taking him to England after the close of the Conference.)

CAIGER, GEORGE, M.A. *Secretary.* General Secretary, A.I.I.A. since June, 1948. Son of Rev. J. S. Caiger, Malvern, England; born January, 1903, Brisbane, Queensland. Educated Denstone College, Staffs., England and St. John's College, Oxford. On staff Sedbergh School, Yorkshire, 1925-27. Travelled to Australia and Japan 1928-29; Sedbergh, 1930; to

Japan across Russia. Lecturer in English, Peers College, Tokyo, 1930-39. Australia, January, 1940, 2nd A.I.F. Major, Military Intelligence, Allied Translator and Interpreter Section, GHQ Manila, Japan, 1945. Chairman and organizer, Nation's Forum of the Air, Australian Broadcasting Commission, June, 1946-48; Commentator on Asian affairs.
Publications: *Tell Me About Tokyo*, 1939. *Tojo Say No*, 1942.
Address: 369 George St., Sydney, N.S.W.

JAMIESON, STEWART W. Born Sydney, 1903. Educated The King's School, New South Wales; St. Andrew's College; University of Sydney (B.A.); Balliol College, Oxford (B.A. Jurisp.). Associate to the Hon. Mr. Justice Gordon, Supreme Court of New South Wales, 1927. Secretary to Chairman, Royal Commission on Coal Industry, 1930. Admitted New South Wales Bar and practised in Sydney and Circuit Courts, 1930-40. Journalistic and Broadcasting Work, Special Foreign Correspondent for Sydney *Morning Herald*, 1938; visited Middle East, Balkans, Russia, Scandinavia, and Central Europe. Appointed Royal Commissioner on Theatres & Film Trade by New South Wales government, 1938. Enlisted R.A.A.F., 1940. Served in New Guinea on loan to U.S. Army Air Forces, 1942-43. Senior Intelligence Officer, Eastern Area, 1943; Northern Area, 1944-45. Entered Department of External Affairs, Canberra, 1946; posted to Ottawa as Official Secretary, Office of Australian High Commissioner, 1947.
Address: Office of Australian High Commissioner, Ottawa, Ont.

WATERMAN, EWEN McINTYRE. Born, December 22, 1901. Chairman, Waterman Brothers Ltd., Adelaide, S.A., until appointment 1948 as Australian Member, International Wool Secretariat, London, England. President, Theatre Proprietors' Council, 1936-48. President, Commonwealth Club, Adelaide, 1948. President, Rotary Club, Adelaide, 1947. President, Australian-American Association, South Australia Branch, 1948. President, S. Australia Adult Deaf and Dumb Society, 1947. President, S. Australia Orchestral Association, 1948.
Address: 40 Marsham Court, Westminster, London, s.w.1.

WHITE, ROBERT SYDNEY. Served in R.A.A.F. during World War II; trained in Canada; overseas service in South West

Pacific Area, Dutch East Indies. Visited for varying periods
England, New Zealand, Ceylon, France, U.S., Canada. As-
sistant to the Personnel Supervisor in Imperial Oil Refinery,
Imperoyal, Nova Scotia. Official Representative in Canada,
Royal Australian Air Force Association. Corresponding Sec-
retary, Chebucto Branch, Canadian Legion, Dartmouth.
Member, Maritimes Bureau of Personnel Relations. Member,
Dartmouth Junior Board of Trade. President, Halifax Re-
finery Social & Athletic Association. Member, United Services
Institute of Nova Scotia.
Address: Imperial Oil Ltd., Box 490, Dartmouth, N.S.

CANADA

FOWLER, R.M. (See under Officers of the Conference.)
Chairman, Canadian delegation.

BAKER, ROBERT PERCIVAL. Assistant General Manager, Huron
and Erie Mortgage Corporation and Canada Trust Company.
Past President, Dominion Mortgage & Investments Association. Past President, Trust Companies Association of Ontario.
Past President, Land Mortgage Companies Association. Past
Vice-President, Toronto Board of Trade. Past Vice-President,
London Chamber of Commerce. Chairman, London Branch
and member National Council, C.I.I.A. Member numerous
clubs (including National Club, Toronto) and other organizations.
Address: 264 St. James St., London, Ont.

BOUEY, G. K. Member of Research Department, Bank of
Canada, Ottawa, Ont.

BRADY, ALEXANDER, Ph.D., F.R.S.C. Professor of Political
Science, University of Toronto. Member, National Council
and National Executive Committee, and Chairman, National
Research Committee, C.I.I.A. Member, Canadian delegations
to I.P.R. Conferences at Hot Springs, 1945, and Stratford,
1947.
Publications: *Canada* (in Modern World series), 1931; *Democracy in the Dominions: A Comparative Study in Institutions,* 1947; co-editor with F. R. Scott, *Canada after the War*
(C.I.I.A., 1943).
Address: University of Toronto, Toronto, Ont.

BREWIN, FRANCIS ANDREW, K.C. Counsel in several constitutional cases before Supreme Court of Canada and Judicial

Committee. President, Ontario Co-operative Commonwealth Federation; member of National C.C.F. Council and Executive. Candidate for Dominion election in St. Paul's, Toronto, 1949, (defeated). Member, Canadian delegation to the Third Unofficial B.C.R.C., London, 1945.
Address: 54 Rathnally Ave., Toronto, Ont.

BUCHANAN, JOHN MURDOCH. President, British Columbia Packers Ltd., Vancouver, B.C. Director, H. R. MacMillan Export Co. Ltd. Educated public and high schools, Bridgeport, B.C.; University of British Columbia (B.A., 1917). In fishing business, Steveston, B.C., 1917-20. With firm of auditors, 1920-21. Cedar's Ltd., lumber manufacturer, 1921-27. Joined British Columbia Packers Ltd., 1928; appointed Secretary-Treasurer, 1932; president, 1946.
Address: 4537 Angus Drive, Vancouver, B.C.

BUDDEN, W. H. Served as National Secretary, War Finance Committee on loan from Bank of Canada. Now Vice-President and Director, MacLean, Budden Limited, investment managers and consultants. Member, National Executive Committee, C.I.I.A.
Address: Sun Life Building, Dominion Square, Montreal, P.Q.

BURCHELL, HON. CHARLES J., K.C., M.A., LL.D. Senior member law firm Burchell, Smith, Jost, Meagher & Burchell, Halifax, N.S. High Commissioner for Canada to Australia, 1939-41. High Commissioner to Newfoundland, 1941-44. High Commissioner to South Africa, 1944-45. Returned to private practice, 1945. High Commissioner to Newfoundland second time in September, 1948, and continued in that position until March 31, 1949. Appointed member of His Majesty's Privy Council in Canada, April 1, 1949. Director, Bank of Montreal, Dominion Steel and Coal Corporation, Halifax Shipyards Limited, and Canada Permanent Trust Company. Vice-President, C.I.I.A.
Address: Chronicle Building, Halifax, N.S.

CAVELL, CAPTAIN R. G. (NIK). Fourteen years Indian Cavalry; service North West and Burma-Chinese Frontiers; also Mesopotamia. Owned and operated sheep ranch, Africa. Business in Europe, China, Japan, Manchuria, Federated Malay. Canadian citizen for last 14 years. Vice-President, Automatic Electric (Canada) Limited and Phillips Electrical Works

Limited. Chairman, Canadian Institute on Public Affairs. Chairman, National Executive Committee, Canadian Institute of International Affairs. Writer on current affairs, particularly Far Eastern.
Address: 515 Vesta Drive, Toronto, Ont.

CHARLEBOIS, COLONEL J. G. Director of Infantry, Army Headquarters. Went overseas with the Royal 22nd Regiment in 1939. Staff College in 1941. Fought in the Italian and Northwest European campaigns.
Address: Army Headquarters, Ottawa, Ont.

DE ROME, COLONEL MAURICE L., O.B.E., E.D. Born and educated in Montreal. Proceeded overseas in 1939 with the Royal 22nd Regiment of the 1st Canadian Division. Staff College 1941. In 1943 seconded to S.O.E. (Subversive Operations Executive) or Special Force for duty in North West Europe (Normandy, Belgium and Holland). In 1945 appointed special military adviser to Netherlands Army and H.R.H. Prince Bernhard. Made a tour of Indonesia in 1946. Canadian Military Attaché to Holland and Belgium in 1947-48. In July, 1948, returned to Canada to become Chief of Staff, Quebec Army Command with Headquarters in Montreal, post at present held. Awards: Dutch order of Oranje-Nassau (commander); Legion d'Honneur and Croix de Guerre avec Palme; American Medal of Freedom.
Address: HQ Quebec Command, 3530 Atwater Avenue, Montreal, P.Q.

DOUGLAS, C. L. MONTEATH. Director, Canadian Tax Foundation. With Bank of Montreal, 1932-46; on temporary Canadian Government Service, Washington, 1942-45. Member, the National Council, the National Executive Committee, and the National Research Committee of C.I.I.A. *Delegation Secretary.*
Address: 194 Inglewood Drive, Toronto, Ont.

FRASER, A. M., M.A. (Edinburgh), 1928. Head, Dept. of History, Economics and Political Science, Memorial University College, St. John's, Nfld. Hon. Secretary, Newfoundland Branch, R.I.I.A., 1938-49. Delegate representing Nfld. Branch, R.I.I.A. at Second Unofficial B.C.R. Conference, 1938. Chairman, St. Lawrence, Nfld., Trade Dispute Board.

Publications: Chapters on external relations in *Newfoundland,* ed. by R. A. MacKay (R.I.I.A., 1946).
Address: 23 Rennie's Mill Rd., St. John's, Nfld.

FRY, HAROLD. (See under Officers of the Conference.)

GIBSON, J. DOUGLAS. Economist and editor of the *Monthly Review* of the Bank of Nova Scotia, Toronto. Economic adviser to the Wartime Prices and Trade Board, 1942-47. Member of the National Executive Committee and the National Research Committee, C.I.I.A.
Publications: Edited and contributed to *Canada's Economy in a Changing World,* 1949.
Address: The Bank of Nova Scotia, 38 Melinda Street, Toronto, Ont.

MACDONNELL, JAMES M., K.C. Resigned from Presidency of National Trust Company and other directorates in 1944 to seek entry into Parliament. Elected in 1945 and served one term; defeated in 1949 General Election. President of Dominion Progressive Conservative Association. Formerly, Chairman, National Executive Committee, C.I.I.A. Honorary Vice-President, C.I.I.A.
Address: 114 Madison Avenue, Toronto, Ont.

McINNIS, EDGAR, M.A. Professor of History, University of Toronto. Member, National Council, National Executive Committee, National Research Committee and *International Journal* Committee, and Chairman, Public Education Committee, C.I.I.A. Vice-Chairman, Canadian delegation to the I.P.R. Conference, Hot Springs, 1945, and Chairman, Canadian delegation to I.P.R. Conference, Stratford, 1947. Chairman, International Programme Committee, I.P.R. Representative, Canadian Council (C.I.I.A.) on Pacific Council, I.P.R.
Publications: *The Unguarded Frontier,* 1942; *The War,* 6 vols., 1940-46; *Canada: A Political and Social History,* 1947; co-author with J. H. S. Reid, *The English-Speaking Peoples: a Modern History,* 1949.
Address: University of Toronto, Toronto, Ont.

McLEAN, JAMES STANLEY. President, Canada Packers Limited, Toronto. Director, Canadian Bank of Commerce. President, Canadian Chamber of Commerce, 1938-39. Chairman,

Board of Trustees, Massey Hall. Honorary Vice-President, C.I.I.A.
Residence: 1225 Bayview Avenue, Toronto 12, Ont.

MICHENER, ROLAND, K.C. Barrister of Ontario Bar and Middle Temple, London. Practising law in the city of Toronto since 1924. Former member of National Council and National Executive Committee, C.I.I.A. Delegate to Third British Commonwealth Relations Conference, London, 1945. One time Progressive Conservative member of the Ontario Legislature and of the Government in the portfolio of Provincial Secretary.
Address: 5 Rosedale Road, Toronto, Ont.

PANET-RAYMOND, REAL. Assistant to Vice-President of Canadian Industries Limited (Montreal). Alderman of Westmount, Quebec. Honorary Secretary, The Canadian Red Cross Society (Quebec Division). Member Executive Committee, Canadian Inter-American Association.
Address: 70 Belmont Crescent, Westmount, P.Q.

SHEARD, TERENCE, C.B.E. Educated Model School, Toronto; Upper Canada College; University of Toronto (B.A., 1921); Magdalen College, Oxford (B.A., 1922); B.C.L. (1923). Called to Bar, London (Lincoln's Inn), 1923; Ontario, 1925. Practised law with G. B. Balfour, K.C., Toronto, 1924-28. National Trust Co. as Estates Officer, 1928-31; Assistant Manager, Montreal Office, 1932-36; Assistant General Manager, 1938; General Manager, 1948. On loan to Department of National Defence for Air, 1940-44; Air Member for Supply (R.C.A.F.), 1942-44. Member, National Executive Committee, C.I.I.A. and Chairman, *International Journal* Committee.
Address: 20 King Street East, Toronto, Ont.

SIFTON, VICTOR. (See under Officers of the Conference.)

SMITH, I. NORMAN. Associate Editor of the *Ottawa Journal*. Covered the United Nations charter meeting at San Francisco. Attended several General Assembly and Security Council meetings in New York. Covered the Dominion Prime Ministers' meeting in London, 1946.
Address: *Ottawa Journal*, Ottawa, Ont.

SOWARD, FREDERIC HUBERT. (See under Officers of the Conference.)

TARR, EDGAR J., K.C., LL.D. President, Monarch Life Assurance Company, Winnipeg. Director, Bank of Canada. Honorary President, Canadian Institute of International Affairs. Chairman, Pacific Council, Institute of Pacific Relations, 1942-45. Member, Canadian Delegation (1933) and Chairman, Canadian delegation, British Commonwealth Relations Conferences, 1938, 1945.
Address: 85 Harrow Street, Winnipeg, Man.

TAYLOR, KENNETH W. Assistant Deputy Minister of Finance and Chairman of Wartime Prices and Trade Board. Formerly Professor of Political Economy, McMaster University, Hamilton, Ont. Member, Canadian group, B.C.R. Conference at Lapstone, Australia, 1938. Member, Canadian delegation, I.P.R. Conference, Hot Springs, 1945. Member, National Research Committee, C.I.I.A.
Address: 308 Clemow Avenue, Ottawa, Ont.

TROTTER, REGINALD GEORGE, A.M., Ph.D., Hon. D.C.L. (Acadia), F.R.S.C. Douglas Professor of Canadian and Colonial History and Head of the Department of History, Queen's University since 1934. President, Canadian Historical Association, 1938-39. Chairman of Canadian Social Science Research Council, 1940-41. Canadian organizer of the biennial conferences on Canadian-American Affairs held at Queen's University and the St. Lawrence University, 1935-41. Member, Canada-United States Committee on Education since its organization in 1944. Member of the National Research Committee of the C.I.I.A. Member of the Canadian Delegation to the Third British Commonwealth Relations Conference, London, 1945.
Publications: *Canadian Federation: Its Origins and Achievements*, 1924; contributions to the Canadian volume of the *Cambridge History of the British Empire*, 1930; *The British Empire-Commonwealth*, 1932; *North America and the War: A Canadian View*, 1940; *Commonwealth: Pattern for Peace?*, 1944; co-author with C. W. New, *Modern History*, 1947; *Charters of our Freedom*, 1946.
Address: 320 King Street West, Kingston, Ont.

CEYLON

DE SILVA, L.M.D. Born Ceylon, April 25, 1893. Educated Royal College, Colombo; Trinity College, Kandy; St. John's College, Cambridge. Senior Optime Mathematical Tripos,

Cambridge, 1914. Called to Bar, 1916; in practice at the Bar of Ceylon, 1916-25. Assistant to Attorney-General, Ceylon, 1925. Deputy Solicitor-General, Ceylon, 1925. Deputy Solicitor-General, Ceylon, 1927. Solicitor-General, Ceylon, 1931-34. K.C. of Ceylon Bar, 1931. Acting Attorney-General and Officer of State, State Council, Ceylon, 1932-33. Also acted as a Puisne Judge of Supreme Court, Ceylon, 1931-34. Retired from Service of Government of Ceylon, 1934. Called to Inner Bar, 1938. Chairman, Commission to Enquire into Law Relating to Mortgage, Credit Facilities and Protection of Lands of Agriculturists, Ceylon, 1943-45. Chairman, Bribery Commission, Ceylon, 1941-43. Chairman, Delimitation Commission, Ceylon, 1946. A Director of the Associated Newspapers of Ceylon.
Address: Park House, Albert Crescent, Colombo 7, Ceylon.

WIGNARAJA, PONNA. Graduate in Economics with B.A. (Honours) at Ceylon University. M.A. Yale University, in international relations, and at present continuing his post-graduate studies at Yale. Was Secretary to the chief delegate from Ceylon to the 1948 Conference of the Economic Commission for Asia and the Far East, held at Octacamund, India. *Secretary.*
Address: "Mangalagiri," Kynsey Rd., Colombo, Ceylon.

INDIA

VIJAYARAGHAVACHARIYA, SIR T. (See under Officers of the Conference.) *Chairman,* Indian delegation.

MUJEEB, PROFESSOR M. Graduated from Worcester College, Oxford, 1922; studied in Germany, 1922-26. Joined the Jamia Millia (National Muslim University) in March, 1926, as Professor of History and Politics, and has been engaged in education work ever since. At present, Sheikhul Jamia (Chief Executive Officer) of the Jamia Millia, Delhi. Represented India at the Centennial Celebrations of the Republic of Liberia.
Publications: *History of Russian Literature, History of Political Thought, Story of the World, etc.*
Address: Jamia Millia Islamia, Jamianagar, Delhi.

RAO, B. SHIVA. Member, Constituent Assembly of India. Special Correspondent of the *Manchester Guardian.* Delegate to the Pacific Relations Conference, Hot Springs, 1945. Represented

India at the United Nations General Assembly in 1947 and
1948 and is representing India in the Assembly during 1949.
Publications: *The Industrial Worker in India,* and *Select
Constitutions of the World.*
Address: No. 4, Hardinge Avenue, New Delhi.

RAO, DR. V. K. R. V. Took his Doctorate Degree at Cambridge.
Principal, L.D. Arts College, Ahmedabad for five years. Now
Professor of Economics and Director, Delhi School of Eco-
nomics, also Dean of Social Sciences, University of Delhi.
Represented India at F.A.O. Conferences in Quebec, Wash-
ington, and Copenhagen. Was Chairman of the United
Nations Sub-Commission on Economic Development.
Publications: Many books on Indian Economics, principally
on National Income of India.
Address: University of Delhi, Delhi, India.

IRELAND

HAYES, MICHAEL. *Chairman,* Ireland delegation. Fine Gael
(United Ireland) Party. Leader for Government in Senate
of Ireland. Member of Dail Eireann, 1921-33. Minister for
Education, 1922. Ceann Comhairle (Speaker), 1922-32.
Chairman, Civil Service Commission, 1922-32. Senator since
1938. Member of Executive, Irish Branch, Inter-Parliamentary
Union. President, Irish Branch, Commonwealth Parliamentary
Association.
Address: 20 Brighton Square, Rethgar, Dublin.

BYRNE, ALFRED. Alderman, Dublin Corporation. Independent
Member of Dail Eireann almost continuously since 1923.
Member of British Parliament, 1914-18. Lord Mayor of
Dublin, 1930-39.
Address: 48 Palmerston Rd., Dublin.

CORISH, BRENDAN. Chairman, Administrative Council, Irish
Labour Party. Member of Dail Eireann. Parliamentary Secretary (Assistant Minister) to the Minister for Local Government.
Address: 1 St. Ibar's Villas, Wexford.

DOUGLAS, HAROLD J. Member of the National Executive of the
Fine Gael (United Ireland) Party. Member of the Dublin
Municipal Corporation since 1945. Commissioner for Irish
Lights. Joint Managing Director of John Douglas & Sons,

Ltd., and Director of several other Irish Companies. One of the Founder Members, and member of the Council of the International Affairs Association of Ireland. Attended International Student Conferences at Geneva in 1934 and 1936 and at New York in 1938.
Address: "Mount Kisco," Hainsult Rd., Foxrock, Co. Dublin.

NEW ZEALAND

CARTER, GWENDOLEN M., B.A. (Toronto), M.A. (Oxon.), Ph.D. (Radcliffe). *Chairman,* New Zealand Delegation. Associate Professor of Government, Smith College, Northampton, Mass., with 2,200 students, the largest women's residential college in the world. Travelled July, 1948 to July, 1949 under the auspices of the C.I.I.A., Canadian Social Science Research Council, Social Science Research Council of New York, and Institute of Pacific Relations, studying British Commonwealth Relations in Great Britain, South Africa, Ceylon, Pakistan, India, Australia, and New Zealand.
Publications: *The British Commonwealth and International Security: The Role of the Dominions, 1919-39* (C.I.I.A. 1947), and co-author with John C. Ranney of *The Major Foreign Powers: The Governments of Great Britain, France, the Soviet Union, and China,* 1949.
Address: Department of Government, Smith College, Northampton, Mass., U.S.A.

NORTHEY, JOHN F. Born 1920; B.A., L.L.M. (New Zealand University). Called to Bar 1942. Employed by Department of External Affairs, Wellington, N.Z.; represented New Zealand at international conferences, including 3rd Assembly I.C.A.O., June, 1949. Now undertaking post-graduate work in Commonwealth Relations and British Constitutional Law, University of Toronto.
Publications: Contributed articles on Constitutional Law to *New Zealand Law Journal.*
Address: 9 Hemalaya Crescent, Khandallah, Wellington, N.Z.

PAKISTAN

BOKHARI, PROFESSOR AHMED, M.A. (Cantab), C.I.A. *Chairman,* Pakistan delegation. Principal, Government College, Lahore. Former Director, All India Radio. Leader Government of India Goodwill Mission to Afghanistan, 1943. Indian Representative and Chairman of Commonwealth Broadcasting

Conference, London, 1945. Pakistan Representative in the Information and Broadcasting Committee of the Joint India and Pakistan Partition Council, 1947. Leader of Pakistan Goodwill Mission to Afghanistan, 1948. Leader of Pakistan Delegation to the Tripartite Committee on the Partition of India Office Assets, London, 1948. Leader of Pakistan Delegation to International High Frequency Broadcasting Conference, Mexico City, 1948-49.

Publications: Author of short stories and critical works in English and Urdu.

Address: Government College, Lahore.

AHMED, AZIZUDDIN, M.A., L.L.B. Born 1900. Educated Muslim University, Aligarh and University of Dacca. Advocate of Dacca High Court, practising at Barisal, East Pakistan. Public Prosecutor of Barisal, 1944-48. Member of Pakistan Constituent Assembly.

Address: Dacca High Court, Barisal, East Pakistan.

HASAN, SARWAR KHWAJA. Born 1902. Educated Nizam College, Hyderabad, Deccan; Muslim University, Aligarh; Peterhouse, Cambridge. Barrister at Law, Middle Temple. Formerly Lecturer in Law, University of Delhi. Member Indian Delegation, British Commonwealth Relations Conference, London, 1945. Secretary, Pakistan Institute of International Affairs. Member, Government of India Delegation to East Africa, 1946.

Publications: Editor of *Pakistan Horizon;* author of numerous papers on international and constitutional questions.

Address: Frere Hall, Karachi.

HASSAN, PROFESSOR MAHAMMAD, M.A. Principal, College of Commerce, West Punjab University, Lahore. Secretary, West Punjab Board of Economic Inquiry. Secretary, Pakistan Economic Association. Fellow of the West Punjab University. Member, West Punjab Tenancy Laws Inquiry Committee. Chief Delegate, Economic Commission for Asia and the Far East meeting in Bangkok, March, 1949.

Publications: Editor of *Quarterly Economic Survey* (West Punjab); author of several reports and articles on agricultural and industrial conditions in Pakistan.

Address: College of Commerce, Punjab University, Lahore.

ZIAUDDIN, MIAN. Born 1901. Barrister-at-Law, 1923. Middle Temple, London. Pathan of North West Frontier Province, Pakistan. At present practising law at Peshawar, North West Frontier Province, Pakistan. Was General Secretary of the Provincial Muslim League. Member of the Pakistan Muslim League Council. Member of the North West Frontier Province Legislative Assembly, 1937-38. Member of the Pakistan Muslim League Council. President of the North West Frontier Province Bar Association.
Address: Barrister-at-Law, Peshawar.

SOUTH AFRICA

MALHERBE, ERNST G., M.A., Ph.D. (Columbia), LL.D. (Sydney, Cambridge, Queen's). *Chairman,* South African Delegation. Principal, University of Natal, Pietermaritzburg and Durban, since 1945. (Lt. Col.) Director of Military Intelligence, South African Army, and Director Army Education Services, 1940-45. Director of Census and Statistics for the Union of South Africa, 1939-40. Vice-Chairman of the Council of the South African Institute of International Affairs, and for several years Chairman of the Natal Branch of the Institute. Chief Investigator, Education Section, Carnegie Poor White Commission of Research, 1928-32. Member of Government Commission to investigate Native Education in South Africa, 1935. Director, National Bureau of Educational and Social Research for South Africa, 1929-39. Member Social and Economic Planning Council since 1946. Member of National Council of Social Research since 1945. Chairman, National War Histories Committee.
Publications: *Education in South Africa, 1652-1922,* 1925; *Education and the Poor White,* 1929; *Carnegie Commission's Poor White Report on Education,* 1932; *Education in a Changing Empire,* 1932; editor of *Educational Adaptation in a Changing Society,* 1937; *Educational and Social Research in South Africa,* 1939; *The Bilingual School,* 1943.
Address: 181 King Edward Avenue, Pietermaritzburg, South Africa.

SCHULLER, MRS. E. (MARY CRAIG McGEACHY). Member of the League of Nations' Secretariat, Geneva, 1930-40. Representative of the Secretary-General of the League of Nations at the Banff Conference of the Institute of Pacific Relations, 1933, and at the First British Commonwealth Relations Conference,

Toronto, 1933. Member of British Ministry of Economic Warfare, 1940; posted to British Embassy, Washington, 1941; First Secretary of the Embassy, 1942-44. Director of Welfare of the United Nations Relief and Rehabilitation Administration, 1944-46. Representative of U.N.R.R.A. at the United Nations Economic and Social Council, July, 1946. Member of the Royal Institute of International Affairs, since 1931; Member of Study Group on "Resources in Africa South of the Sahara for British Strategy"; rapporteur for Study Group on "Immigration into South Africa."
Address: "Vale Cottage", Sandown, Johannesburg, South Africa.

SOLOMON, MRS. BERTHA, M.P. Barrister and United Party member of Parliament for Jeppe, Johannesburg. Member Transvaal Provincial Council, 1933-38. Led South African delegation at the Conference of the International Council of Women, Paris, 1934. Elected to House of Assembly, 1938; re-elected, 1943, 1948.
Address: 726, His Majesty's Buildings, Johannesburg, and 4, Riviera Mansions, Killarney, Johannesburg, South Africa.

WILLIAMS, W. TREVOR, M.C., B.Sc. (Engineering). Managing Director of Ussher Industries Ltd., Northern and King Ltd., Creteweld Ltd. President, Natal Institute of Engineers, 1948. Member of Durban Rotary Club. Member of Committee, South African Economic Society, Natal Branch. Member of Royal Institute of International Affairs, Durban Branch. Member of Institute of Race Relations (South Africa).
Address: Box 563, Durban.

UNITED KINGDOM

BUTLER, THE RT. HON. RICHARD AUSTEN, P.C., M.A., F.R.G.S. *Chairman* of the United Kingdom Delegation. Member of Parliament, (Conservative) Saffron Walden since 1929. Chairman, Conservative Research Department. Deputy Chairman, Conservative Parliamentary Foreign Affairs Committee. Educated Marlborough; Pembroke College, Cambridge. Fellow Corpus Christi College, Cambridge, 1925-29. Hon. Fellow of Pembroke College, Cambridge, 1941. President, Union Society, 1924. Under-Secretary of State, India Office, 1932-37. Parliamentary Secretary, Ministry of Labour, 1937-38. Under-Secretary of State for Foreign Affairs, 1938-41. Minister of

Education, 1941-45. Minister of Labour, June-July, 1945. Member Indian Franchise Committee, 1932. Chairman Scientific Advisory Committe and Engineering Advisory Committee, 1942. Chairman of Council National Union of Conservative Associations, 1945. President Modern Language Association, 1946. Chairman of Council Royal India Society, and of Anglo-Netherlands Society, 1946. Leader of the Parliamentary delegation on the occasion of the Speaker's visit to Rome, 1948. Address: 24 Old Queen Street, London, S.W.1., England.

BONHAM-CARTER, LADY VIOLET. A Governor of the Old Vic. Vice Chairman of United Europe Movement. Hon. President United Nations Association. Elder daughter of Rt. Hon. H. H. Asquith, 1st Earl of Oxford and Asquith; m. 1915, Sir Maurice Bonham-Carter. Governor of B.B.C., 1941-46. President of Women's Liberal Federation, 1923-25, 1939-45. Member of Mr. Churchill's Focus in defence of Freedom and Peace, 1936-39. Member of Executive of League of Nations Union up to 1941. President of Liberal Party Organization, 1944-45. Member of the Royal Commission on the Press, 1948-49. Address: 40 Gloucester Square, London, W.2, England.

BRAND, THE LORD, C.M.G., D.C.L. (Oxon.) Educated Marlborough; New College, Oxford. Fellow of All Souls College, Oxford. Served in South Africa, 1902-9. Secretary Transvaal Delegates at the South African National Convention, 1908-9. Member of the Imperial Munitions Board of Canada, 1915-18. Deputy-Chairman, British Mission in Washington, 1917-18. Financial Adviser to Lord Robert Cecil, when Chairman of Supreme Economic Council, Peace Conference, Paris, 1919. Vice-President, International Financial Conference of League of Nations, Brussels, 1920. Financial Representative, South Africa, at Genoa Conference, 1922. Member of Expert Committee advising German Government on Stabilisation of the mark, 1922. Until May, 1944, Managing Director of Lazard Brothers & Co. Ltd. Head of British Food Mission, Washington, 1941-44. Representative of H. M. Treasury in Washington, 1944-46. Chairman, British Supply Council in North America, 1942 and 1945-46. U.K. delegate at Bretton Woods and Savannah Conferences. Director of The Times Publishing Co. Ltd., Lazard Brothers & Co. Ltd., Lloyds Bank Ltd. Chairman of the North British and Mercantile Insurance Co. Ltd. Hon. Fellow of New College, Oxford, 1948.

Publications: *The Union of South Africa,* 1909; *War and National Finance,* 1921.

Address: c/o Lazard Brothers & Co. Ltd., 11 Old Broad Street, London, E.C.2.

CURTIS, LIONEL GEORGE, C.H. Fellow of All Souls College, Oxford. A President of Royal Institute of International Affairs. Born 1872. Educated Haileybury and New College, Oxford. Called to the Bar. Served in South African War. Town Clerk, Johannesburg, 1901. Assistant Colonial Secretary, Transvaal, 1903. Member, Transvaal Legislative Council, 1908. Beit Lecturer in Colonial History, University of Oxford. Secretary to Irish Conference, 1921. Adviser on Irish Affairs, Colonial Office, 1921-24. Delegate to British Commonwealth Relations Conferences, 1938 and 1945.

Publications: *The Problem of the Commonwealth,* 1916; *The Commonwealth of Nations,* 1916; *Dyarchy,* 1920; *The Prevention of War,* 1924; *The Capital Question of China,* 1932; *Civitas Dei,* Vol. I, 1934, Vols. II and III, 1937, (in one volume as *The Commonwealth of God,* 1938); *The Protectorates of South Africa,* 1935; *Decision, Action,* 1942; *Faith and Works,* 1943; *The Way to Peace,* 1944; *World War: Its Cause and Cure,* 1945; *War or Peace?* 1946; *World Revolution in the Cause of Peace,* 1949.

Address: Hales Croft, Kidlington, Oxford, England.

FITZGERALD, SIR WILLIAM FITZGERALD, M.C., K.C. Educated Blackrock College, Trinity College, Dublin. Barrister-at-Law, King's Inns, Dublin, 1922. Nigerian Administrative Service, 1920. Police Magistrate, Lagos, 1921. Crown Counsel, Nigeria, 1924. Solicitor-General, N. Rhodesia, 1932. Attorney-General, N. Rhodesia, 1933; Palestine, 1937-43. Chief Justice of Palestine, 1944-48.

Address: 22 Egerton Gardens, London, S.W.3, England.

GAGE, CONOLLY HUGH. Member of Parliament for South Belfast (Ulster Unionist). Chancellor of the Diocese of Coventry. Principal Official to the Archdeacon of London. Born 1905. Educated Repton, Sidney Sussex College, Cambridge. Occupation Barrister-at-Law. Enlisted 1939. Served in Europe with 1st Canadian Army. Mentioned in Despatches.

Address: 4 Paper Buildings, Temple, London, E.C.4.

HALL, JOSEPH ARTHUR, C.B.E., J.P. President, National Union of Mineworkers, Yorkshire Area, since 1936. Left Elementary School at 11½ years of age to commence work as pony driver in the coal mines. Financial Secretary of the Yorkshire Mineworkers Association, 1924-36. Member of the National Union of Mineworkers Executive Committee since 1928. Member of the National Miners' Welfare Commission since 1935. Auditor of the National Labour Party since 1928. Chairman of the Yorkshire Regional Council of the Labour Party since 1949. Assisted in rescue work of 38 major colliery explosions and enquiries.

Address: National Union of Mineworkers, Yorkshire Area, Miners' Offices, 2 Huddersfield Road, Barnsley, England.

HEALEY, DENIS WINSTON, M.B.E. Secretary of the International Department of the Labour Party since 1946. Born 1917. Educated Bradford Grammar School, Balliol College, Oxford. Harmsworth Senior Scholar, Merton College, 1940. Royal Engineers 1940-46. Member of Council, Royal Institute of International Affairs since November 1948.

Publications: Author, Labour Party publications on foreign policy. *Approach to Foreign Policy*, 1947; *Cards on the Table—an Interpretation of Labour's Foreign Policy*, 1947; *Feet on the Ground—A Study of Western Union*, 1948.

Address: International Department, The Labour Party, Transport House, Smith Square, London, S.W.1, England.

HODSON, HENRY VINCENT. Assistant Editor of the *Sunday Times*. Educated Gresham's School; Balliol College, Oxford. Fellow of All Souls College, Oxford, 1928-35. Staff of Economic Advisory Council, 1930-31. Assistant Editor of the *Round Table*, 1931, Editor, 1934-39. Secretary to U.K. delegation at 1st British Commonwealth Relations Conference, 1933. Conference Recorder at 2nd British Commonwealth Relations Conference 1938. Director Empire Division, Ministry of Information, 1939-41. Reforms Commissioner Government of India, 1941-42. Principal Assistant Secretary, and later head of Non-Munitions Division, Ministry of Production, 1942-45. Chairman, British Commonwealth Relations Committee, Royal Institute of International Affairs.

Publications: *Economics of a Changing World*, 1933; *Slump and Recovery 1929-37*, 1938; (Editor) *The British Commonwealth and the Future*, 1939; (Part) *The Empire in the World*,

1937; *Twentieth Century Empire,* 1948. Sections in annual *Survey of International Affairs,* and many articles in reviews, etc.

Address: 26 Mount Street, London, W.1, England.

JACOB, MAJOR-GENERAL SIR IAN, K.B.E., C.B. Director of Overseas Services of B.B.C. since 1947. Educated Wellington College; R.M.A. Woolwich; King's College, Cambridge. Staff College, 1931-32. Brigade Major, Canal Brigade, Egypt, 1936-38. Military Assistant Secretary, Committee of Imperial Defence, 1938. Military Assistant Secretary to the War Cabinet, 1939-46. Retired 1946. Waziristan, 1922-23 (medal and clasp), U.S. Legion of Merit (Commander).

Address: 69 Melton Court, London, S.W.7, England.

LLOYD GEORGE, MAJOR THE RT. HON. GWILYM, P.C., M.P. Member of Parliament (Liberal) Pembrokeshire, 1922-24 and since 1929. Educated at Eastbourne College; Jesus College, Cambridge. Served with the Royal Artillery in France, 1914-18. Mentioned in despatches. Parliamentary Secretary, Board of Trade, 1931 and 1939-41. Parliamentary Secretary, Ministry of Food, 1941-42. Minister of Fuel and Power, 1942-45. Member of Parliamentary Mission to Ceylon in January, 1949.

MANSERGH, PHILIP NICHOLAS SETON, O.B.E., B.Litt., M.A., D.Phil. Abe Bailey Professor of British Commonwealth Relations, Royal Institute of International Affairs since 1947. Born 1910. Educated College of St. Columba, Dublin and Pembroke College, Oxford. Research Worker and Tutor in Politics, Pembroke College, Oxford, 1937-40. Ministry of Information, 1941-46. Director, Empire Division, 1944-46. Assistant Secretary, Dominions Office, 1946-47.

Publications: *Ireland in the Age of Reform and Revolution,* 1940; *Britain and Ireland,* 2nd edition, 1944; *The Commonwealth and the Nations,* 1948; *The Coming of the First World War,* 1949.

Address: Chatham House, 10 St. James's Square, London, S.W.1, England.

ROBINSON, EDWARD AUSTIN GOSSAGE, C.M.G., O.B.E., M.A. Fellow and Lecturer of Sidney Sussex College, Cambridge. Member of Economic Planning Staff since 1947. Secretary, Royal Economic Society since 1945. Joint editor of *Economic*

Journal since 1944. Educated Marlborough; Christ's College, Cambridge. R.N.A.S. and R.A.F. (Pilot), 1917-19. Tutor to H.H. The Maharaja of Gwalior, 1926-28. Member of Economic Section, War Cabinet Office, 1939-42. Economic Adviser and Head of Programmes Division, Ministry of Production, 1942-45. Member of British Reparations Mission, Moscow and Berlin, 1945. Economic Adviser to Board of Trade, 1946.

Publications: *The Structure of Competitive Industry,* 1931; *Monopoly,* 1941. Contributor to *Modern Industry and the African,* 1933; Lord Hailey's *An African Survey,* 1938. Articles in *Economic Journal,* etc.

Address: 62A Grange Road, Cambridge, England.

SUTHERLAND, MISS LUCY STUART, C.B.E., M.A. Principal of Lady Margaret Hall, Oxford, since 1945. Educated Rodean School; University of the Witwatersrand, S. Africa; Somerville College, Oxford. Fellow and Tutor, Somerville College, Oxford, 1928-45. Temporary Assistant Secretary, Board of Trade, 1941-45. Chairman, Lace Working Party, 1946. President Girls Public Day School Trust. Member of Portal Committee on the Distribution of Films.

Publications: *A London Merchant (1685-1774),* 1933; edited (with M. McKisack) *Mediaeval Representation and Consent,* by M. V. Clarke, 1936, and *Fourteenth Century Studies,* by M. V. Clarke, 1937; edited (with H. Cam and M. Coate) *Studies in Manorial History,* by A. E. Levett, 1938. Contributions to *English Historical Review, Economic History Review, Economic History, Transactions of the Royal Historical Society,* etc. (Joint) *Report of the Lace Working Party,* 1947. Address: Lady Margaret Hall, Oxford, England.

WEBB, MAURICE, M.P. Labour Member of Parliament for Central Bradford since 1945. Chairman, Parliamentary Labour Party since 1946. Political journalist and broadcaster. Educated Christ Church School, Lancaster. Propaganda Officer for Labour Party Headquarters, 1929-35. *Daily Herald* staff, 1935-44. *Sunday Express* staff, 1944-45. Has done considerable home and overseas broadcasting for B.B.C. Has served as Chairman of Parliamentary Lobby Journalists and Press Gallery Committee. Member of National Executive Council of National Union of Journalists.

Publications: *Britain's Industrial Front,* 1943, and various political pamphlets.
Address: Willow Cottage, Pinner Hill, Pinner, Middlesex, England.

Secretaries to United Kingdom Group

ASTOR, HON. JOHN JACOB, M.B.E. Légion d'honneur and Croix de Guerre. Parliamentary candidate (Conservative) for Sutton Division of Plymouth, Devon. Concerned with Thoroughbred Breeding Partnership, (Partner) and Mixed Farm. Address: 88 Marsham Court, London, S.W.1, England.

HUNTER, LESLIE DAVID STEVENSON. Managing Editor, Central News Parliamentary Service since 1942. Born 1909. Educated Wilson's Grammar School; Selwyn College, Cambridge. G.S.O. 2 Allied Liaison Staff, G.H.Q., M.E.F., 1943-46. Officer of the Royal Order of King George I.
Address: Brookham Green, Betchworth, Surrey, England.

MANSERGH, DIANA MARY. Educated, Queen Anne's School, Cavisham; Exhibitioner, Modern Languages, Lady Margaret Hall, Oxford, 1937-39. M. 1939 Dr. Nicholas Mansergh. Assistant Principal, Ministry of Supply, 1941-44.
Address: c/o Chatham House, 10 St. James's Square, London, S.W.1, England.

CONFERENCE SECRETARIAT

MACADAM, IVISON STEVENSON, C.B.E., M.V.O. (See under Officers of Conference.) *Acting Secretary-General.*

MACLENNAN, DOUGLAS A. (See under Officers of Conference.) *Organizing Secretary.*

NEALE, MISS EDNA. Assistant National Secretary and Office Manager, C.I.I.A. Attended Canadian Conference at Montebello, Quebec, 1943, and I.P.R. Conferences at Mont Tremblant, 1942, Hot Springs, 1945, and Stratford, 1947. *Assistant Organizing Secretary of Conference.*

LINGARD, C. CECIL, B.A. (Hon.), M.A. (Queen's), Ph.D. (Chicago) in History. Research Secretary, C.I.I.A., 1946-50. Editor, C.I.I.A. *International Journal,* 1946-50. Member, Canadian delegation to Hot Springs Conference, I.P.R., 1945. Publications: *Territorial Government in Canada,* 1946; Part

One of *The New Northwest,* 1947. "Canada's External Relations and War Effort, 1937-46," in *Ten Eventful Years,* Vol. I, 1947; co-author with R. G. Trotter, *Canada in World Affairs, 1941-44* (C.I.I.A., 1950). *Assistant Secretary.*

CAMPBELL, DUNCAN C. Aluminium Limited, Montreal. Honorary Secretary, Montreal Branch, C.I.I.A. *Secretary to International Committee and special Executive Assistant.*

GARDNER, DONALD H., B.A. Public Information Secretary, C.I.I.A. *Transportation and Speakers' Secretary.*

SAUNDERS, MISS BEATRICE, B.A., B.L.S. Chief Librarian, C.I.I.A. *Librarian and Documents Officer.*

BLYTH, MRS. W. D., B.A. *Private Secretary to Organizing Secretary.*

Précis Writers

HORNE, HAROLD REGINALD. Foreign Service Officer, Commonwealth Division, Department of External Affairs, Ottawa.
Address: 1 Cornwall Street, Ottawa, Ont., or Department of External Affairs, Ottawa.

HYNDMAN, PATRICK ROBERT. Foreign Service Officer, Legal Division, Department of External Affairs, Ottawa, Ont.
Address: Department of External Affairs, Ottawa.

McGILL, ALLAN S. Foreign Service Officer, Department of External Affairs (European Division), Ottawa, Ont.
Address: 128 Genest Street, Eastview, Ont.

McILWRAITH, KENNETH DOUGLAS. Foreign Service Officer, Personnel Division, Department of External Affairs, Ottawa, Ont.
Address: 289 Nelson Street, Ottawa, or Department of External Affairs, Ottawa.

Secretarial Staff

McCREARY, MISS BETTY A. (Membership Secretary, C.I.I.A.)
CHAMBERS, MISS MARGARET
FRY, DAVID
GREER, MRS. JESSIE
HASLER, MISS NORMA
PETTAPIECE, MISS MYRA
SPOTTON, MISS RANDA
WADDELL, MISS CATHERINE M.

Appendix F

ADDRESS BY LIONEL CURTIS

Prevention Of War[2]

You have done me a great honour, which I did not expect, in asking me to speak to this informal meeting of delegates. You have also given me a great privilege. I must however make it emphatically clear that I speak for no one but myself. What I am going to say does not express the view of the United Kingdom delegation.

In 1935 Lord Lothian gave a lecture which was published under the title "Patriotism is not enough nor pacifism either." He pointed out that the rule of law could only exist inside a sovereign state. The world is divided between sixty or seventy sovereign states and between them there is no rule of law—there is anarchy, a word derived from two Greek words meaning "no government." Where there is no rule of law and therefore anarchy, world war is inevitable. This state of affairs can only be terminated by merging national sovereignties into an international sovereignty.

In August, 1939, Lord Lothian went as British Ambassador to the United States. In December of 1940 he died of overwork and I was called upon by the Oxford Press to edit the speeches he had made in the United States. I was amazed to find that, although he was speaking as an official, he had kept repeating what he had said in his lecture, notably in his speech to the Virginia Legislature, which I understand is the oldest in North America. Had he lived, I am certain that Lord Lothian would have gone on to show how national sovereignties could be merged into an international sovereignty. I knew his mind and, now that he was gone, I felt that it was up to me to work this out.

I did my best. In 1941 I published *Decision*. Then, in December 1941, came Pearl Harbor and the United States, with other free countries, came into the war. American troops and those of other nations were sent to England. The British War Office started a scheme under which men of all the United Nations, of all ranks, were sent to Balliol College for one week and I was asked to give one lecture on the prevention of war. The subject so interested the

[2] Delivered at Bigwin Inn before the members of the Conference on the evening of September 14.

group that I was asked to come again next day to continue the discussion. The management then realized that the men in uniform attending these groups were thinking first and foremost of how to save their children from going through what they themselves were going through and their fathers had gone through 25 years before. I have kept in touch with the men whom I met at Balliol and know that some of them afterwards lost their lives in the war. For three years I addressed leave groups nearly every week for two days in which we threshed out a policy for stopping war once and for all! The most important sections in these groups were soldiers from the United States, Canada and Australia, because they were the only people who understood a federal system. They knew how it worked and what it is. The United Kingdom with its centralized government has no notion of what federalism is nor of how it works.

In their private lives most of the men who came to Balliol were scholars and lawyers. I was impressed with their eagerness to raise every difficulty, but always from the point of view of seeing how to overcome it. As a result, I found that the policy we were discussing was growing, week by week. For example, in my pamphlet *Decision* I confess that I had funked the question, where the capital should be. My reason was that I remembered how, when the constitution of South Africa was near completion, it came within an inch of breaking down on the location of the capital. The groups insisted that we go into this problem. We reached unanimous agreement that it should certainly not be in the United Kingdom, and not in the United States, where it would be overshadowed by the American government. Much the best place would be Quebec where French and English civilization meet, where the fleet could lie in safety and where there was space to train mechanized forces, on land and in the air.

When peace approached, the Oxford University Press asked me to write down the results of these studies in time for them to be printed so that members of the groups could take them home. More than 3,000 service men had passed through these groups. So, working against time, I wrote a rather dull book called *World War; Its Cause and Cure*, which was published in 1945. In 1946 I brought it up to date in a short book called *War or Peace?*, the last chapter of which is headed "Canada's Century." I will explain this presently.

By chance, a copy of *World War; Its Cause and Cure* fell into the hands of Mr. Justice Owen Roberts, now retired from the Supreme Court of the U. S. A., whom Mr. Roosevelt had sent to inquire into the loss of the American fleet in Pearl Harbor. Mr. Justice Owen Roberts showed it to Professor Einstein and said, "Here is the first policy for preventing war that makes sense." They got together a group of influential Americans and published an edition in the United States.

When this conference came in sight, and I was invited to attend it, I felt that the best thing I could do would be to write and print a short account of the conclusions I had reached after forty years' study of the question of how to prevent war. So I wrote *World Revolution in the Cause of Peace.* [3]

Mr. Justice Roberts wrote a foreword to the American edition of *World Revolution in the Cause of Peace,* in which he said:

The prevention of world war has become the first essential for our survival. War, as one of our most distinguished soldiers has said, has become like a fire—you cannot win a fire, but you can prevent fire. And this is what we have got to do. This book tells us how it can be done, and in my opinion the only way it can be done.

I ask your particular attention to the last words of this great American.

Macmillan, the American publisher in New York, at my request, sent one hundred copies to the Secretary of the Canadian Institute for distribution to the delegates.

My case is that war can be prevented, but in one way only, as the Americans prevented it in 1787, by transferring the responsibility for peace and war from sovereign governments to the whole people. Let me give you two illustrations. In the first election after the constitution had been adopted the whole American people selected as President George Washington, the man who had won the war, as the man most likely to win the peace. They elected a congress authorized to provide him with the funds necessary to win the peace. In our own time, a vastly greater electorate, in defiance of all precedents in American history, gave four terms to Roosevelt as the man most likely to win the war and the peace.

My book shows that the War of Independence in starting the American Revolution, really started the world revolution which we are now facing. That is why I have called it *World Revolution in the Cause of Peace.* We can only end World Revolution in the same way as Americans ended their revolution, by placing the responsibility for peace and war on the people themselves. We are thus facing the final crisis in the growth of democracy, and its final

[3] New York, London: Macmillan, 1949.

consummation. We have still to give free peoples the responsibility for the maintenance of peace and the power to maintain it.

A number of problems have been raised at this conference by delegates who gave the impression that these problems were insoluble. My case is that all problems are insoluble so long as the world goes in fear of a third world war. Once end that fear and all the secondary problems will be comparatively easy to solve. For example, one delegate said that, once security from war was assured, American bankers would immediately lend their capital all over the world, especially to backward countries.

This conference has brought out one thing and that is the baffling confusion of the situation we are facing. Mr. Justice Owen Roberts simplifies this when he says that we have got to prevent war once and for all, if mankind is to survive. This tremendous task is laid on us; but Roberts says it can be done and how it can be done. We can only do it by merging sovereignties on the largest scale. We cannot do it for the Commonwealth; we cannot do it for Western Europe, as the views of the United Kingdom delegates here have shown; nor can we do it for the British Commonwealth and Western Europe together. The United States must be included from the outset. The difficulties can be overcome, but only by treating them on the widest scale. The last war has changed our whole perspective. The British Commonwealth and the United States are now acting together like twins in the world situation. Have you noticed that the Union Jack and Stars and Stripes are flying together everywhere here at Bigwin? It is the same in England and all over Canada. This shows the change which has taken place since the 1945 Conference.

Since the war the whole position of Canada has been changed by the inclusion of Newfoundland. Since I first looked at Canada forty years ago it has been a nightmare to me that we should one day wake up to find that the oldest British colony had yielded to tremendous economic temptation and included itself in the United States, so that American territory lay across the Atlantic gateway to Canada. That nightmare can haunt us no longer. Canada is no longer a middle power. If not a major power, she is the key power. I believe that it rests with Canada more than any one else to do what Roberts says we must do if we are to save mankind from the unspeakable disaster of a third world war. That is why I called the last chapter in my book, *Peace or War?*, "Canada's Century."

This brings me to my final point. What is to be the outcome of this Conference? It may be just a debating society, which will be forgotten. It may, and will, I believe, be remembered as a milestone in history. If two or three members in each delegation, seized with Mr. Justice Roberts' view, induced their governments to face and solve the one problem that dominates all others, that is to say to secure peace once and for all, then they can solve all the secondary problems we have discussed here. With the control we now have of natural resources we can start an era of plenty and happiness beyond the dreams of poets who have sung of the Golden Age. Winston Churchill, the most practical statesman of the age, has said this in words of eloquence in the pamphlet by which he launched the United Europe movement.

I see in this room men who can do this, leaders in industry, in thought, in politics and above all in journalism. It only needs, as Churchill said, "one spasm of resolve." You in this Conference can give that impulse, and those who give it will be regarded by after generations all over the world for all time with that kind of devotion which Americans bestow on leaders like Washington, Lincoln and Roosevelt, who gave them peace.

After his speech, Mr. Curtis signified that he would welcome questions, and the following discussion ensued:

A DELEGATE—

In a surrender of sovereignty in the present world, how could one deal with Soviet Russia when the kind of worldwide merger conceived by Mr. Curtis seems beyond the practical bounds of hope? Where should we be if Russia were left out?

MR. CURTIS—

I cannot conceive of an international state not based entirely on democracy. It passes the wit of man to devise a constitution for an international state to include democracies and despotisms side by side. Either the constitution would crumple in a year or all would become despotisms. When I hear Smuts and others talk of wiping out the iron curtain, I recall the words of a Roundhead in the Long Parliament: "You cannot build a bridge between heaven and hell." You cannot build a bridge between constitutions built on the validity of the sense of right and wrong and a constitution built entirely on material values. If you are to get anything done, you must see clearly your ultimate objective —a world state. To get it, you must first make the free system of the world inviolable, and that can only be done by merging national sovereignties in one system so strong that no aggressor would dare to attack it. In the nineteenth century, every one thought that in time democracy would spread to Germany, Russia, China and everywhere, because they thought that the democratic system was inviolable. In the twentieth century all this changed because democracy was threatened. Totalitarian systems began to spread. After the first world war, Soviet Russia, Germany and Japan did not learn democracy. Democracy did not come and as a result totalitarianism spread. I believe that once we have an inviolable system of freedom, the process will begin again. The example of freedom has a longer range and a greater power of penetration than bullets. It is not bullets but ideas of freedom that will then go through the iron curtain. People in Russia will envy our freedom, shake off their chains, learn to govern themselves and in the course of time join the community of free states.

A DELEGATE—

How can de jure governments approve the establishment of "a constituent assembly of the peoples" to work out a constitution?

MR. CURTIS—

I don't think they could. In the United States there stands a resolution supported by over 100 Congressmen which calls on the President to invite the signatories of the Atlantic Pact to send representatives to Washington to discuss what the constitution of the Western Union should be. The events of 1787 offer a parallel on a smaller scale. Such a meeting could prepare a workable constitution. Obviously the several electorates could not do it. My point is that if we want to secure peace to consummate the progress towards democracy, we must have a congress to do for the world what was done for the United States by the Congress of Philadelphia. We must have a constitution which will transfer the issues of peace or war from sovereign governments to the shoulders of the electorate itself.

A DELEGATE—

Would every person have a vote?

MR. CURTIS—

I have no opinion on that point. I would nevertheless go so far as to say that if I were on the drafting conference, I would propose letting each component state settle its own franchise, subject to the franchise being a democratic one.

A DELEGATE—

Would the world government have under its jurisdiction a police force?

MR. CURTIS—

Certainly. That is my whole point. Pearl Harbor demonstrated that the most powerful state could not keep itself out of war. Under the leadership of Roosevelt and Churchill, the United Nations pooled their forces. Had they pooled their forces ten years before, say in 1935, there would have been no second world war. It is much easier to pool forces in time of war than during peace. We can for certain prevent war if in peace we pool our land, sea and air forces and make ourselves so strong that the Russians dare not attack us. I know there are difficulties—I know this well from my experience during the drafting of the South African constitution—but with leadership it can be done. The greatest man I ever knew was General Botha, backed up by Dr. Jamieson, who loved him. The friendship of these two men was the secret of that miracle, the Union of South Africa.

A DELEGATE—

The United Nations seems to be failing us and the blame cannot be placed entirely on the U.S.S.R. Could Mr. Curtis say what quality his idea possesses that the United Nations lacks? There is still evident in the United Nations a strong sense of individual sovereignty. There are 48 members that have still not started to think of themselves as an organization.

MR. CURTIS—

The Covenant of the League of Nations did not refer to sovereignty, whereas the Charter of the United Nations did, especially with respect to the great powers. I have come to the conclusion that there were principles governing human relations and especially politics, as certain in their operation as those governing physics, chemistry and engineering. A world divided into a number of national sovereignties would always be subject to world wars, which could only be prevented by merging them into one international sovereignty. Before the American federation, the delegates of the thirteen states never agreed, and were on the brink of civil war, and the U. S. A. was bankrupt.

I consider that the League of Nations, although it has done useful work in the fields of health, white slavery and drugs, has been a major cause of war, because it misled the British people into believing that they could rely on collective security. The United Nations Organization is attempting to create a similar illusion. If democratic peoples believe that U. N. is a guarantee of peace, then another war would surely follow. Only a world government, only an over-riding sovereign authority can prevent war. The League of Nations, the United Nations Organization, the O.E.E.C. are all examples of "chartered impotence." I hope that this Conference will not suggest the creation of more examples of "chartered impotence."

The solution was first found in the American Constitution drafted in 1787, but it was not completed until the civil war. By transferring responsibility from the State governments to the peoples themselves, it made America the greatest peace area in the world. What party or statesman in the British Commonwealth advocates such a policy? I feel that Disraeli, had he lived in our times, would have had the vision to realize that democracy must be consummated by giving the people themselves power to decide the issues of peace and war.

A DELEGATE—

As a representative of a new nation, I would like to believe in the ideal expounded by Mr. Curtis, because I do not want my country to follow the footsteps of the nation-states of Europe, which has led them to wars and destruction.

If one looks at the prospects of a Federation, there are two questions to be faced:

(1) What would be the nature of the franchise in the Federation? Would it be one vote for one man? If so, undeveloped countries, with a large population would have greater weight than highly developed and richer countries which had a small population, and I doubt that they would accept such a solution.

(2) How would the economic functions be distributed in this new state? To what extent would the more advanced countries be willing to surrender part of their income to the less developed countries?

MR. CURTIS—

The draftsmen of a federation should hold in mind the object in view, which in this case is to secure peace once and for all. The power of the federal government would at first be kept as narrow as possible. The constitution should be more flexible than the American constitution and the method for amending it should be simpler, so that it could be changed according to experience. There should be a clause, however, that, in case of war, all powers necessary to win the war should be temporarily handed out to the Federal authority.

Federation was brought to America by soldiers led by Washington and Hamilton. The policy we are now discussing for winning the peace was worked out by the 3,000 soldiers in the leave-groups.

At the outset, the proposed Federation should only include experienced democracies. If states like the South American Republics were brought in at the beginning the federal structure would crash. The American Confederation, too, started with thirteen states, and after getting stronger felt its way to the 48 states it possesses today. Furthermore the experienced nations are also the nations who would have to find most of the money.

The distribution of political power should be based on the taxable capacity of the various states. The power of spending money should be also distributed according to the taxable capacities of member nations.

INDEX